YESTERDAY IN PARADISE

1950-1974

CYPRIAN FERNANDES

BALBOA.
PRESS
A DIVISION OF HAY HOUSE

Balboa Press books may be ordered through booksellers or by contacting:

Balboa Press
A Division of Hay House
1663 Liberty Drive
Bloomington, IN 47403
www.balboapress.com.au
1 (877) 407-4847

Print information available on the last page.

ISBN: 978-1-5043-0343-9 (sc)
ISBN: 978-1-5043-0344-6 (e)

Balboa Press rev. date: 09/14/2016

Sources

Kenya Parliament *Hansard* 1960-1974

Alex de Figueiredo for having the courage and patience in telling me a most horrific story.

Anne Thurston OBE for use of her interviews, parts of which are also published in *'A Path Not Taken'* compiled from transcripts of Joseph Murumbi by Alan Donovan.

Excerpts from (pp.123 & 124) from *Exporting American Dreams: Thurgood Marshall's African Journey* by Mary L Dudziak (2008). By permission of Oxford University Press, Inc.

Benegal Pereira for access to his conversations with Emma Gama Pinto.

Gerry Loughran (author of *Birth of a Nation: The story of a newspaper in Kenya*) for considerable assistance and contribution.

John Kamau and the *Nation* for access to his published material and his vast experience in land-grabbing in Kenya.

The Truth, Justice and Reconciliation Commission, Kenya.

Audrey da Gama Pinto for sharing her father's tribute to her uncle Pio Gama Pinto.

The Swynnerton Plan, various.

I am indebted to the Kenya-born Goan academic **Clifford Pereira** for an excerpt from his study *Cogwheels of Two Empires: Goan Administration within Nineteenth century British Indian Ocean Empire.*

Very Special Thanks to **Vijay Badhwar** and **Anya Odhiambo** for editorial assistance.

Corina Palmer and Everyone at Balboa Press for all your help.

Dedicated to my late wife
RUFINA
And our children: Andreanna, Leon and Carl

For my siblings: Hippol (deceased), Peter (deceased), Johnny (David Joseph), Rose, Flora and their spouses, children and grandchildren.

For the Goans of Kenya and their descendants, the Kenyans who enriched my life so much and folks I met around the world and who showed me kindness.

CONTENTS

Pioneers of the Railway Goan Institute. *Photo from the Mervyn Lobo collection.*

A historic photograph: From left Vincy D'Souza, the greatest Goan athlete sprinter Seraphino Antao, Rosendo Abreu, Marcel Brunner (boxing pioneer and snooker lover, hotelier), Sebestian Gomes (sports administrator, treasurer, sportsman), Archie Evans (Colony Sports Officer and the founder of organised athletics in Kenya), Saude Georg (Kenya soccer and hockey international, sports administrator, journalist). Vincy, Rosendo and Saude were members of the Kenya Goan Sports Association.

Kenya government at Independence in 1963: key players in the front row, from left Ngala Mwendwa, Oginga Odinga, Jomo Kenyatta, Njoroge Mungai, Joseph Murumbi, Tom Mboya

No copyright

Pictured is a more
recent version
of the dhows
that brought the
earliest visitors,
among them Arabs
and Indians, to
East Africa

*Photo courtesy of
Coastweek*

INTRO

This book is about people originating from the state of Goa, India and the Republic of Kenya, East Africa. This book is also about growing up in colonial British East Africa, the Mau Mau rebellion and the illusion of freedom after independence. A brutal war was fought between Kikuyu tribesmen - dubbed the Mau Mau - fighting for the return of their confiscated lands, and the British armed forces, backed by the mighty Lancaster bombers from World War II and supported by the colonial police force. It is also about insights I garnered from the Mau Mau while growing up before Kenya's independence. It is sadly ironic that a tropical paradise like Kenya has joyful beauty at one end of its spectrum and pure evil at the other, evolving into a place where murderers roam free.

Kenya was blessed with what was once the greatest collection of flora and fauna in Africa, never-ending beaches with the softest of milky white sands, a winterless climate, only moistened with dew and rain and tortured by periodic droughts. Kenya is also graced with soil that brings forth bountiful harvests and mineral wealth. Endowed with a network of world-class game reserves and game lodges, producing some of the finest male and female middle- and long-distance runners, and a people who, to this day, despite scarcity, unemployment, and tough lives in shanty towns, continue to blossom. Oddly, despite considerable negativity, there is also a huge amount of progress. All this is occurring in spite of the corruption that appears to be eating away at the country's soul. Independence gave birth to a Kenya elite (which replaced the colonialists), a middle class and improved quality of life, education, health and much of what the developed world has taken for granted for centuries. That is the new life for a comparative few. But for the majority, independence continues to mire them in poverty, poor health, and very few opportunities amid life's daily struggle for survival, shanty town-based crime cartels and endemic corruption.

Goa is but a tiny speck on the western coast of India. But what a speck! For centuries it has been a paradise to visitors and conquerors from all over the world. The Portuguese colonialists (1510) stayed for 450 years, until India kicked out their tiny contingent of soldiers and annexed the state. The Portuguese left without a whimper, but not before they had imprinted their influence on Goa to the point that most Goans actually valued their colonisers and adopted many aspects of Portuguese culture and custom. Initially, the conversion to Catholicism was forced, but Goans remain to this day amongst the most devout of Catholics. The Portuguese brought religion, music, cuisine, theatre and a life of wine, women and song. A very, very relaxed lifestyle developed to the point its description, *susegaad* ('relax'), in the Konkani language of Goa, is embedded in the Goan DNA. Even though there was a considerable lack of industry and job opportunities, Goans did not protest much. Instead, they left home to seek fresh opportunities, initially to British-ruled Bombay (Mumbai), Bangalore, Belgaum (in Karnataka state, India) and Karachi. They excelled as barmen, waiters, stewards, cooks and musicians in the Royal Navy and on various European, American and British passenger liners and cargo ships.

The British seemed not all bad, if you were not an African. In 1807, the British government outlawed the trade in humans in the Atlantic, but not beyond the Cape of Good Hope. The slave trade in the Indian Ocean was distinct from that of the Atlantic. It was an ancient trade dominated by Muslim Afro-Arab slave traders in collaboration with local tribal chiefs, some of whom are reputed to have sold their own villagers into slavery. By the nineteenth century the trade was financed primarily by Hindu and Muslim Indians, and the enslaved Africans (who were mainly young children) were transported to Western Asia, India, the Mascarene Islands and the Americas by vessels flying the flags of Oman, Brazil, Portugal and France. The British Indian Ocean anti-slavery campaign was led by the Royal Navy and the HMS *London* base-ship moored at Zanzibar.

Goans, a few Arabs, free Africans and ex-slaves served in the campaign alongside British crewmen. But it was the abolitionist Sir Bartle Frere, governor of the Bombay Presidency, who was to champion the qualities of Goans and the Bombay Africans as potential players in the development of Eastern Africa. There was naturally strong opposition from the Sultan of Zanzibar and coastal Sheikhs who accused the British of interfering in local affairs. The antislavery campaign eventually merged with European colonial plans and led to the dismantling of the Sultan's realm into British and German rival spheres of influence, and to the establishment of the Imperial British East Africa Company (IBEAC). The British colonial government took over from the IBEAC and built the Kenya-Uganda railway, opening the highlands to European (mainly British) settlement, leading to resentment from the Kikuyu and Kalenjin peoples.

The British were cognizant of the fine qualities of the Goan workers and, when they needed clerical and manual labour for their East African colonies, they encouraged Goan migration. Goans were Christian, spoke English, and were loyal, honest and very trustworthy. As a result, in the early 1900s Goans dominated in the colonial administration of British-ruled Kenya, Uganda and German Tanganyika which, after World War I, became a British-mandated Tanganyika. Goans even formed a voluntary force in World War I in Uganda, while thousands of African soldiers of the Kings African Rifles and Indian troops fought against the Germans in East Africa. The end of the war in 1919 brought the assisted settlement (to the exclusion of African and Asian land ownership) of British ex-servicemen into what became known as the White Highlands.

Many have said that the colonial administration would have collapsed but for the skill and management of the Goan clerks and accountants. Later, doctors, chefs, musicians, dentists, motor mechanics, coolies, carpenters, tailors and workers with other skills joined the growing Goan and other South Asian communities in East Africa. In semi-tropical Kenya, Uganda, and Tanganyika they found an even larger paradise than they could have ever imagined. Until 1963 they enjoyed life with a gusto that could only have been found in their beautiful Portuguese-ruled Goa.

The British introduced modern medicine, hospitals and education, Westminster system of Parliament, established game reserves, modern roads, the telegraph, postal service, radio, competitive sports, large-scale farming, local government and animal husbandry. Some of the jewels in the British crown in Kenya were the wildlife reserves and the attendant game lodges which more than quadrupled in number after independence. Tourism has been a big money-earner for the country. Sadly, elephants and rhinos continue to be murdered for their horns, prized for their medicinal qualities and as an aphrodisiac in the Far East.

Christianity improved on the provision of education for both Africans and Europeans, sometimes with a very heavy hand. Most of Kenya's leaders at independence went to church schools and people like Jomo Kenyatta enhanced their skills by actually going to Britain. They brought law and order and a colonial kind of justice which was not always fair to darker skinned people. They brought aviation and built aerodromes. They introduced automobiles and that changed the mode of transport forever. They brought the sciences, including some world class anthropology. They brought aspects of modernity that suited the settler and the colonial government as quickly as they could. Most of all they built the required infrastructure, a little bit at a time.

All these wonderful elements of the modern world did not make an iota of difference to the thousands of Kikuyu and other tribes who had been run off their lands to make space for the white settlers. For Goans and Asians in general, the British were no problem. Apart from work, we did not interact at all. The colonial whites infected Kenya with what is the worst in people and they anointed them with what is the best in humankind.

Land consolidation - the brainchild of Roger Swynnerton in the colonial department of agriculture - was originally designed to place Kikuyu lands in the hands of a few and was correctly considered a cruel British plot. However, it has since been recognised as the basis for land reform in developing countries. Even today, there are rich and powerful Kenyans who wish the British had done more land consolidation. One forward-thinking chief in Meru was reputed to have owned more than 1000 acres and smaller plots were owned by various members of his family. The chief paid for this land. Those Kikuyus who could afford it also bought small plots.

For the first time, the colonial administration, through the Swynnerton Plan, allowed Africans to not only buy land and acquire titles to land in the White Highlands but also, facilitated the acquisition of credit, and removed the restriction on the cultivation of export crops by Africans. However, the plan had serious flaws. The plan provided for, among other things, a process of land adjudication, consolidation and registration of adjudicated parcels of land in theof those identified as owners. Absentee owners, especially the Mau Mau, were not considered.

Kenya's independence was won primarily with the blood of the Mau Mau, ordinary Kikuyu people, loyalist chiefs and African policemen, comparatively few white settler families, soldiers and a few South Asians. Kenya is a land of warrior tribes, the more charismatic being the nomadic Maasai whose tradition it was to kill a lion with a spear to attain manhood. The Kikuyu were not far behind, and if they needed any reminder of their prowess as warriors, the Mau Mau is proof enough. Around 1950 a fight for the return of confiscated Kikuyu lands occupied by British settlers in Kenya was gaining momentum. The campaign was led by Kikuyu soldiers who had just returned from fighting in Burma for the British 'king and country' in World War II. The Mau Mau rebellion was a vicious guerrilla war and, as more and more people were killed, the British Government declared an emergency in 1952. By the time it ended in 1960, Kenya was well on its way to independence, not solely because of the Mau Mau but because the British Government sensed the coming 'winds of change' and the end of colonialism.

Just before and after independence, there were several land resettlement schemes. Most of them like the Million acres scheme, the Haraka sand Shirika were somewhat successful. Most of the large farms and arable land bought by the new elite were in the Central Province and the Rift Valley and, of course, the coast. The land pillage of the choice beach front, urban and rural land is pitiful and deserves a book in its own right. This is one Kenya's sorriest stories.

Independence came to Kenya in 1963 and signalled the exodus of virtually anyone who was not prepared to take up Kenyan citizenship. The enigmatic Jomo Kenyatta led the Kikuyu politically. Before that the British tried to break him and thousands of other Kikuyu by locking them up in detention or killing them. The incarceration not only failed but also inspired Kenyans to push on for independence. Kenyatta's eventual rival was the leader of the Luo, Jaramogi Oginga Odinga, who was a self-styled African socialist at a time when no one had actually defined what African socialism was. Odinga had very strong communist connections and was supported by both China and Russia. On the other hand, Kenyatta and the Kikuyu - with the help of Britain, USA and the World Bank - exploited the opportunities that flooded the country in the months after independence with the result that quite a few black people became extremely rich overnight. While land was the main reason Kenyans fought for their independence, very few enjoyed the 'fruits' of freedom. Jomo Kenyatta and his well-placed Kikuyu colleagues made sure that they grabbed thousands of acres vacated by departing British settlers. That was the beginning of a cancer of corruption that continues to eat into Kenya from the core. There were other successful Kenyans from other tribes as well but the richest were the Kikuyu.

Kenya's first President, Jomo Kenyatta, brought prosperity to the country and continued to improve facilities for education, health, farming, jobs, industry and the general well-being of Kenyans. Foreign aid, foreign investment and foreigners flowed into Kenya as a result. There was a daily procession of locals and foreigners to State House, Gatundu, for the privilege of shaking Jomo Kenyatta's hand and giving him millions of shillings, supposedly for the construction of his pet project, Gatundu Self-Help Hospital. Under Kenyatta's patronage, all the top jobs in the Kenyan Civil Service and other Government departments and organisations were reserved for the Kikuyu. It seemed as if Kikuyus ran every major industry and organisation including local government and the more lucrative provincial administration. He also masterminded the distribution of land, favouring Kikuyu ownership mainly in the traditional Kikuyu stronghold of Central Province and encroached on non-Kikuyu areas where the landless Kikuyu had settled in the Great Rift Valley. The traditional owners of the land in the Rift Valley, mainly the Kalenjin, wanted it back and the Kikuyu out.

The genesis of Kenya's post-independence land issues lies in the secret deals Kenyatta made with the British, especially one in the final steps towards independence. That Kenyatta made a secret pact with Michael Blundell (leader of the European settlers) comes out clearly in the notes of the former Vice-President Joseph Murumbi (confirmed also many years later with the release of the Blundell papers). During one of the plenary sessions of the final Lancaster House Conference in London, Jomo Kenyatta made a blistering attack on departing colonialists and indicated that their place would *depend very much on the readiness to admit liability on past mistakes and be ready to work with the African government in effecting immediate reforms'.*

Murumbi reckoned that while Kenyatta's statement went down well with radical Africans, the whites saw red in what was a clear indication that the fire-spitting of old had not disappeared.

That night at a secret meeting, Blundell told Kenyatta that kind talk was unacceptable to the British Prime Minister the colonial Governor in Nairobi. Blundell accused Kenyatta of reneging on agreements made earlier in Kenya at Lodwar and Maralal. Kenyatta replied that he had been provoked by whites and their African supporters at the conference who were talking as if they did not accept that black people would be the ones to decide the destiny of the country after independence.

A hint on the exact content in the secret pact reached between Kenyatta and the colonialists can be glimpsed from Murumbi's notes on a meeting held between him, Odinga and Dr Munyua Waiyaki on August 16, 1964 in regard to the growing agitation over the land question, nearly a year after independence. The trio had particularly sought Kenyatta's position on the distribution of the 10 million acres arable land occupied by white settlers.

According to Murumbi, Kenya told them that his hands were tied and he had committed himself to the white settlers that all land in the country would change hands on a willing seller, willing buyer basis.

In another entry in Murumbi's notes, before he resigned as Vice-President in 1966, he expresses disappointment that President Kenyatta "had no political will to direct the Settler Transfer Fund (STF) to benefit millions of landless Africans as has been stated in the KANU manifesto at Independence."

Instead, Murumbi noted that the STF 'had been hijacked by a new elite Africans (replacing the white elite) who were loaning themselves money meant for the landless at the expense of the majority of the poor.' (*Nation 2008*)

In 2013, *the Nation* reported: "The regime of Kenya's first president, Jomo Kenyatta, was riddled with land grabbing which was perpetrated by him for his benefit and members of his family. The *Truth Justice and Reconciliation Commission* report says that the injustice also benefitted other political leaders from other tribes.

'One-sixth of European settlers' lands that were intended for settlement of landless and land-scarce Africans were cheaply sold to the then President Kenyatta and his wife Ngina as well as his children. Throughout the years of President Kenyatta's administration, his relatives, friends and officials in his administration also benefitted from the vice with wanton impunity.

'Other leaders who engaged in the practice were Daniel arap Moi, Mbiyu Koinange, Ronald Ngala, Oginga Odinga, through the Luo Thrift and Trading Company, Gikonyo Kiano, J.M. Kariuki, Masinde Muliro and Paul Ngei.

'Kenyatta himself appears to have benefited immensely from irregular allocations of land that should have benefited those who lost land to Arab and British colonisers.' By 1965, Kenyatta bought numerous settler farms in the White Highlands and also excising and allocating to himself and family government forest land in Kiambu.

'President Kenyatta's direct engagement in irregular land allocations compromised his position to prevent or remedy similar cases of land grabbing by his close associates. Kenyatta personally approved the purchase of large farms by his family in the Rift Valley, exempting the transactions from review by the respective land control boards.'

'Kenyatta and his family owned several beach plots and hotels on the Coast where, as previously stated, many African communities lost their land, first, to Arabs and later to Europeans, rendering many landless, to this day.' (*Daily Nation 2013*)

This continues to be a serious problem to this day. Investigative reporter John Kamau, of Kenya's *Daily Nation*, exposed the Z-plot conspiracy in 2016, in which 100 acre plots with a house on each block were given to ministers, members of parliament, ambassadors, permanent secretaries, provincial commissioners, civil servants and prominent national personalities.

Kenyatta did not trust the administration of areas to politicians, and soon prosperity was concentrated in the hands of a few. Kenyatta's own family, government ministers and associates were soon amongst the richest people in Kenya. An American scripted Parliamentary Sessional Paper No.10 crafted Kenya as a capitalist country in which the majority was robbed of equal opportunity. Despite everything, Kenyatta's 15-year regime was generally pretty good. He kept a very tight rein to ensure both that there were no issues and that people were too frightened to challenge the status quo. The saddest irony is that the Mau Mau fought and died for land, yet most of the survivors got not even a single square metre.

In the strangest of ironies, Europeans and Americans continue own swathes of Kenya. Here is one prime example: 'Laikipia Plateau, estimated to be about 10,000 sq km or 2.5 million acres, has the biggest number of white landowners. It stretches from Mt Kenya in the east to the Rift Valley in the west. The Laikipia Maasai, who number approximately 35,000, are squashed on different patches of land, which measure about 1100 sq km or an equivalent of 281,587 acres of land.

On the other hand, foreigners comprising mostly the British and American "aristocratic" class and a few influential local politically well-connected barons, occupy thousands of acres of land on an individual basis. Only 20 own 74 per cent of the total land in the Laikipia District. In the Laikipia Plateau, private ranches range from "small" concerns of 5,000 acres to endless horizons of massive land properties that are over 100,000 acres. There are approximately 36 estates. Two of the 18 estates are owned by multi-millionaire Hollywood A-list types who entertain tourist guests. Many of the private farms and ranches are today being converted to wildlife sanctuaries.' (realtor Edith Makena Mbwiria, 2016)

Since gaining independence from Britain, in 1963, there have been some high profile unsolved assassinations and massacres in Kenya. Thomas Joseph Odhiambo ('Tom') Mboya was killed in the centre of the Kenya capital Nairobi on a Saturday morning (July 5, 1969). He was a Luo from Nyanza Kenya who worked with the majority Kikuyu cabinet of Jomo Kenyatta. He was highly regarded in the West by many and touted as the likely successor to President Jomo Kenyatta. But Mboya was a Luo, the other dominant tribe that was challenging the Kikuyu for power in Kenya. The man accused of killing Mboya alleged 'a Mr. Big was the real killer'.

Another Luo, Dr John Robert Ouko, was killed in 1990 with a single shot to the head. In a short-lived but stellar career, Ouko was Foreign Minister. His killers have never been caught. In 2008, G.G. Njuguna Ngengi was hacked to death in full view of the public at a meeting he was addressing. In 2015, George Muchai, a Member of Parliament, was murdered as well as his driver and two bodyguards. There have been others: Ronald Ngala, a leading politician from the Coastal region, was killed in a suspicious car crash. One of the few white men to serve in Kenyatta's cabinet, Bruce McKenzie, died after a bomb exploded in the aircraft carrying him.

Kenyan forces allegedly carried out massacres of North Eastern Kenyan Somali tribes in Garissa (3,000 dead), in the Wagalla massacre at Wajir (approximately 5,000 killed) and, in 2015, the Somali terrorist organisation Al-Shabaab killed 148 people, most of whom were non-Muslim students at Garissa University. In an earlier attack on a shopping mall, they had killed more than 71 people. In 2016, Al-Shabaab killed 180 Kenyan soldiers on a peacekeeping mission in Somalia. And, of course, there is Pio Gama Pinto, Kenya's first political martyr whose assassination I deal with at length in this book.

Virtually all the killers roam free in Kenya.

This book is as much a tribute in wonderment of Kenya as it is about the Kenya I remember, and some of the people and places that filled my life there. Most of these stories have enjoyed considerable readership as part of my blog. People have often asked when I would write my book. Well, here it is. I have written it most in the first person because it is an eye witness account. I was there. I knew most of the people involved. I lived much of the story. I have hit my memory recall button and I hope I have done it justice.

The Portuguese-built Fort Jesus in Mombasa. *Photo courtesy of Coastweek.*

CHAPTER 1

GOAN MIGRATION

The British in India always had issues with racial mixing. The explorer Richard Francis Burton expressed prejudiced views on half-castes, calling Goa a strange mélange of European and Asiatic peculiarities, of antiquated civilization and modern barbarism. British Victorians struggled to understand the relative lack of racial discrimination even among the higher classes in Goa and were shocked by God's images painted in ebony in the churches and convents.

For the British the concept of empire was based on visions of Europeans settling in large tracts of thinly populated areas (e.g. Australia, Canada, and New Zealand), where the indigenous peoples could be easily overcome, and assimilated or exterminated, and thereby creating model copies of the motherland. The West Indies and India were anomalies in this scheme. The aim here was to keep the 'natives' separate from the Europeans. The 1857 'Sepoy Mutiny' in India only supported this British perspective. For the Portuguese, empire was based on a Roman model (i.e. Latin speaking and aspiring to the dictates of Rome) and was multi-ethnic, with a hierarchy built on Lusitanisation: i.e. Catholic, Portuguese speaking and culturally orientated towards Lisbon. The Catholic Goan was therefore socially near the apex of the Portuguese concept of empire, in stark contrast to British view of Indians as noted in 1896 by Oskar Baumann, when he was watching a religious procession in Goa: 'Since there are Christians, Hindus and Mohammedans, Europeans, Asians and Africans in a colourful series, it is a curious sight for everybody coming from British India, where the distinction of races is so strictly carried out'.

The British proclaimed specific racial traits, regarding such peoples as the Sikhs and Pathans as 'martial races' and regarding others such as the Tamils as 'docile races'. Goans could not be regarded as a business-like group like the Hindu and Ismaili Gujarati merchants they encountered in India and Zanzibar. To them, Goans represented an anomaly or failure of the social/racial policy designed by the Portuguese.

Wherever the late nineteenth century European administrator wandered in Eastern Africa, the Goan had either already ventured or was soon in his footsteps. David Livingstone was keen to stress that any 'half-caste' Portuguese he encountered in South-Central Africa was not a legitimate sign of Portuguese presence. The truth is that in the Portuguese Eastern Empire, the European presence generally stopped where it had always been: less than ten miles from the safety of the coastal forts. Inland and up the rivers it was the Goan or the Afro-Portuguese merchant, agent or district officer who flew the Portuguese flag, and since these were not 'white' Portuguese, this provided the excuse for British expansion in Central-Southern Africa.

In East Africa, Goans initially headed for Zanzibar. Their role was primarily to serve the Sultan and the European community composed of the various consuls, missionaries and endless expedition leaders. It was only by the early twentieth century that the stereotypical Goan clerk or 'Bwana Karani' came into his own in East Africa. This increased with the completion of the Uganda Railway, and Zanzibar was gradually overshadowed by British Uganda and particularly Kenya, and after 1919, the mandated Tanganyika. The Goans increased their migration to these territories, replicating the socio-economic role they previously held within British colonial India. In terms of pathways to migration, the Goans now brought their kinsmen directly from their villages in Goa, and fewer Goans sought to return to Goa for retirement. The shipping agency of Mackinnon McKenzie & Co. acted as an agency in Bombay for the recruitment of Goans for the East African civil service. Goans reached their highest numbers in Zanzibar around 1931 when there were over 1700 of them there. In Tanganyika, Uganda and Kenya their numbers would quadruple over the next twenty years. Much of this growth was within East Africa and not due to new immigration.

The social development of East Africa offered Asians little infrastructure. So, like other Asians, Goans established their own churches, clubs, schools, surgeries and even hospitals within the prescribed 'Asian' areas of towns and cities. The eighteenth and nineteenth century Goan cook or steward was the maritime cultural interface between the European crew and other Asian (Muslim, Sikh and Hindu) or African (Siddi or Swahili) crew, and was also the broker between crew and passenger. As clerks in the civil service, Goan men held another brokering position, as the interface between those who held colonial power (the British and Germans) and those Africans whose lands were being colonised. Goans in East Africa therefore held a distinct and precarious position in the social hierarchy, below Europeans but above all other Asians, who themselves were above Arabs and Africans.

Referring to the eighteenth century Pombaline Reforms and the sense of equality by which Goans regarded Europeans in the nineteenth century, Burton stated that it is 'No wonder that the black Indo-Portuguese is an utter radical, he has gained much by Constitution'. The Goan attributes of public philanthropy and community service grew out of the pre-Portuguese Goan concepts of *communidade* (community) and were revisited by the European enlightenment. This concept was very important to the community in Bombay and was carried to the segregated highlands of Kenya by such people as Dr. Rosendo Ribeiro and Dr. A.C.L de Sousa. Arguably the same sentiments may have been part of the reason Goans were relatively less supportive of the independence movements in East Africa than some Asian communities, providing such freedom fighters as Oscar Fonseca, Fitz De Souza, Pio Gama Pinto, Eddie Pereira, John Nazareth and the part-Goan Joseph Zuzarte Murumbi. This is not surprising given that Goans were never numerically more than four percent of the total Asian population of East Africa, themselves less than three percent of the total East African population. Additionally, Goans were constrained by being Portuguese citizens in British colonies. Though predominantly employed in the civil service, they were not allowed to strike, demonstrate or generally be politically active.

As 'Lusitanised Indians' (i.e. Catholic and European cultured) from a Portuguese colony, Goans considered themselves socially distinct from the British Indians, many of whom initially arrived in Africa as indentured railway workers. The British accorded Goans a separate non-Indian census grouping. The different history and special social, religious and occupational attributes left a mark in the psyche of the East African Goans, who are unique among the South Asian Diaspora for changing their working and in many cases their home language from Konkani to English, so that by 1951 Goans were considered an English-speaking community in East Africa. In all African countries their numbers plummeted after independence, due to a combination of the Africanisation of the civil service, citizenship restrictions and social factors.

The statement that 'poverty sends forth thousands of Black Portuguese (i.e. Goans) to earn money in foreign lands' was an over simplification of the push factors, and does little to explain why the overall majority of these migrant Goans were Catholics, and why, or how, they migrated to Bombay. There is not one specific date that marks the large-scale migration of Goans from Goa to British and German East Africa in the nineteenth century. Rather, this migration can be regarded as a gradual process, marking the fading of the Portuguese Empire and the rise of the British Empire and the transition and expansion of the industrial revolution. During this process Catholic Goans, who had come to see themselves as equals of Europeans, migrated to areas where their cultural endowments as Lusitanised Asians made them particularly valuable as cultural brokers, becoming the interface between Asians or Africans and Europeans. In the case of British East Africa, this role was held within a strict racially based socio-political hierarchy.

Sins of Caste and Prejudice in Goan Migration

In colonial Kenya's Goan communities, the 'war' between North (Bardez) Goa and South (Salcete) Goa was perhaps most pronounced, at least in vitriol and prejudice. There were similar experiences in the coastal protectorate city of Mombasa, the island of Zanzibar, the Ugandan capital Kampala and other towns with sizeable Goan communities. The Nairobi Goan Institute restricted membership to those who could read and write English. It was designed to keep the lower class Xasticars out. People from North Goa were called Bardezkars and from the South, Xasticars. The Goan Gymkhana reputedly restricted membership to Bardezkars but preferred Brahmins (upper class Goans). The Railway Goan Institute restricted membership to Goan employees of the railways. The Goan Tailors Society, as the name implies, catered to tailors and their families but it allowed entry to all Goans, especially at their famous trouk (card) tournaments, where the prizes were often gold chains.

Up until 1955, Xasticars were made to feel inferior to their northern cousins. They were dismissed as ill-bred and lacking in the airs and graces. They were frowned upon because they did not eat with forks and knives. Worse, most Xasticars in Kenya were branded as foul-mouthed drunks. Not many spoke English and most did blue collar or menial jobs. English speaking Xasticars had long deserted their 'uncouth' country cousins. Most tailors, shoemakers, cooks, butlers and others came from Salcete and were of a lower class and lower caste, remaining fairly isolated from the other upper classes. The Portuguese had done little (if anything) to change the class and caste culture. Hindu Brahmins became Christian Bammons, *Kshatriyas* became noblemen called Chardos, and *Shudras* became Sudirs. Landlords were called *bhatkars* and came only from the upper classes and castes. The serfs, who came from the lower classes with no standing in society, were called *mundkars* (non-persons); most came from Salcete. Aboriginal Goans are called Gavddi and are of a higher caste. Converts, called *Kunbis*, came mostly from Salcete.

By 1960 the prejudice and divide had disappeared, and most Goans born and raised in East Africa not only spoke English but had adopted the British way of life, becoming little English men and women. It is at this stage that the first fractures became evident, especially in the devotion and total loyalty to Goa. Another contributing factor was the 'annexation' of Goa by India in 1961. The so-called independent Goan persona had dissipated.

Kenyan-born academic, Clifford Pereira, writes:

'The Initial Goan migration to Eastern Africa in the early to mid-nineteenth century was mainly from Salcete, where Portuguese-medium schools provided for the administration in Mozambique. Early Bardezi migration was to Zanzibar in the mid-nineteenth century, but as the communication between Goa and Bombay improved, English-medium schools developed in Bardez and the migration from Bardez to Zanzibar increased. By the last decade of the nineteenth century Goan migration to East Africa (German Tanganyika, Kenya Colony, Kenya Coast Protectorate and Uganda Protectorate) increased through the Imperial British East Africa Company (IBEAC). This was more from Bardez than Salcete. Migration from Salcete to British East Africa increased again after World War I. Goans in East Africa were mainly male, transient and initially too few for divisions based on *taluka* (provincial) origins. The system of hiring people to replace those on leave was based on village contacts. It was quite normal to find that employees working at a bank, or government department originated from the same village or taluka. All evidence suggests that the middle and lower castes were predominant in the early days. This system of village contacts and contracts brought the Goan caste system into the work place in British East Africa.

'One thing is for sure, when men made contact with other Goan men of the same caste in East Africa, the request for brides from Goa was rarely across the *taluka* lines. However as more Goans were born in British East Africa (after World War I) they increasingly chose partners from the East African Goan community, mainly (but not exclusively) from the same caste, but from different *taluka* origins. So Bardez-Salcete (i.e. trans-*taluka*) relationships became more common. This is especially true for those born in East Africa from the 1930s onward.

'The *taluka*-divisions appear to have been more a point of honour, than a marital issue. Of course, the issue of geographical origin became less pronounced as more people were born in East Africa, and linguistic differences (i.e. between Bardez and Shasti Konkani) mattered less. As the community indigenized, making a language switch from Konkani to English evolved. By the 1960s a second East African born generation with no knowledge of Goa or the Konkani language came into existence. *Taluka* and even caste become irrelevant. The shrinking of the Goan communities after 1964 further decreased the *taluka* identity.'

Photo by Brian McMorrow

When the Kenya-Uganda railway reached mile 327 in 1899, a basic camp and supply depot was set up in the uninhabited swampland but the herding Maasai were driven off. It was a central spot between Mombasa and Kampala. It was an ideal spot: a cool climate, plenty of clean water supply and with an elevation of 1661metres safe from malaria carrying mosquitoes. It grew quite rapidly but the shanty town had to be destroyed because of an outbreak of plague. However, the rebuilt town soon replaced Mombasa at the capital of British East Africa.

This minor Basilica of Nairobi had its humble beginnings as a tiny Holy Family Church with the Catholic Parochial School attached, which I attended as a very small child.

Photo courtesy of Brian McMorrow

CHAPTER 2

NAIROBI, THE EARLY DAYS

The name 'Nairobi' comes from the Maasai Enkare Nyorobi and translates to 'the place of cool waters'.

I was born a war baby in Nairobi on 16 September 1943. My father eked out a living as a tailor. My mother was an illiterate housewife. In the early 1950s Nairobi was a comparatively small city. We lived on the western fringe of the city's small central business district. My brother Hippol and I were born when we lived in the Central Hotel, behind the National and Grindlays Bank. My brother Johnny would be born in Goa and my brother Peter was born in the suburb of Eastleigh, Nairobi, as were my sisters Rose and Flora.

This story begins one day in December, many decades ago. We were returning home at midday from St Teresa's Boys' School in Eastleigh. When we passed Tracey Benoit's (not her real name) home, three doors away from ours, all hell seemed to break loose. Hell indeed! The devil himself, it seemed, was raining havoc on the humble home. Crockery was smashed, glass shattered into fragments and fine powder. Wooden chairs and tables were splintered against the stone walls and shredded into the air. The noise was frightening. 'A poltergeist is the problem,' the local Catholic priest told us. The priest and two altar boys in their red outfits and white tops were timidly trying to enter the pandemonium. They were armed with incense and holy water, hoping to perform an exorcism of sorts. They gingerly took a step forward and five steps back, ducking and crouching as the poltergeist's splinter bombs exploded eerily around them. In the end they gave up and waited for advanced Catholic reinforcements.

The kids, unperturbed, simply explained that a ghost had gone madly wild. We peered in and inched closer. We huddled against each other, and then tottered backwards in a panic at the sound of the next crash. Our forced laughter was a feeble ruse to hide our fear. High anxiety filled the air. 'What if the ghost decided to come after us?' I thought. We resolved to not be afraid of a ghost.

Our mothers calling us interrupted this false bravado against the phantoms of occult and devilry. We prayed that the splashes of holy water, accompanied by the Lord's Prayer and our fervent chorus of Hail Marys in various decibels, served as shields against the devil at work. As they prayed incessantly, the old women looked like hens with their heads chopped off. It was a funny sight for the kids. There were mums chasing the kids, round and round. My mother, flaunting and flapping her wings like some Olympian butterfly swimmer, chased us. It was an intense effort to gather her brood under the safety of her wings so she could later shepherd us home. Not even the threat of 'I will tell your father' could stop us kids. Even though we appeared tough, we felt fear, real fear. This was the stuff of nightmares. This fear had been fed and nurtured by myths and legends from lands far beyond the horizon. We kids knew very little about this, yet the little that we did know would surely bring pain, nightmares and tears as darkness fell.

Tracey Benoit was many years my senior. With blue eyes, honey blonde locks and long sexy legs she was, to me, the most beautiful girl in the world. After the ghost had destroyed their home, we never saw or heard of Tracey or her mother again. Seychellois friends used to swear that Mrs. Benoit sold black-magical potions for any occasion, including some strange powder to bewitch a girl or boy to marry their son or daughter. Seychellois served it with tea, coffee, soft drink or liquor as well. She was called "*bonom di bwa*" (a seer) in Creole. By the time the Catholic artillery (several bishops and an army of clergy) had arrived, the poltergeist had become bored and the home was quiet again.

Eastleigh, a few kilometres east of Nairobi, was founded in 1921. The British colonial government established the suburb for Asians and elite Africans as part of its segregation policy introduced in 1920. I never knew any 'elite' Africans in Eastleigh except John Kasyoka, who was president of the Kenya Football Association, and pharmacist for the Goans Dr. Charlie Paes. The Royal Air Force Base at Eastleigh Airport and the St Teresa's Boys' and Girls' schools adjoining the St Teresa's Catholic Church were the outstanding elements of the neighbourhood. In the 1950s it was the poorest man's paradise, but it was a pretty peaceful place. The only crime was a little thieving and pole fishing of homes. The families who could afford it employed maids and houseboys for very low wages. These families complained incessantly about the pilfering of sugar and coffee or alcohol. Nobody was actually very rich but some fared better than others. Few families owned a car; even fewer owned their own homes. In the early 1950s most families lived in rented homes. We had never heard of the word mortgage. The bus was the primary mode of transport: the service was good and the buses were always very clean.

Today in 2016, Eastleigh and its surroundings are called Little Mogadishu where it is rumoured Somali Al-Shabaab terrorists come for R&R. It is alleged that one can also buy any kind of part, including body parts. Notoriously, one can buy any kind of ammunition. In recent years, almost exclusively Somali immigrants have dominated it. The shopping is pretty good, the traffic insane. Eastleigh remained a large Kenyan Asian enclave until independence in 1963.

My mother, Rosa Maria Fernandes, never grew over five feet. She was a walking skeleton. Blackened by nature of skin and darkened by nature of heat and dust, her skinny legs carried her with a precision of step that translated into a type of motorised speed. She was fast. Her bony hands had a vice-like grip. Her brow was unfurrowed. Only her eyes betrayed her: little round balls of dynamite waiting to explode. Such was her determination. She was a little woman, but she was a living rocket. On the other hand, those balls of dynamite lit her face up like lamplight when she smiled or laughed, which was rare. In her low or quiet moments, there was also silent resolution.

Picture then, the sight early one morning with Christmas just around the corner. This steely woman with her brood of six - including a girl barely a month old - all wrapped in the warmth of her wings and at rest in a large square chair that had been abandoned in the hallway. An uncaring husband and father who was a victim himself had thrown us out of our home. In those days folks rented rooms and shared common toilets and bathrooms. Nobody knew whose chair it was, but it had become a permanent fixture. My father, unable to come to terms with the ills that dogged him, took the easy way out in a drunken frenzy. He thought he was getting rid of his problems. So there we were hanging on to this tiny woman who said not a word, murmured not a sound, but in her silence her determination grew by the minute.

For some of us children, the episode came almost as a relief. It was an end to the beatings, the abuse, the belittlement, the pain, the tears, the shame, the madness, the lunacy, the despair and always the poverty. We, who had nothing, had never known anything other than our pitiful world. We knew that but not many people did, and if they did, they did nothing to help. Yet there was never any hate in any quarter, or any regret. 'You all go to school, I will find a place by the time you get back,' was all my mother could say after we had breakfasted on mouthfuls of tap water. It was the end of our life with father. It didn't matter what was in store, from here on whatever happened to us would be of our own making, because we made it so. We would survive. She would make certain we survived. We had only the clothes we stood in, we four boys, the oldest 11, and two infant girls. Mum had nothing, not a single cent. She was less than nothing. Uneducated, untrained, her only tools were her feet and hands, her eyes and, above everything else, her faith in God and an unshakeable belief that nothing was impossible.

Soon she found a place for us. The Adela family was just two short of a soccer team but now they had a couple of reserves as well. Like us they were survivors, but extremely disciplined and happy. There was plenty of laughter and lots of God. Each Sunday morning we would be up at 4:30 and walk single file for an hour to St Peter Claver's Church at the bottom of River Road, on the outskirts of Nairobi. Along the way we would say a couple of rosaries and many prayers. On the way back, we would stop at the nearby Mincing Lane Market and pick out the cheapest vegetables. There were always more prayers at home including the daily rosary. Here we would survive until that distant day we would find a home of our own. Right then such a thought was further away than the moon or the stars.

To feed us, Mum ran errands, cleaned homes, did grocery shopping, babysat, ironed and cooked, dressed corpses, wailed at funerals and performed other menial tasks. She never turned down any job. Lines of injured football players would stand outside waiting for her healing massage. Her fingers, they said, made miracles. She also treated thousands of children with Goan traditional medicines. Many still remember her for the relief from pain she brought to many young children. She also dabbled in traditional Goan exorcism in which salt and dried red chillies are used to remove the evil eye and similar evils. The hand with the salt and chillies makes circles, anti-clockwise, above the victim's head while the exorcist chants. Most Goans swear by this.

Unable to read or write, she developed an uncanny ability to pick winners in the local horse races. Tiffin boys who biked lunches into the city would come round to pick up her bets and follow her tips. She only bet 10 and 20 cents but the winnings did come, supplementing her dawn-to-dusk work. It was not long before we rented our own home. Later in life, she would take her scrimping and saving to new heights. Many years later, she would visit my two sisters and me who had migrated to England. She would return to Nairobi with tons of suitcases full of second hand clothing that sold like hot cakes in Nairobi. She did not become a millionaire, but she had a bob or two of her own. It seemed all so silly, the effort did not seem rational but there was a bottom line, however small. It did not stop for a very long time. She never spent a cent on herself, not for gold or jewelry, pearls or the classier things in life. She never needed them, never had them, never knew them. All she knew was her children and everything she did in life was for her children. But she was also tough, very tough with the children, almost as hard as she was with herself. She said farewell to the world after a short stay in hospital in Sydney, Australia, following a motoring accident in which she was a passenger. What a lady, what a mother. She found peace at last.

Two views of the Mathare Valley slums. *Photos courtesy of Ian Cross*

CHAPTER 3

EASTLEIGH, UNFORGETTABLE

Eastleigh was a melting pot of non-whites: Muslims (including Ismailis, Pakistanis, and Punjabi Muslims from India), Somalis, Kutchies, Gujaratis, Sikhs, Seychellois, Mauritians, and a host of other communities. Each community stuck firmly to themselves. The Sikhs were great carpenters and builders and drank neat scotch three or four fingers deep. They were also good motor mechanics. Muslims worked in a variety of jobs mainly with their hands, especially as motor mechanics and electricians. Somali men were renowned as house and business guards. Goans, also referred to as 'Brown Portuguese,' felt superior to other brown and black skins. They were a large community whose life was dominated by the Catholic Church. The only white people in Eastleigh were the nuns and priests and the Royal Air Force personnel stationed at Eastleigh Airport.

A lot of families relied on credit till the end of the month. There was Martin's butchery, a couple of fish shops, Babu's big grocery store, Kania's shop (Kania, because he had one bad eye), Dr. Charlie Paes' surgery and Kajani's small goods store (the owner's son was a brilliant Ismaili snooker player). There were D'Costa's grocery store, the barber shop, John D'Souza's little store, Cyril's Hollywood laundry, the Sikh shops in front of the church and a whole bunch of others.

The Indians are legendary shopkeepers, and in Africa they turned that into an art form. They were also among the original stonemasons, carpenters, builders, auto mechanics and much more. The Goans were mainly tailors, accountants, clerks and worked in private business or the civil service. The Africans performed menial tasks or were housemaids, houseboys, gardeners and cooks. The Seychellois were brilliant motor mechanics. The Goans owned bars; the Indians had little shops called dukas and teahouses. They were known throughout Kenya as the *dukawallah* (little shop owner). The desperate pawned whatever little gold they had, mainly from their dowries. While we lived and grew up there some had it tough, but it did not matter. Between church, school and sport, and clubs for the elders, life was okay.

Clearly the British segregation plan flopped. Goans congregated by the local church. Much later, as other churches came into being, they migrated to the newer suburbs, of which chief among them were Nairobi West, South C and B. Some even ventured into Langata and Karen. Holy Family Cathedral in the city attracted Goans living in the Railway Quarters, Riata Road and River Road, while Parklands Church catered to folks living in Forest Road, Parklands, High Ridge and Ngara.

There was a lot of prejudice in Eastleigh, the Goans among themselves, and everyone else was prejudiced against everyone else. But Africans and other darker skinned people suffered the greatest prejudice. Nevertheless, each community survived within the confines of segregation. The bottom line was that we all went about our lives in a blissful, happy kind of way. Life was tough, but what could you do about it? Generally speaking, Eastleigh, Pangani and the other suburbs with a Goan community were happy places. The truth was that the colonial government appeared to keep law and order pretty tight, at least to Indian eyes. What's more, most suburbs were pretty clean, neat and tidy, with lots of flora and wide open roads with no traffic jams or any road rage, except when a couple of drunken whites thought they were rhinos and tried locking horns with each other.

Just a kid

In Nairobi, I attended Catholic Parochial School attached to Holy Family Church, which later became Nairobi Basilica. The school was outgrowing itself and they closed down both the primary and secondary streams.

When we moved to Eastleigh initially, I attended the primary section of St Teresa's Girls' School while the boys' school was being built, and later the boys' school for the last four years of my primary education. I loved the school: school was fun, with great teachers and great pals.

Mathare Valley stretched from the edge of a tiny suburb called Pangani chini (Lower Pangani) in the east to the edge of Ruaraka in the West, past Eastleigh. It was at this exact junction that Eastleigh ended and Ruaraka began. At this point Eastleigh Road, from Section 1, naturally forked. It was more like the road continued into the airport and a new unnamed extension headed for Ruaraka. While the airport road was bituminised with kerb and guttering, the extension was just a mud road.

My life was centred on a two-mile stretch of the valley with Mathare Mental Hospital towering on the southern ridge. The hospital consisted of several buildings with gardens whose rich, green grass sparkled clearly on the other side of the valley. We would sneak up to get a closer look at the 'mad' people in white. We were a horrible lot and we laughed loudly, jeered, poked fun at them and pretended to throw things at them. We were really very unkind. Fortunately, they took no notice of our antics and we eventually tired of them. As young *totos* (boys) we soon understood from older friends that the people we saw wandering somewhat aimlessly on those green patches were in fact mentally ill. We did not know any better in those days.

On the northern ridge stood St. Teresa's Girls' School, one of the finest complexes in the area. Eastleigh Road separated the Girls' and Boys' schools. Before the Emergency in 1954, this section of Eastleigh, the surrounding suburbs and Mathare Valley were my paradise. I also liked the African suburbs of Shauri Moyo, Starehe, Kariobangi and especially Kariokor market where you could buy some amazingly barbecued meat (*nyama choma*). To the east of the school there was a dilapidated mansion in more than 40 acres of land. The land was empty except for another abandoned house. Further east from the mansion were homes forming the start of the Upper Pangani suburb. With the exception of the hospital, the northern ridge had nothing else but virgin land. It was easy to understand that barely 40 years ago a variety of the country's wildlife roamed freely all over the area. The animals had since been restricted to Nairobi National Park. Only snakes were left as residents of a bygone era.

Children all over the world tend to have their own special secret spots, and Mathare Valley was our favourite place. A small stream at the bottom of the valley ran from east to west. There were tiny fishes in it, as well as a selection of frogs and toads and other amphibians. I met my first tadpole there. And it was there I first recorded the itchy agony of a mosquito bite. We used to play happily in that tiny stream, unaware that the snails we teased were in fact carriers of the deadly disease called bilharzia, a disease caused by parasitic worms and spread by snails. Soon teams of men from the Nairobi City Council's health department swarmed the place spraying any stagnant or running water to kill the snails. For a long while we had to give the stream a wide berth. We turned our attention then to trapping rabbits and squirrels. Those whose parents could afford an air gun took to shooting doves and partridges for supper. One of the Mauritian boys had an air gun, and he let most of the gang have a go. The gang, by way, was made of mostly Mauritian, Seychellois and Somali boys.

Sometimes, I would meet up with the Pangani chini gang who were mainly Goans or adopted Goans. Their interests were mainly fishing, camping and biking on rented bicycles. They were a great bunch. The Goan boys were scared to come into the valley; however, some of the older Goan boys would go swimming in two out-of-bounds places. It was forbidden to swim in the two disused quarries filled with water, aptly named Big Doom and Little Doom. Two Goan brothers, Romulus and Remus, had drowned there. Their parents built a house directly opposite St Teresa's Catholic Church and named it Romulus and Remus in their memory. My gang ventured to the two dooms but we did not dive in. In my case I could not, because I did not know how to swim. One time one of my Seychellois friends did strip and jump in and he only came out after we screamed in frenzy for him to get out. We spent our school holidays and whatever spare time we had idling in the valley.

By 1953, the whole valley had transformed into a wall-to-wall squatter camp of mud huts and corrugated iron sheets. This was a complete shanty town of mostly displaced Kikuyu families. A lot of those who had been evicted had been labourers from white farms or squatters in the Rift Valley and had been sent to the Kikuyus' Central Province where they were like strangers. Some of them had never been to Kikuyu country, having been born on white farms. They were then moved to Mathare Valley which had evolved into the Nairobi chapter of the Mau Mau, the toughest and most fearsome guerrilla force anywhere in Africa. The eviction of the angry and normally loyal Kikuyus drove them to join gangs or go into the forests where the Mau Mau had their strongholds. The newcomers strengthened the Nairobi chapter. A few huts started appearing as early as 1952. Soon the valley morphed into a hovel of the worst kind, with no running water, medical facilities or sewerage. The little stream was no more. In its stead was a cesspit. Thousands of people displaced by the colonial government called the shantytown home and lived peacefully. The valley had an economy all of its own. Illegally brewed local beer was plentiful, as were bicycle mechanics and a whole generation who pioneered recycled motor parts. There were barbers, charcoal makers, hut builders, thatched roof repairers, tailors, *karanis* (Swahili for clerks) who could read and write in English, and many other significant occupations. Spirals of smoke from cooking hearths wafted in the evenings, suffusing the air with aromas of meat roasting and maize meal (*ugali*) being cooked on charcoal burning stoves called *jikos*. Vegetable dishes of varying sorts were plenty including *irio* (mashed vegetable mixes), *maharagwe* (beans), *sukuma wiki* (a local spinach) and very rarely the Kikuyu equivalent to Scotland's haggis, *mutura*. My favourite were *mahindi* (corn cobs), sweet potatoes or *muhogo* (cassava) roasted over a charcoal fire.

I was in Mathare every day after school. Later, some of the African boys of my age befriended me and we would meet regularly and do the things boys of that age did. They would invite me into their mud huts and I was adopted by various parents. I used to see groups of men sitting down and talking. I asked one of my young friends what they were doing and they explained the men were the elders of the various Kikuyu clans. My life with the Mau Mau first began when a group of Kikuyu elders took kindly to me and told me their history. Historically, the elders were the leaders of each village. I spoke a lot to the father of one of my friends. It was from these elders that I understood some of the Kikuyu traditions, especially their songs and dances. I also came to learn some of the Kikuyu language.

What struck me most was that most of the elders were very serious men. I never saw any one of them smile or laugh or joke. They spoke in soft tones and gestures to the children and the women. One day I asked one of them why they were so serious. He explained with a bitter heart that the reason most of the Kikuyu were living in the valley was because the colonialists had confiscated their lands and given them to white settlers. He explained that no Kikuyu could find peace until their lands were returned to them. They were convinced that the white man would leave Kenya one day and then the Kikuyu would return to their traditional lands. Another Kikuyu told me that this would happen because their god Ngai, who lived on the snow-capped Mount Kenya, had willed it. They did not admit to being Mau Mau, but it was easy to see the fire in their eyes, and their passion. Typically, at around 5:30 pm they would ask me to go home. One of the elders, Macharia, told me it was not safe be in the valley after dark. Several months after they had come to know me better and were aware that I knew a little about the Mau Mau, one of them told me the elders were involved 'in serious men's business'. He would not explain further. Much later, after I started working, I realised that the 'serious men's business' was in fact Mau Mau oathing and induction ceremonies.

Everyone, it seemed, was a businessperson. The women maintained that they were the best at it and that they made the money that their men spent. The women, too, wore cheery natures and brilliant smiles on their faces. Whenever misery befell, it was the women who masked their deep pain with laughter and smiles, while the faces of the men wore hurt and anger. The elders spoke of the past nostalgically, when they were free, without the white man and his sanctions. Life under the State of Emergency brought fears and blinded their futures. It was here that I learnt of the Kikuyu's unshakeable faith in Jomo Kenyatta. Even as a kid I sympathized with their frustrations and felt the outrage that white domination had rendered. It was a human issue.

The name 'Mau Mau' itself as reported was never used by the Kikuyu themselves, and did not exist in their language. The urban legend is that some white journalist invented it, for what reason, I know not. The British were frightened by the oathing ceremonies so they mandated the taking of the oaths into a capital offence. As a result, over a thousand Africans were publicly hanged for alleged Mau Mau crimes.

The Mau Mau campaign resulted in a protracted guerrilla war fought mainly in Central Kenya, which included the Mount Kenya and the Aberdares forest range, the towns Nyeri, Nanyuki, Embu, Meru, Mount Kenya, the Rift Valley and the White Highlands: all choice farming lands which had been usurped by the colonialists. The Mau Mau did not target whites only. They also exterminated *askaris* (African policemen) and those in collaboration with the British, including village chiefs and others who resisted the Mau Mau. The most frightening thing about the Mau Mau was the stories of their alleged atrocities. The British tried very hard to demonise the land army (aka Mau Mau) as being a part of an international communist conspiracy. Instead they 'presented them as straight out of the heart of darkness – as gangsters who indulged in cannibalism, witchcraft, devil worship and sexual orgies and who terrorised white settlers and mutilated women and children. This deceit conveniently masked the Mau Mau's true struggle: a quest for the return of confiscated land. They were even rumoured to eat the hearts of their victims in their oathing ceremonies. The colonial administration was fully aware that the Kikuyu used oathing ceremonies to settle all sorts of disputes. The colonial administration was known to use the oathing ceremonies when settling their disputes with Kikuyu villagers.

My teachers in Mathare Valley assured me: 'We have been taking oaths, swearing to our creator god, Ngai, forever. It is nothing special. Every community swears by its God. The Christians swear by their Almighty God. Even the colonial administration has an oath for everything' was the simple explanation. Apparently the Mau Mau oathing involved drinking the blood and eating the flesh of a sacrificed goat. One of the oaths was, 'we swore we would not let white men rule us forever. We would fight them even down to our last man, so that man could live in freedom.'

The oath was taken in the name of Ngai. The Mau Mau killed all oath breakers. They were enforcing the oath but to everyone else it was murder or massacre. The demonizing of the Kikuyu oathing ceremonies was simply a propaganda ploy. Virtually every rebellion or revolution in history required every single member to take an oath to kill the enemy or traitors from within.

One of the first British conscientious objectors against the colonial warfare, commenting on the compensations the British government made to Kenya's victims, stated confidentially: 'With these expressions of "regret" by our foreign secretary, I now feel vindicated for being pilloried as a "conchie" (conscientious objector). Young soldiers were brainwashed into believing they were fighting in Kenya for their glorious empire. In reality we protected land-grabbing British farmers and enriched UK companies. Senior officers offered prize money for every death. I was told to shoot down unarmed women in the forests because they were carrying food to the so-called Mau Mau – a word they never called themselves. Very few white people were killed by Africans'.

In the valley there were many Africans who spoke brilliant English. One of the men could quote Shakespeare by heart. Another taught me bits of philosophy; yet another gave me insights into pre-colonial history. Though many of the shantytown dwellers were well educated, the government restricted them to menial labour.

I must confess, despite the injustices against the Africans, many Goans thought well of the British. Goans must be the only race of its kind to have loved its colonial oppressors and thought them close to God. Unlike other South Asians, Goans had made no substantial bid (country-wide) for freedom from Goa's colonial masters, the Portuguese, in the twentieth century. There was a group of freedom fighters in Goa who did their best. In colonial Kenya, for everyone else but the African, life was orderly and safe. As a child I did not actually experience any of the colonial yoke, nor did most South Asians. Most Goans and other South Asians went about their lives as if they lived in some kind of paradise, seemingly oblivious, unable or unwilling to react to all the death and destruction around them.

Yet the colonial prejudice preyed on all non-Europeans. Most South Asians were slightly favoured above the Africans, and were loyal subjects who considered themselves more civilised than most Africans. South Asians - Catholic Goans, Ismailis, Sikhs, Punjabi Sikhs, Hindus and others - kept to themselves except in sport. The Goans lived a lifestyle somewhat mimicking the Europeans, drinking, wining and dining. All the social events came alive in their three main clubs: The Goan Institute, Goan Gymkhana and the Railway Goan Institute, as well as in the low-caste and low class Tailors Society Club. There were similar clubs in Mombasa, Kisumu, Nakuru, Tanga, Dar es Salaam, Entebbe, and Kampala: almost everywhere in East Africa there was a small Goan community. And they had one other thing in common with the European: they were Christian and deeply religious. Goans did not consider themselves politically or culturally Indian, but rather as Portuguese citizens.

If the Goans were the British favourites, Pakistanis, Ismailis and other non-Anglo Saxons quietly went about amassing fortunes over the next few decades. Assimilation within the South Asian community was not openly allowed. Consorting with someone outside the community often resulted in death or being shipped off. Sikhs and Muslims were said to enforce this with menacing and fatal brutality. Marriage with an African was not even an idea. It was the one truly impossible act in Kenya. Africans were dismissed as being on a par with the magnificent wildlife. A small handful of South Asians joined the fight for freedom even though the British gave Asians six seats in the Legislative Assembly many years before an African entered the hallowed halls of government.

You did not see many Asians in Mathare Valley. One afternoon, just before 1pm, the whole valley was overrun by hundreds of British soldiers who rounded up every male in the valley. Unfortunately I was too, as young as I was. Mothers screamed in terror and shots rang out all around us. After I was rounded up we were marched up the valley and were made to sit with our hands on our heads on Eastleigh Road, stretching for several kilometres, four deep. I tried to explain to a soldier in English that I was not an African. All I got was a huge kick that doubled me up. Before the trucks arrived, a Kikuyu elder who knew me spoke to an African policeman and explained that I was an Asian. I was numb and I just could not think, except for one thought: 'I wish I was big enough to kick that bastard back.' We boarded the trucks and headed for detention. I was officially, at twelve years old, a detainee, suspected of Mau Mau activities.

My head was hurting from the kick and invisible, kind hands were soothing my head and drying my tears. 'Don't worry,' I was assured by my fellow detainees, 'we will defend you as much as we can'. After travelling a few kilometres the truck stopped, and I was dropped off at a police station. I sat alone in a cell until my father picked me up just after 6pm and we walked back home in silence. My father and I did not speak at all about the incident but my mother almost killed me without raising her hand. Her words and that look of steel were deadly.

Over the next few months, you would see Africans hung by the neck from the honeysuckle trees that lined the northern boundary of our school. I never returned to my beloved valley again. Set against my own miserable life, it was easy to empathise, and even be at one with their suffering. I was traumatised and scared shitless. I mourned the rape of Mathare Valley. That British soldier's military-issue boot haunted my nights for a long time. I lost my teachers, my friends, the smiles, the laughter, the tribal elders and the magic of seeing the shanty town survive against huge odds. The raids continued sporadically over the next few years but the valley never lost its numbers: for every thousand people detained, another thousand moved in.

The Catholic Church built by Goans in Eastleigh: St Teresa's
Photo courtesy of Nizar Hassanali, ex St Teresa's Boys' Secondary School

CHAPTER 4

ST TERESA'S

Losing my connection with the African community forced me to focus on school. I enjoyed English, history and maths. I was a bookaholic, reading on average between two and three books a day. Reading was probably the best thing I ever did. I thought highly of my headmaster, Father Patrick Hannan. He had an Irish twinkle in his eyes and a sense of humour. He could be harsh too, almost cruel. Yet, he was a dedicated educator. The secondary school began with four classrooms; by the time he retired the school was several buildings and facilities larger.

A friend and I once wrote a play consisting of one word:

"Rumours"

Did you know that Fr Hannan nearly tripped and fell as he came through the school gates?

What happened?

Thirty impromptu rumours by various classmates later, it ended up with Fr Hannan falling from the equivalent of the Empire State building and miraculously escaping without a scratch. Hannan sat with the teachers in the front row and laughed his head off.

My close pals nicknamed me Skip. The school had shown an American movie starring a boy called Skip. At the end of the movie the name Skip stuck. My best pal Vincent and I got into all sorts of mischief. One year we hooked off from school every Wednesday afternoon to watch Flash Gordon at the movies. We saw every single episode. We were also regulars at Kontiki, a banned Rock n Roll joint. We even got caught once. If there was any mischief about, Vincent, Gaby and I were usually in the middle of it all.

My streetwise savvy came from the many Africans, Somalis, Muslims, Punjabi Sikhs, Gujaratis and Ismailis I knew, but mostly from the Seychellois and the Mauritians. After leaving school, I spent all of my time with these Francophone friends, even learning to speak pretty good creole, and I developed a fierce reputation for head-butting. Personally I liked the girls; they were a lot more fun. I was a favourite with their mums and dads. I think it was the creole that charmed them. I started my first band, 'The Wheelers', with Steve Rodrigues, Godfrey Agricole, Vernay and Lewis Arissol, David Lobo, Benjamin Lopez, Robert Cecile and Maurice 'Kanada' D'Silva. Brian Fernandez, who resembled Elvis and was a great dancer, sang with the band occasionally. I took to being an MC like a duck to water and later produced two of the biggest variety shows in Nairobi: one at Nairobi City Hall with a cast of more than 100 people; the other at the Railway Goan Institute with just as many participants. My true education came outside of school and from the hundreds books I read so fervently. My friends called me the Walking Dictionary. In diction I learnt to give due emphasis to the letters R and L, so my accent was slightly different. Many years later, a newspaper colleague reviewing a music show I was presenting on local television called my accent a 'fraudulent American accent from no American state'.

The radio brought music and lots of stories, but very little politics. The British Forces Radio used a lot of stuff from the BBC; Sports Round-Up at 9:45 pm was a favourite program. Keith Skues from British Forces radio was a great inspiration. School was a breeze. I rarely did any prepping, but I wanted to impress Fr Hannan and I was doing a lousy job of it… that is, until the first term of 1956.

Funds that had been raised from regular evenings of whist and raffles helped expand the building programme. The Whist Drive was a big event that required a large team - some 20-30 school kids - to set it all up and later put away all the chairs and tables. This time Fr Hannan put me in charge of the team. Everything had gone smoothly and, elated, we began the task of dismantling and putting everything away, looking forward to a barbecue around the huge bonfire. We had brought our sleeping bags and would spend the night on the floor of one of the classrooms. As we were packing up, one of my classmates brought a cupful of liquid to my mouth and said with a broad smile, 'taste this'. It was sweet red wine. I recognised it and asked where he had found it. He showed me a huge, huge, bottle. I snapped at him and said: 'Don't touch another drop or I will kill you.'

I did not know that half the class was already pretty merry. As we sat around the bonfire joking and laughing, Fr Hannan and a visiting priest came round to say well done and good night. I swear I must have pissed in my pants from the sheer guilt that was choking me. I prayed and prayed that the priests would not notice that some of the kids were not quite themselves, laughing and stumbling about, some unable to get up. Fr Hannan did not notice anything unusual and must have thought the kids were frolicking after a successful night. They fell asleep pretty quickly, and pretty quickly woke up with their first hangovers, and were sick for most of the next day. Fortunately it was a Saturday and the beginning of the Easter school holidays.

The great thing about holidays was fishing and books, lots and lots of both. On one of these fishing trips - to a dam in Ruaraka, about 10km from Eastleigh - I walked across Mathare Valley to Muthaiga and followed the road to Ruaraka. I had caught seven or eight bass and was readying to return home when a white guy - loaded down with two or three fishing baskets, umbrella, fishing net, and chair and dressed in full khaki, including an oval khaki helmet - trudged his way to the bank and began setting up. He looked like a one-man trawling ship with all that equipment. I watched him fish without success for 30 minutes or so, getting more and more impatient by the minute. I used to tie my own flies and I took one and told him in English to try this.

He shooed me away in Swahili. *'Kwenda, kwenda'* (go away!)

I tried again slowly, almost one syllable at a time: 'I speak English', I told him. 'Try this fly. I have already caught seven or eight.' I showed him my catch.

'Oh, wow. OK.' He tried five or six casts, but caught nothing.

'Drop the fly into that little waterfall and let the current take the fly into the reeds, and tighten your line slowly,' I said.

Within a few moments mayhem erupted. His rod doubled up and in frenzy he started screaming 'Get the net! Get the bloody net!' like a mad man.

I told him to calm down. He did not need the net. He could easily land the fish on the little sandy beach a few feet away. 'Let the rod do the work,' I told him. 'Work the fish, don't fight it. You will land it.'

When he landed it he looked inebriated with sheer ecstasy. It was the biggest bass I had ever seen. As he bent to unhook the fish, he asked me to take out what was in his left breast pocket. I did. It was the biggest roll of cash I had ever seen, thousands of shillings, more money than I had ever seen in my whole life. 'Take it, it's yours,' he said, his eyes still glistening.

'No I don't want your money, the fly only cost me a few cents,' I told him.

'Take whatever you want,' he insisted. So I took 10 of the 100-shilling notes, a fortune. I doubt if my father had earned that kind of money in a month.

'This is the greatest fish I have ever caught. Thank you. Can I keep the fly, please?' he asked.

'Sure.' Then he gave me his card: J. J. Williams, Chief Accountant, National and Grindlays Bank, Nairobi.

'If you ever need any help, of any kind, come and see me,' he told me.

With that we both set off for home. I do not recall whose euphoria was the greater but I know my mum was the happiest person on earth that day, after I had reassured her that I had not stolen the cash.

Back to school

I was happy to be back in school after the holidays. I had scored a First Grade in the Kenya Asian Preliminary Examination in January that year and was still privately basking in that glory. Just after 9 am the teacher told me to go to Fr Hannan's office. I went expecting some sort of congratulations.

Instead: 'Sit!' he barked. 'I trusted you and you robbed me of my altar wine.'

To say that I was shocked is an understatement, but I was not going to take that lying down. 'Father, to rob you I would have needed to use some force or cause personal discomfort in taking the wine from you. And I did not steal your wine either,' I told him, still shaking in my boots and my knees knocking. I was not far from pissing in my pants.

The fire in his eyes burned hotter than the Saharan sun and he fired back: 'Who are you to argue with a man whose knowledge of English is like an ocean compared to yours which is less than a drop? You took the wine.'

'I did not,' I stood my ground.

'You are a liar,' he shot back.

'I am not,' I said somewhat feebly, my strength seeming to drain out of me.

He pointed to the sofa that had been in his office for what seemed like centuries and had been the curse of every boy who had ever been asked to bend over. 'And drop your pants,' he commanded.

I told him: 'I will not. My father never dropped my pants and I am certainly not going to do it for you.'

With that he began chasing me around the sofa, his reddening eyes spotlighting his complete loss of control and his fury. His whip-like bamboo cane did not touch me, but the sofa looked like a heavyweight after going 12 rounds with Muhammad Ali. He was not bad looking but his reddening eyes made him resemble one of those lovesick vampires in a ghoulish cinema plot.

'Go back to class,' he ordered after catching his breath.

I went back with my usual cheery smile. Everyone was normal except the teacher, who looked truly perplexed. Soon it was recess and I received another message to see Fr Hannan. I went into his office. Sitting there was my mother, tears running down her cheeks, her skinny fingers clutching at her rosary beads. We lived less than five minutes from the school.

He was waving his bamboo cane again and virtually screamed, 'Now drop your pants, I have explained to your mother what you have done.'

I shouted back with the tears gushing down and my nose running, 'No. I am not going to let you hit me for something I am not guilty of.'

'Yes you are. Yes you are. By God you are!' he said ferociously.

With that we started another game of round the sofa. Ten or 12 rounds later, my mother intervened. The sofa had lots of stuffing sticking out in various places where the cane had struck.

Fr Hannan flopped into his chair, in rage. My mother's face was wet with tears, still clutching her rosary beads. Her lips trembled in prayer.

'What am I going to do with you?' he asked.

'You are going to do nothing with me. I quit,' I said, somewhat calmly.

'No you don't. Over my dead body you will,' he said, somewhat resignedly. There was virtually no conviction in those words. With that he got up and tried to slap me. I put up my fists and looked for an opening for a head butt.

My mother intervened. She told him in Swahili and broken English, 'You won't stop him, Father. If he has made up his mind to leave, he will leave. If he says he did not steal your wine, he did not steal your wine. You must believe him.'

A little more calmly, Fr Hannan asked, 'So you want to leave school? What are you going to do to earn a living? Become a beggar? Continue to live off charity? Beg, borrow and steal? You are 13, what kind of a job could you get? You are not only a robber; you are also a complete idiot. Now go back to class.'

'No. I am going home and I am never coming back,' I sobbed. I felt utterly betrayed and let down.

'OK,' he said. 'I will make you a deal. If you can get a decent job within seven days you can leave school permanently. If not, come back and all this will be forgotten.'

The next day, just before the start of school, I was at the southern gate, dressed in a brown double-breasted suit, the only one I owned. I felt like the original matchstick man, all bone but very tall for my 13 years. Lighting the single cigarette I had bought from Kajani's shop with the only matchstick I had, I puffed arrogantly as I headed towards the church, and just as I turned toward the bus stop I caught Fr Hannan's glance. We both nodded, more out of habit.

That was the last time I went to St Teresa's, the school or the church. I lost school, and all contact with my school-friends until 50 years later, and I was convinced God had deserted me that day. More than 50 years later one of my school buddies, an altar boy, told me, 'the wine, it was me.' And we laughed till our guts hurt.

Chapter 5

My first job

With freedom from school, I knew what to do. I caught the No. 44 bus and headed for the city centre via Pangani Chini. At the National and Grindlays Bank I had to do a lot of fast-talking before I was allowed to see Mr. Williams, my fishing buddy. When I got to his office his secretary condescendingly told me that the 'office boys entrance was at the back of the bank'.

'Madam, I am not an office boy, I am here to see Mr. Williams,' I told her quite politely.

'Do you have an appointment?' she asked, quite angrily.

'No. He said I could drop in any time,' I said, keeping my fingers crossed.

'You cannot see him without an appointment. He is much too important a person to see you…' Before she could finish her sentence, I had already opened the door with her in hot pursuit.

'He just barged in. I am sorry. I will get the office *askaris*,' she pleaded with Mr. Williams.

'No, no. I know Mr. Fernandes. I will see him,' Williams told her. He motioned me to the chair in front of his desk.

'How are you Mr. Fisherman, thank you for seeing me on such short notice,' I said somewhat cheerily but I was actually nervous as hell.

'How's the fishing? What can I do for you?' he asked, somewhat informally, putting me at ease.

'I am at the lowest point in my young life. I am desperate beyond words and I have come to you because you are my last resort,' I told him.

'What do you need, money? Are you in any kind of trouble?' he asked, seemingly very concerned.

'I need a job to save my life,' I begged.

'That's easy. How old are you?' Hearing his words my face lit up.

'Twenty-two,' I lied.

He got up from his chair and said, 'Follow me.'

He led me to an amazing large room filled with 35 white girls all busy typing away at their accounts register business machines. The closest I had come to a white person were the priests and nuns at school and, of course, those British soldiers. Working in a room full of beautiful white girls seemed a very unnerving prospect. The arrogant part of me thought, what the heck, they are only people, even if they are white.

He introduced me to the head of the department, a medium-sized, matronly red haired woman called June. He told June, 'This is Cyprian Fernandes your new recruit.' Turning back to me he said, 'Good luck. Here you can take your first steps to a brilliant career in banking.'

Nobby Rodrigues, a fellow churchgoer, would give me a lift to and from work on his Vespa scooter. He lived a minute or two from our place in Eastleigh.

I spent a blissfully happy nine months at the bank, rising quickly to be June's assistant. There was no socializing; we kept our distance in that department. Then disaster hit. I allowed the girls to go home early one trial balance day provided they all finished their work. They had pleaded with me so that they could see the final performance of a show.

At first glance the trial balance looked OK, but when we looked in detail there were a million shillings missing. June and I checked and rechecked and in the end we were forced to call Mr. Williams. While he was checking our work, I walked around the room flicking the files on the desks and there were the little blighters, a million shillings worth of cheques that had not been debited to the relevant accounts. The girl responsible had created a kind of mirrored suspense account that fooled us. She put the cheques into her secret place. She planned to deal with them first thing the next morning.

The next morning, I was in Mr. Williams' office. 'Well, Mr. Fisherman, it would seem the figures that are going on in your head are not the type that would suit the bank. You can hang around until you find a new job. Sorry, it has to be that way,' he said somewhat regretfully.

I went back to my desk and telephoned a family friend and a fellow Goan, Oscar D'Mello, Kenya's then star soccer goalkeeper, who worked for Oxo, a canned food wholesaler. Oscar was a family friend and a special kind of guy. Oscar called me back later that day and said I had a job as a stock clerk in the warehouse in Nairobi's Industrial Estate. So there I was, seated at my desk in this vast warehouse of canned foods. Lunch was on the house: we just opened any can and noted it in the stock book. After four months, I treated myself to a beautiful, Italian-made, creamy white sports jacket with spots of black. It was stunning and looked almost like a dinner jacket. I paid for it from the little savings I had been putting away.

The next month I was out of the place. The reason for my dismissal, apparently, was that the guys were jealous of my white jacket. I finished at Oxo on a Friday and I started at the Kenya Probation and Remand Home Service as a clerk on Monday. Within a few months I had my own office and the lofty title of Colony Statistical Officer. My tasks were to produce the annual reports and to keep a monthly review of each probation officer. The probation officers came from all over Kenya. Some were young, some not so young, some were closing in on their 60s and there I was at 14 years old demanding they 'explain this continued trend of absconders' and asking 'what do you propose to do to arrest the situation?' Soon things improved and the job became routine.

I also filled in as a juvenile probation officer. My first day in court was a classic. In the dock was an exile, snot running down his lips and chin. He was 12 years old but looked more like eight and scared out of his shredded pants. He was nabbed for repeatedly stealing candy from the local Woolworths. He was a street kid like so many thousand others in Nairobi.

The magistrate, Mrs. Riceborough, was almost five feet square, with no neck, a mop of greying hair and a voice that was straight out of some London drama school.

The Police Prosecutor began, 'Your Honour, the boy has admitted to the offence and as you can see he is in a pretty poor state. I recommend probation.'

'I agree entirely' Mrs. Riceborough said. 'Why is there never a probation officer on hand when we need one?'

I put up a finger and slowly got up and said, 'If it pleases Your Honour ...'

Mrs. Riceborough boomed, 'What is it, are you related to the accused?'

'No your Honour, I am the probation officer,' I replied rather sheepishly.

'My God! They do breed them young these days, don't they? Report back in two weeks.'

I said, 'Your Honour, might I humbly suggest a remand home or an orphanage since the accused is homeless and a street kid?'

Mrs. Riceborough said, 'Mind your lip young man; I will do the suggesting around here. You just do what I ask of you. Yes, liaise with the Police and find a suitable shelter.'

'Thank you your Honour, Madam,' I said.

'By the way, how old are you?' she asked.

'Twenty two,' I lied again.

'You don't look much older than the thief. Oh, well.'

Mrs. Riceborough became a real friend and taught me as much as she could about everything that went on in the Kenyan court system. That gave me a head start when I became a court reporter. She was brilliant.

It was also during this phase that I regularly met some of Kenya's greatest legal minds, among them Madan Lal and A. R. Kapila.

For the rest of my life living on the edge was the only way for me. I was addicted to living by my wits and by the seat of my pants.

CHAPTER 6

AN INSTANT JOURNO!

During one of Fr Hannan's absences, a relief headmaster had been impressed with my essays and compositions. He asked if I wanted to be a writer when I grew up. I said I wanted to be a criminal lawyer. He gave me a copy of the *London Times* and the *Sydney Morning Herald*. 'See what you think of that,' he had said. 'That's newspaper reporting, journalism' he added. I was fascinated with the quaint rigidity of the *Times* but felt a lot happier with the *SMH*. The *Times* sounded many centuries old, while the *SMH*, although rough around the edges, seemed more alive. From that moment, the thought of becoming a journalist would stay with me until I achieved it.

As the Colony Statistical Officer, bored with my job, I had gone on a walkabout for a week without reporting in. When I reported back, the sombre, almost statue-like Principal Immigration Officer simply shook his head and held out his hand to say goodbye. Suddenly living on the edge or by my wits seemed a load of crap at such an early age. I was not that disappointed with losing the job. I had been telling myself for months that I was only acting the part. I was neither old enough nor experienced to put those probation officers on the carpet.

Being jobless was the hardest time for me. My younger brother had to quit school and find a job to care for the family. He never forgave me. For the next four or five months I bludged and lived off my friends and their folks, until a wonderful day in 1960 in the snooker parlour at the Queens Hotel.

The snooker parlour remained a regular haunt for a long time. Besides the snooker, they served the best rare roast beef sandwiches, the crispest chips and Heinz tomato sauce, the expensive brand.

I was sitting with Julio Menezes who was at university, and he asked me what the heck I was going to do with my life. 'What do you really want to do?'

I wanted to become a criminal lawyer, I told him.

'You won't be able to do that without a High School Certificate and years at university, besides you can't afford it,' he said.

I shot back, 'Well, the next best thing would be journalism.'

He said, firmly, 'Get off your butt and go and become a journalist. Do it today.'

The Aga Khan Media Group owned the *Daily Nation* and *Sunday Nation*. Both were in their infancy in 1960. The *East African Standard* was supposedly the best newspaper in Africa but they did not employ African or Asian reporters. It had to be the *Nation*. That afternoon I went into the typesetting and compositing room of the *Nation* in Victoria Street. I asked to see the editor and was pointed to the works manager, Stan Denman. A former British Royal Commando, he was a tough and imposing guy.

'What do you want?' he asked.

I told him, 'I need a job in journalism.'

He asked what my age was and I told him, '22'. I was 16, skinny and tall.

'Come with me,' he said, and I followed him into what turned out to be the paste up room. The *Nation* was the first newspaper in Africa to use computer-generated copy. This proofread final computer print came in long strips and had to be trimmed perfectly to fit the page designed by the sub-editor. The composed page was proofread and finally approved to be photographed. The negative produced an aluminium plate that fitted onto a drum of the litho-offset printer. One drum, one page. Computer generated printers were more expensive, though faster, and the *Nation* also used linotype originated lead type and the pages were composed in the traditional fashion.

'Do you think you could do that?' he asked, pointing to the composition of the computer type.

The first thing that flashed through my mind was: this is not the kind of journalism I am thinking about. I told him, 'No thanks. I didn't come here to paste up little bits of paper. I want to be a journalist.' Perhaps a simple 'no' might have done the trick. He kicked me out of the place. As I licked my wounds it struck me that I could have been a lot more diplomatic. Never mind. There is always Plan B. The next morning I awoke and went to church to find God again. I think I found Him, because I cannot think of any other reason for what followed. I went back to the *Nation*. Only this time I went to the Editorial department where Marina - an angry looking-receptionist with her eyebrows seemingly permanently arched - interrogated me.

'What do you want?' she asked.

'I would like to see the editor, Mr. John Bierman,' I told her, somewhat meekly.

'You can't. Go away,' she insisted, almost like swatting a pesky fly. Political correctness had not been invented.

'But I have to see him,' I pleaded.

'In what other language can I tell you? You cannot see him; he is a very busy man. At best leave him a note.' She was getting a bit tired with me, I could tell.

'Mr. Bierman wants to see me,' I persisted.

'Are you sure of that?' she asked with those raised eyebrows.

'Yes,' I said somewhat meekly, but grinning broadly.

'Speak to his secretary,' she ordered.

The secretary, a gorgeous red head with whom I fell head over heels in love instantly, sat in a little cubicle just behind the reception desk. 'Yes, what can I do for you?' she asked, those pretty red lips moving elegantly.

'I have an appointment with the editor,' I told her quite confidently.

'Which editor?' she mused.

'John Bierman,' I beamed back.

'No, you don't have an appointment.'

'Yes I do. I spoke to him yesterday.'

'I make all the appointments,' she said. 'No one else makes them, not even he. There is no appointment.'

'Yes there is, I spoke to him.'

'No you didn't. No one speaks to him without first talking to me.'

'You must have been away from your desk.'

'"You have an appointment, do you? You are sure of that? What time is your appointment?'

'10 am,' I replied.

'It is 9:45, you are too early.'

'I always come at least 10 minutes early for an appointment.'

She was smiling a little now and said, 'Well, Mr. Bierman is right behind you.' I turned around and there was a guy with movie star looks, his hands hanging on to part of the metal frame above the doorway. And he was smiling.

'Cyprian Fernandes, Mr. Bierman.' I stuck out my hand.

'Ten minutes early, I like that,' he said, a full moon smile pasted on his face.

'Thanks for seeing me,' I said.

'So you spoke to me yesterday and I agreed to see you today? I must be suffering from amnesia because I cannot recall talking to you yesterday or ever,' he said quite firmly but the smile was still there.

'I lied,' I confessed.

'What, you little bleeding blighter ...' he said, pretending to be very angry.

'Well, I am getting my interview, aren't I?' I said rather cheekily, smiling back at him.

'So what can I do for you? By the way, how old are you?' he asked.

'Twenty-two.' That lie again.

'Education?' he queried.

'High School Certificate,' I said. Another lie.

'What would you like to do in journalism?' There was the question I had been praying for.

My 18 point by-line flashed in front of me: by Cyprian Fernandes. I blurted out, 'court reporter, municipal reporter, social reporter, political reporter, general news reporter,' and a myriad of other titles.

'Got nothing like that,' he said.

'What have you got?' I asked with terror in my eyes, the golden opportunity seemingly disappearing, when he said, 'a sports reporter, maybe.'

'I will take it,' I said, even before he had finished talking.

'Hang on, hang on, not so fast. Come with me.' He led me over and introduced me to Sports Editor Tom Clarke, one of the most wonderful guys I have ever met. 'Tom, this is Cyprian Fernandes, your new sports junior or the biggest conman I have ever met,' he said with that smile even larger now.

I had played a little soccer as a child, a goalkeeper in full black from head to toe, copying the great Russian goalkeeper Lev Yashin. I knew very little of the other sports. Tom went through the introductory ropes of how the Sports Department functioned. He was the boss and I was his only reporter. Freelance contributors provided some copy; the rest came from news agencies. He gave me a sheet of wire stories and said, 'rewrite one of these and make it bright and interesting, use a little fiction if you need to, just this once.'

I wrote something like this:

'United's babes boot Spurs out of the park

A bunch of kids, some not old enough to be out of school, ran circles around the older professionals of Tottenham Hotspur in the English League yesterday. Manchester United's Busby's babes, led by the genius of Bobby Charlton, the only survivor of the 1958 Munich air crash that killed eight United players, won 3-nil. It could have been 10 or 12.'

Tom had a quick look and took it to John Bierman, who was standing a few feet away and they both cracked up in hysterics. Tom came back and asked how good I was on cricket.

Know the game, know the rules, can report, I answered.

'OK. Tomorrow there is the annual Asians v Europeans match at the Nairobi Club. I want you to cover it and write a trial report. Take the rest of the day off and prepare for tomorrow. By the way, you are hired,' he said with a broad grin on his face. We shook hands, but that was not the only thing shaking: so was the rest of my body. 'Thanks a million,' I said in a quiet voice. 'I won't let you down.'

'Don't worry, I will look after you,' he promised.

As I passed Marina, I said, 'I got the job.'

'Good for you,' she said, with a smile I have never forgotten and from that moment we became friends for life.

I ran outside and jumped for the sky. Yes!

But, cricket! The only cricket I knew, having never played, was listening to Test cricket on British Forces radio, BBC's Sports Round-Up, or commentary on my tiny crystal set. I never missed a Test, especially the Ashes. I went to the nearest bookshop and asked for a comprehensive book on cricket. There was only one, a fairly thin one but it was just what I needed.

It contained the MCC (Marylebone Cricket Club) Rules of Cricket. The MCC was the supreme authority on the game. It also contained an outline of the various fielding positions, which I drew on the first page of my notebook and to which I was to refer again and again with each shot and until I had learnt it all by heart. It explained taking guard (lining up with the three stumps at the other end of the pitch), 1, 2 and off stump, with a short commentary on the different guards; the art of batting, including cutting, driving, square, through the covers, and the various fielding positions; fast and medium pace bowling; and spin bowling. One of the rules was a lengthy piece on no-balls.

As I was to learn in later years, the booklet provided only the basics and was really meant for cricket ignoramuses like me. For the moment, I thought that was enough. Cricket in Kenya was played on jute matting, as opposed to turf wickets which were mowed down to almost dirt. What else could I need to know?

Next I called the Kenya Cricket Association. I eventually got the names of the two teams and the respective captains. The match was due to start at 10 am; I got there at 9 am. I was the only one there; as other folks arrived I introduced myself and gleaned their thoughts on the games and various players. At 9:30 I got into the dressing rooms and spoke to the individual captains, asking: how is it looking for your team? What is the batting like? Who are your main stays? What is your attack like, pace and spin, and who are you looking to for the breakthroughs? What would be a good score? Which batsmen are you looking to get out quickly? If I was writing a preview, I thought, I had enough for a half decent story.

It was a fine day and the weather would not have any effect on the game. There was no such thing as a press box. You just sat where you thought was most comfortable, especially from the sun. I did not know if there were other journalists there. I met a couple of guys at lunch but they did not identify themselves as journalists or contributors. I was fortunate enough to sit with a couple of die-hard former cricketers and gleaned much for my notes. At the end of the match I copied the scores and interviewed the two captains. I went back to the office, said a prayer, and typed my story on a typewriter chained to the desk. Before the chaining, typewriters had ghosted away regularly.

When I handed Tom my story, he asked me to hang around. A few minutes later he showed me some of the sub-editing changes he had made. 'Be back at 9 am from now on,' he said. 'By the way you are no longer a junior, you are a senior sports reporter.' Thus began a journey that would take me to the four corners of the world, allow me to meet presidents and prime ministers, cabinet ministers, dance with a princess and become a household name in print, radio and television.

Reporting soccer came easily. Writing came fairly easily as did asking the tough or awkward questions. In my reports I was complimentary as much as I was critical and was never afraid to question the form of a player or why he should not be dropped. I was also never afraid of challenging the establishment or seeking out fraud, or indiscretions like nepotism or tribalism. I always made sure I knew the answers to the questions I was asking, making further investigation more fluent. I was never put off by the proverbial 'no comment'. I got to the bottom of the story after digging and digging, one source after another.

I got caught out once on the radio when I had accused the Football Association of misuse of funds after they had shown a strange loss. Reg Alexander, who was affiliated to the association, asked me, 'have you got any proof?'

'I have an eyewitness who has seen the evidence. Let me have the books and I will have them independently audited,' I said.

I had been told by 'my sources' that not all the gate-money taken at the matches was ending up in the Football Association's coffers. The problem had persisted for several decades. Reg was dismissive. I never got caught out like that again. I had not based my allegations on the fact that corruption was institutionalized. Most people in high positions or power had their hands in something or other. Consequently, the association canned my press facilities. Undaunted, as a paying customer I reported on the match from the grandstand. A few months later, the ban was inexplicably lifted.

I had never played hockey and remain indebted to international hockey umpire Oscar D'Souza for tutoring me in the rules of the game. I am also grateful to international Hilary Fernandes for teaching me the finer points of the game. I refined my knowledge by picking the brains of various international players and coaches. I was lucky enough to ask the right questions most of the time. But it was an unforgettable time. The 1960s were the heyday of the classic hockey stick work game, unlike today's long-passing, boring power-hitting game. Today, those deft dribbling skills continue to impress in the women's game (2010). Argentina's Luciana Ashmar and the Netherland's Van As are brilliant exponents. India and Pakistan dominated the game then and Kenya usually gave them a good run for their money. Among the Kenyan players I will remember most are: Alu Mendonca (the best Goan player), Hilary Fernandes, Silu Fernandes,

Edgar Fernandes, Egbert Fernandes, Avtar Singh, Surjeet Junior, Franklin Pereira, Anthony Vaz, Reynolds D'Souza, Dunstan Rodrigues, Leo Fernandes, Pritam Singh and Cajie Fernandes (with Alu arguably the greatest). Bringing my soccer style of reporting to hockey was unheard of before, but I soon earned respect from the players and from my editor Brian Marsden, who rewarded me with a weekly column on the subject. I didn't make too many friends in the management of the sport, which was dominated by Sikhs. Nevertheless, I fought for and won selection for players who were not on the selectors' radar.

Soccer, hockey, athletics, cricket and tennis gave me great pleasure, but I also reported on rugby until Michael Wright took over, and golf or any other sport on a slow day. Sports also gave me instant access to several ministers, many of whom I had already known before, and going to the top on any issue was not a big deal. For example Seraphino Antao, a Commonwealth Games double gold medallist, was Kenya's greatest athlete before Kenyan African athletes dominated the world. On one occasion, weeks before the then Commonwealth Games, the athletics chiefs had denied him the services of his regular coach, Ray Batchelor. I spoke to the relevant Minister and the problem was resolved in a couple of minutes, with the Minister making the funds available immediately.

Life as a young sports reporter was one of perpetual learning. My addiction to reading several books a day had come in handy. I had contacts who regularly tipped me off. One blemish was that in December 1963, the Ghana All Stars wrecked Kenya's Uhuru soccer celebrations. The All Stars were 6 or 7 to Kenya's nil at half time. Jomo Kenyatta left in disgust at half. I was stunned. Every Kenyan was stunned. Back at the office I froze at my typewriter. Thankfully sports editor Brian Marsden helped me save the day as he wriggled the story out of my shell-shocked brain.

CHAPTER 7

THE NATION

The news and nothing but the news

I moved to the General News department. The transition was smooth. I brought Norman Da Costa from the lowly *Sunday Post* and later Polycarp Fernandes joined the Sports Department. Michael Wright had joined the sports department many months before. As the new boy, I had to cover the bottom of the diary (the jobs for the day) stories, which often did not make the paper. I covered the Rotary and Lions Club lunches, openings, launches, minor motor accidents, chased fire engines and sometimes wrote the horoscopes. I made a brief attempt at writing about youth, music and the nightclub scene. Work started around 8 in the morning and I rarely went to bed before 3 or 4 the next morning.

The first real story I covered was the murder of an Ismaili family in Nairobi West. I heard it on the radio and headed for the scene of the crime. As I entered the home and saw the corpses, I was emotionally smashed. It was like a scene from the horror movies screened today. The parents and two children were dead. To this day, I don't think the killer or killers have ever been caught. After that story, my situation improved considerably. The late Brian Tetley was an alcoholic but a wonderful and very humorous writer. He birthed the 'Mambo' column and all its hilarity: it was an instant success. When he left, I inherited the column but I doubt I ever matched Brian's brilliance. His interview with British comic genius Spike Milligan, published in the *London Guardian*, remains the best I have read anywhere. Spike spoke with the speed of lightning, a joke, a funny line, and hilarity every nanosecond. It was impossible to have a serious interview with him, but Brian Tetley managed.

Some other folks who changed my life were Michael Parry, a proof-reader with the *Nation*. Another self-taught journalist, Mike went on to adorn journalism in his own, very special way. He was also good with the camera. He and I were appointed to lead the court reporting team at the same time. Thus began many years of intense rivalry. We also headed the teams that covered the annual gruelling East African Safari, which attracted many international drivers. Kul Bhushan was another outstanding member of the *Nation* team.

My best pal at the *Nation* then was Philip Ochieng. I admired his intellect and his speed in finishing *The Times* and *Daily Mail* crosswords. Philip remains a respected author and political analyst. Later, the ever smiling and funny Joe Kadhi and I always met for a beer at the nearby Sans Chique. Not far behind was the handsome Adrian Grimwood, who has had an eternal affair with Kenya's coast, especially Mombasa, Malindi and Lamu, and who continues to edit *Coastweek*. He is a walking, talking encyclopaedia of everything coastal Kenyan. Adrian is one of life's gifts: a great journalist, he is generous, very funny and a pleasure to have a beer with. I met him after 40 years and he had not changed a bit, just clocked up the years.

The best journalist at that time was without a doubt Hilary Ng'weno. In today's parlance he was a cool dude; in journalistic terms a clean skin. He was the man for Kenya's tomorrow, not tied down by the rampant tribalism or the rampant corruption. Hilary has gone on to carve out a career that has him at the pinnacle of African and international journalism. He was appointed Editor-in-Chief of the Nation Group in 1964 but left a few months later. Hilary would not tolerate crap from anyone, certainly not from a white guy or a black politician. He was never comfortable at the *Nation*. He was too brilliant for the *Nation* of that era.

Azhar Chowdhary, a brilliant photographer, was another special friend. He lost a leg that had become infected from the coral at a Mombasa shoot of

President Jomo Kenyatta. Azhar was a wildlife essayist as well as a brilliant news photographer. He had this uncanny knack of seeing the subject in a unique way, frame by frame. While his cousin, Akhtar Hussein, was a creative genius of the set up picture and went on make a name for himself as a Royal Photographer, Azhar was always better in the moment. The ornamental Sashi Vassani, the Nation's first Chief Photographer, preceded them. A quiet man without the flamboyance of Hussein or Chowdhary, Sashi was Mr. Reliable. He had a heart attack while sitting in the sofa opposite the News Editor's desk and died in hospital. Anil Vidyarthi was another special photographer and a can-do kind of guy who would not let anything or anyone stop him from getting the gun shot.

Boaz Omori, the *Nation's* Editor-in-Chief, was a gentle man. He gave me some huge breaks and also enabled me to travel the world. Joe Rodrigues and I rarely spoke about work. We used to have a beer at the Lobster Pot at 7 o'clock each evening. I think he was quietly proud of me. Many years later when I showed him my debut features page design, he said 'wonders will never cease'. He never was one for handing out compliments. But I still think he was a great Goan journalist with few, if any, flaws. Henry Gathigira, as News Editor, was a gentle but grand journalist, especially his knowledge of local politics. He was a Kikuyu. He assigned me to some of the best, if sometimes the toughest, stories. It was Henry who appointed me the *Nation's* representative on VoK television's 'Meet the Press' program. To say that I got the plum jobs is an understatement.

Karo, our office driver, and I travelled thousands of miles, chasing story after story. He became my honorary assistant because he was a big help talking in Kikuyu with people at the scene of an incident. He brought potential witnesses to me. He was a beautiful man who had a heart as large as the horizon and the greatest smile in the world.

My single most unforgettable memory of Kenya was driving through an African village in Central Kenya (Kikuyuland), Nyanza (Luo), Western Province (Abaluhyia), Rift Valley (Kalenjin) or any village in Kenya and seeing the welcoming smiles from everyone, especially the women and children. Those smiles live in my heart.

Chief Sub-editor, the late Allen Armstrong (a Geordie from England's North), was my biggest fan. If we were short of a Page One lead or a major story, he would say 'don't worry, Skip will turn up with something.' As I passed his desk and briefed him, he would say 'ten pars please.' Ten paragraphs he would get and not a word more, another very special person.

Northern Irishman Jim Glencross, Editor of the *Sunday Nation*, was a real pal. First, he gave me a real column, 'Fernandes on Sunday', and later taught me the art of editing. Features editor Trevor Grundy had a lot of faith in me, and after I had had enough of news, he introduced me to the art of page design. Neil Graham was another special friend. Jack Beverley, founding Editor of *Sunday Nation*, was a hard man to like but he had an eagle eye for detail and was a respected journalist. In one of my stories, I had begun, 'In a brief five minute interview...' He asked 'How brief is five minutes?' Touché! Jack's sidekick, Gerry Loughran, was probably the most likeable person I knew and a grand journalist to boot. Buddy Trevor was a great beer drinker.

Nostalgia aside, I will tell you about just one more guy, and what a guy! Mike Chester was hired from England as news editor. Mike was a revelation. A suave guy, he was also a tough taskmaster. Above all he was a brilliant journalist. He taught me the art of writing a crisp, 25-words or less intro, the first paragraph of any story. The opening paragraph said what the story was all about and usually provided the sub-editor with an instant headline. Mike also brought me to tears one day. He made me rewrite the intro to a story 25 times. In disgust I told him after the 25th time, 'that's my best and if it is not good enough you had better find someone else to write it.' I went to Chief Sub-editor Allen Armstrong and asked if he had received the story. 'I sent the story off over an hour ago,' he said. He had used my original story. So I asked Mike why he had put me through those 25 attempts. 'You zip into the office, light your cigarette and speed-type your story. Think how much better it would be if you gave it a little more thought before you rushed into type.' What he did not know was that I was in the habit of doing all my thinking on the way back to the office and usually had it pat by the time I got to my desk. A few weeks later, he said, 'forget all that stuff I told you. You are an intuitive reporter, stick with it.'

The first week Mike was there, I handed in an expense chit for 20 shillings. 'Come over here,' he said as he headed for my typewriter, 'let me show you how a white man writes his expenses.' My humble 20 shillings chit was turned into 200.

'Here you are,' he said. 'You are in the chair.'

'What chair?'

'You are buying the drinks at the Sans Chique'. The back door of the *Nation*, across a lane, led to the back door of the SC. He called me his shotgun rider. If there was a troublesome story, he sent me. He loved his Tusker lager as much as he loved women. I had some of my best times with Mike as a journalist and was sorry to see him wrongly deported. He was a stringer for the *London Financial Times* and had for a long time chased the story of the Kikuyu Mau oathing ceremonies that had begun surfacing.

If John Bierman was the polished diamond, Mike was a rough one, though a diamond nonetheless. John Bierman was truly a fearless editor, even a renegade of sorts. But he did it with a heart and soul that was dedicated to the greater good of man and the truth. As brilliant as he was, he, too, was flawed. But during his tenure, the *Nation* was as fearless as he could make it. When the clinically true history of Kenya is written, it may judge him to be a mere mortal at a time when history demanded him to be immortal. I loved the man.

Individually, I did not think that George Githii was the best man for Editor-in-Chief, not only because of his strong connections to President Kenyatta. He saw in me someone who needed taming and to toe his flawed line. I could never do that. When George was good, he wrote brilliant editorials. He was not afraid to challenge the government or minsters. When he was bad, it was pretty obvious. He had two stints at the job and he was sacked during the second.

Editors, in my mind, are inspirational flag-bearers, guardians of the truth, innovators, brilliant analysts, warrior ambassadors leading where others followed. I always felt that George was something of a thug. Thugs do not make good editors. Besides, he broke the first rule: he had personal agendas. He was blessed with some moments of brilliance when he fought for the truth like a crazed warrior. I always felt it was a little bit like the devil fighting for something good, godly even. He was an impostor, a mad man, unpredictable and dangerous. The handgun he a carried was known to fall from his person on more than one occasion. He was a huge opponent of Foreign Minister Njoroge Mungai. I had worked closely with Mungai on several UN and Commonwealth campaigns. Mungai was part of the GEMA group that wanted to stop Vice President Daniel arap Moi from succeeding Jomo Kenyatta. Quite rightly, Githii, himself a Kikuyu and a former right-hand man for Kenyatta, opposed this with considerable help from the so-called black Englishman Charles Njonjo. Githii was like a man possessed. I left after few months. I could not work with him.

If the cancer of corruption emitted a purse of money, millions and millions, then the worst corruption was political corruption. To this day, that is the legacy that generations of Kenyans will have to live with. But life goes on and many beautiful and wonderful things continue to bless Kenya.

Gerard Loughran, in his brilliant book *Birth of a Nation: The Story of a Newspaper in Kenya*, focused on what he thought was the journalist's hard news revelations, but in the process forgot all the small people who made the *Nation* what it was. Without them there would be no *Nation*. Notice that there is no mention of the Features section especially the gorgeous Barbara Kimenye, who is now a famed Kenyan author, or the sports writers (including me) Norman Da Costa, Polycarp Fernandes, the late Monte Vianna who died young in a plane crash near Voi, Alfred Araujo, a sub-editor who went on to greater things in the UK, Olinda Fernandes the first Goan woman to venture into journalism, Kul Bhushan who was always busy, and the greatest gentleman or journalist Sultan Jessa who was our man in Dar es Salaam. Sadly, there has been no celebration of the people who made the *Nation* what it was: a world where most everyone lived and worked in harmony.

Yet *Birth of a Nation* is a testament to Gerry's brilliance as a journalist. He burrowed deep into the soul of archival and reportage material to write on issues we never dared to speak of let alone write. For anyone who has the slightest link with Kenya, *Birth of a Nation* is required reading.

Kipchoge Keino on his victory lap in Munich 1972. *Photo courtesy of IOC*

CHAPTER 8

BIRTH OF THE GOLD RUSH

At the heart of the British colonial plan to build the American funded Jeanes School at Kabete, just outside of the Kenyan capital of Nairobi, was a conspiracy that had 'noble aspirations' towards the enhancement of the colonists in the country. The school was named after an American philanthropist, Ann Jeanes, who had done much work in helping African-Americans in the US. One observer described the noble conspiracy as, 'The school trained teachers who were to be change agents, acting with tools of the social sciences to radiate social transformation throughout their communities. The target of the Jeanes School intervention was the rural villages of Kenya Colony's Native Reserves. There, Jeanes' teachers would not merely teach the "Natives" the "3Rs (reading, 'riting and 'rithmatic)," but also the "4 essentials" of civilization - industry, health, recreation, and domestic life. To these essential needs, the Jeanes Teachers would adapt education, making the kinds of students who would become agents of change themselves, carrying social transformation to all corners of the colony until all natives were uplifted and social progress assured.'

The plan was for all members of the colonial provincial and district administration, chiefs and sub-chiefs, headmen, headmasters and teachers to be trained to become change agents to perpetuate the presence of the British in Kenya. Provincial administrators, District Officers and teachers would also be encouraged to introduce sport in schools. In the Rift Valley, where young students ran anything up to 20 km to school and back, the introduction of athletics was given a high priority. In 1949, the Arab and

African Sports Association, recognising the growing popularity of athletics in both urban and rural areas, asked the colonial government to appoint a colonial sports officer. A.E. (Archie) Evans got the job and he quickly set about organising a system of athletic competition beginning with schools and comprising local divisional, district, provincial and national competitions. Also planned were inter-territorial athletics meetings for East Africa and other British territories.

One of the teachers to be put through the Jeanes School system was Daniel arap Moi, who was destined to become a leader in the battle for Kenya's independence, Kenya's second Vice President and President. He was no change agent, but he, like so many of his Kalenjin teaching colleagues, quickly saw the value of athletics in the life of the natural young runners in the Rift Valley schools. After all, Moi served as vice president of the Arab and African Sports Association which was eventually replaced by the Archie Evans-engineered Amateur Athletics Association of Kenya. An organisation like the AAAK was required to facilitate Kenya's participation in international events. Setting up the AAAK meant that competition among Asians, Africans, Arabs and Europeans was sort of legal. Evans was the inaugural Secretary and Derek Erskine, a Nairobi businessman, became the first chairman and the partnership lasted 10 years. Moi was also one of the first Kenyan African athletics officials. Archie Evans went on to coach and manage subsequent pre-independence Kenyan athletics teams, both at home and abroad. He was joined by his brother Edward, who I think worked in the Central Province, and by Ray Batchelor who looked after the Coast and Rift Valley. He was particularly successful in the coastal city of Mombasa where he coached the Achilles Club, comprised mainly of Goans and which included the future double Commonwealth Games Gold medallist Seraphino Antao. It is interesting that the Goans in Mombasa were considered more successful in track and field than their Nairobi counterparts and not only because of Seraphino Antao. I think the difference was Batchelor.

Batchelor was only interested in winning the hearts and minds of sports men and women at the Kenya Coast for athletics and other sports. He was not a civil servant or a colonial. I spent a lot of time with Batchelor all around Kenya. There was no room for colonial politics in his life, he lived only for sport. Unlike Archie Evans, who was not very popular with African athletes, Batchelor was very easy to get along with, especially among the Goans.

Archie Evans was also a principal of Jeanes School which later became the Kenya Institute of Administration and played an important role as the country came to grips with the challenges of post-independence, especially in the need for well-trained people.

In those pioneering days, competitions were restricted to first past the post because nobody could afford stop watches, and the long distances were run on the mud roads close to the athletics venue. Everyone ran in bare feet. We all did, except for the children of the rich, and the white kids. Ironically, it is an accident of British colonial conspiracy that really gave birth to Kenyan African athletes and laid the foundation for the country which would go on to dominate the World, Commonwealth and Olympic scene. Yes, it all began with a British colonial plan.

It was not long before Nyandika Maiyoro, Arere Anentia and Lazarus arap Chepkowny were flying the Kenyan flag on the world's athletic stages. Antao would win the Perth Commonwealth Games sprint double; Naftali Temu would become the first African Kenyan to win an Olympic Gold Medal at Mexico in 1968; Kimaru Songok would win the 400 metres hurdles bronze in the 1966 Commonwealth Games and Kipchoge Keino would rewrite the record books and astound the world with his charismatic, front-running style. Europeans thought he was mad to hare off like a cheetah hunting down prey, but he had the last laugh. Among the early pioneers there were names like Stephen Chelimo, Peter Francis, Anthony Ngatia, James Wahome, Kanuti arap Sum, Joseph Leresae Naftali Bon, Charles Asati, Daniel Rudisha senior and Munyoro Nyamau. The first woman to represent Kenya was Diana Monks who won a silver medal at the 1958 Kingston, Jamaica Commonwealth Games.

The first qualified athletics coach to work in Kenya was Geoffrey Harry George Dyson, the man who is often credited with being the 'father of British athletics'. Dyson was among the first to train as coach at the now famous Loughborough College where he is said to have 'learnt much about the athletics coach's art'. In 1939 he arrived in Kenya and was attached to the Kings African Rifles in Nakuru. His mission was to prepare men mentally and physically for battle. He combined a regimen of physical education and athletics training to achieve this. His stint in Kenya also improved his coaching skills. He set up impromptu athletics training centres wherever he was posted, returning to Loughborough in 1945.

Another respected British coach, Dennis Watts, visited Jeanes School and was impressed with the athletics program.

So, long before Archie Evans, Edward Evans, Ray Batchelor and much later John Velzean, who were all Physical Education teachers in the first instance and developed themselves into athletics coaches while in the job, Kenya's entry into the world of international athletics had already taken many, many steps via the humble school teachers, chiefs, sub-chiefs, rural colonial administration and especially the District Officers. The children were especially delighted with athletics because they were running naturally every morning, noon and night. Receiving small gifts for coming first or second or third was a bonus.

In my book, the white coaches were better motivators, providing a lot of physical training, discipline, and some advice on tactical running. Perhaps Ray Batchelor with Seraphino Antao was the best coach. No man can take credit for 'coaching' Kipchoge Keino. With the help of advice from the many international athletes he ran against, especially Ron Clarke of Australia, he developed a training regime all by himself. Occasionally he would consult a coach in Kenya. In a1960s *Nation* interview, I asked him if there was any single person he owed his success to, and he said, 'No, but lots of people have helped me to get where I am today.' These included American 800 metres Olympic gold medallist Mal Whitfield (who was based in Nairobi at the time), John Velzean, British long distance runner Mike Wiggs (who was training in Kenya at the time), and from observing other international opponents doing various exercises. Naturally, his favourite long distance star was Australia's Ron Clarke. John Velzean's contribution as an athletics coach is also undeniable.

At the time in Kiganjo, at the Police Training School, his routine was to run 10 to 14 kilometres each morning, helping him stay in trim while concentrating on extending his stride. Monday was warm-up exercises for 10 minutes and the same for other evening sessions, with 8x400 metres interval training, taking around 64 seconds each and with about 2.5 minutes rest between laps. Wednesday was 4x800 metres, taking 2 minutes 10 seconds each, five minutes' rest and 30 minutes exercise. Friday was warm-up, 4x750 metre laps of 3 minutes 25 seconds each, with exercises for 30 minutes.

Archie Evans was a product of the colonial era when whites did not treat Africans well at all and interaction was limited to master and servant. He had the typical stiff-upper lip, and was a starched, staid individual. He always wore a suit and carried a briefcase with him wherever he went. His great skill was forward planning, vision and organisation. He was not particularly good with people nor did he enjoy talking to the press. He was not a media animal by any stretch of the imagination.

Arere Anentia and Nyandika Maiyoro spent some time with Evans but they soon tired of his dogmatic discipline. At a meeting in Madagascar, for example, Maiyoro missed the start of a distance race and realised what was happening when the runners were a hundred yards down the track. He took off after them, in the process disrobing, much to the amusement of the spectators. He won the race anyway. Seraphino would not have anything to do with Evans and I was told that things between Batchelor and Evans were never sweet.

The first time Kenyans knew they had a potential world-beater was when Kip Keino finished a commendable 5th in the 5,000 metres in the Rome Olympics in 1960. From then on there was no stopping him.

The good, the bad and the ugly was what it took to bring Kenya onto the international athletics scene.

A glorious athletics day in June 1966

On Saturday, June 4 1966, at the Kenyan Students' Games (in their infancy at the time), being held at the Kenya Institute of Administration athletics track in Kabete, two things happened. The first was that Kipchoge Keino, who was already a household name in Kenya, ran the fastest mile by an African, clocking 4 minutes and 0.2 seconds, 2.8 seconds faster than his first Kenyan record for the distance. He had run his first sub-four minute mile in August the previous year at London's White City where he clocked an amazing 3 minutes 54.6 seconds. A truly fast time was difficult at Kabete which I think was a grass track at the time. Keino eventually ran 3:53.1 to lock in the first sub-four minute mile on Kenyan soil at Kisumu, on the shores of Lake Victoria, in September 1967.

The second was the emergence of a young schoolboy, Daniel Rudisha. Rudisha senior is the father of the Daniel Rudisha you might be thinking about who in recent years (since 2008) has been setting the 800 metres track alight and is currently (2016) working his way back to competitive running following an injury a year or two ago. Rudisha senior won the hearts of his fellow students when he was narrowly beaten by the legendary Wilson Kiprugut Chuma in the quarter mile (440 yards). The young man was so full of promise and so exciting that the crowd reserved its loudest cheers for him. Both runners made the Commonwealth Games standard on their first outing.

Wilson said of the then young Rudisha, 'Daniel will be a man to watch. He ran very well and might have beaten me. It was a good race.' Wilson had every reason to be apprehensive because Rudisha beat him in the 220 yards sprint. John Velzean, the Kenya coach at the time, was perhaps his biggest fan and told me at the time that if continued to develop as his early promise showed, there was no reason he would not one day break the 400 metres world record, or even the 800 metres world mark. Rudisha senior was a quiet achiever and a quick learner, and Velzean said he was a very easy athlete to coach.

Rudisha senior went on to win a silver medal in the 4x400 relay at the Mexico Olympics in 1968. I lost track of him after I moved to the News section at the *Nation*. I had almost forgotten about him until world record breaker Rudisha lit up the world's athletic tracks.

To this day, I still think that Kip Keino is Kenya's greatest athlete. I say that because Kenya smashed the international athletic scene in the 1960s and 1970s, coming out of the athletics wilderness. The developed world had had a huge head start on the developing world. In 1965, Kip stamped his authority on one of the two great rivalries of the 1960s. First, he set up a new 3,000 metres world in Helsingborg, Sweden of 7 min 39.6 sec. Next, he smashed the 5,000 metres record held by his great nemesis, Ron Clarke. Kip beat the Australian in Auckland, and set a new mark of 13 min 25.8 sec. He beat the other great rival, Jim Ryun, in the 1,500 metres at the Mexico Olympics in 1968. Clarke smashed almost every long distance record but never won Olympic gold.

Kip went on to win the Mile and 3 Mile events at the Empire Games in Kingston, Jamaica in 1966. Besides the gold medal in the 1,500 metres at the 1968 Mexico City Olympics, Kip won silver in the 5,000 metres. In 1972 he won silver in the 1,500 metres, and the 3,000 metre steeplechase gold medal in the Munich Olympics. Mexico was frighteningly dramatic. In the 10,000 metres in Mexico, Kip collapsed and was knocked out of the race by what turned out to be a gallbladder inflammation. Doctors ordered him not run in the mile but Kip ignored the advice and went onto win in style. His silver in the 5,000 metres was equally painful to watch, wondering if the gallbladder would get the better of him. That was one medal he was really desperate to win. After the steeplechase in Munich in 1972, I sat with Kip for nearly two hours while he prepared to give a urine sample for a regulatory drug test. He was ecstatic about his gold medal because he went over the jumps 'like a *punda* (donkey)'. Since 1966, Kenyans have gone on to win glory consistently at subsequent world events and in some instances to completely to dominate track and field, especially after the women athletes finally made their breakthrough.

CHAPTER 9

MUNICH

In 1972 of my junkets took me to Germany, to the Olympic stadium in Berlin which had been the scene of Jesse Owens' 1936 Olympic four gold medal success. Jesse, a black athlete, was the man Hitler would not recognise or shake hands with. Jesse won the 100 and 200 metres double, the long jump, and was part of the winning 4x100 metres relay team. In Munich, I spent a whole morning with the great yet very humble man. The junket, which would end in Munich just before the start of the Olympics, was made up of journalists from many parts of the world including Australia and New Zealand.

Once we got to Munich, I realised I would be the only one going home. I thought it would be a shame to have come so far and miss being at the Olympics. I was not supposed to be in Munich; Norman Da Costa was covering it for the *Nation*. I went into the Press Room and sought out the Chief-Press-Officer, a likeable guy called Wolfgang, and asked if I could get press facilities. He was sorry but every available press pass had been issued months before. In that case, I said, could I have somewhere to stay since all the hotel accommodation in Munich was booked out? No problem, he said, but it would be expensive. I took the offer.

That afternoon I attended a press conference by the African head of Olympic organisations. I asked him, 'Now that Idi Amin has thrown out all the Asians and killed any chance of multiracial sports, will you ban Uganda from taking part in the Games?'

There was numbed silence followed by an uproar of sorts, including cries of 'answer the question'. I asked a few more touchy questions before the African chiefs left in disgust. A lot of English speaking journos tapped me on my shoulder and said 'good question'. Later that afternoon there were a couple more press conferences and I made a similar impact. At the end of these, Wolfgang came and put his arms around my shoulder and led me away. When we had reached a certain point, he said, 'stand here and smile.' He stood a little away from me. Moments later he handed me my premium press pass, press kit and a whole bunch of other stuff, free of charge. 'You are a good journalist, I wish you good success,' he said.

I had worked for the German radio station Deutsche Welle off and on for a while, mainly political reporting and daily commentary and analysis whenever I was in Bonn. The next day I headed for the DW studio and they welcomed me by handing me a couple of large tape recorders. I also contacted the BBC World Service and their Africa Service and they agreed to take any feeds I could provide. Eventually, I would go from station for them to copy material from my tape recorders. My plan was simple: I would interview former greats like Jesse James, Emil Zatopak (one of the greatest long distance runners of all time), Mal Whitfield (an Olympic 800 metres gold medallist who had been attached to the US Embassy in Nairobi) and ask them how they would run their pet event/events, who were their likely opponents, and what tactics would best suit the Munich track. I had to find my subjects and update the tapes after the finalists emerged following the heats. I also spoke to a whole bunch of coaches.

The stations would use sound bites in their previews of races to come and also slot them in during the actual races. Almost every broadcasting unit bought my tapes. Some used the material unchanged; others used the model to create their own stuff relevant to their audiences. Most of them paid cash in US dollars. I did not talk to many of the Kenyan athletes but provided my own analyses.

On September 5, 1972 every man, woman and child in the Munich Olympic Games complex died a little that day. While most people in Munich were happily asleep, eight members of the Palestinian terror group Black September scaled a wall in the Games Village. They headed for the dormitory consisting of five apartments which housed the Israeli men's team. In the process of taking hostages, wrestling Coach Moshe Weinberg and weightlifter Yossef Romano were killed. Nine people were taken hostage. It was 4:40 in the morning.

What happened next is history. At 11:30 pm the next day, during a series of ill-fated attempts to rescue the 11 hostages at Munich airport, all the Israelis and five Palestinians were killed. Three kidnappers were arrested but later set free in exchange for passengers taken prisoner in a Lufthansa plane.

From the moment we first heard of the siege at the Israeli dormitory, a dark cloud seemed to descend on the Games Village. The day before it seemed everyone was full of smiles, laughter, expectation, and anticipation and was happy to be there. The smiles were gone. Athletes, officials and other people gathered in groups, spoke in low voices, and many could not stop crying. The whole place looked like some kind of zombie land. The first thought was the Games would be stopped. But the tragedy did not seem to matter.

I spent most of the day with the London *Daily Mail*'s internationally renowned columnist (and one of my heroes), Ian Woolridge. He would start by putting his thoughts down on paper sometime in the morning, and he would improve on the writing during the rest of the day until it approached his idea of perfection a few minutes before the earliest deadlines. Ian was a stunning writer with a great gift of entertaining, informing and educating his readers with a style that was exclusively his. On this day, however, he did not start writing. For a few hours, he simply sat down and tried to grasp what had happened, the enormity of it all. Was this going to be the new norm for sportsmen and sportswomen all around the world? Would more of them have to die at the hands of terrorists?

I had watched many athletes alone in their thoughts. There was lots of green space in the complex and each athlete found his own space to be alone, do a few warm-up exercises and not talk to anyone, especially pesky journalists. This was the darkest day for many people, but especially the

Israelis. As the German police spent the day attempting to seek the release of the hostages, most people prepared to go home as they were certain the Games would be cancelled. At 10 am on September 6, a memorial service was held in the Games Village. That afternoon, the Games continued.

The Israeli siege followed by the massacre opened up an opportunity to provide live feeds to several stations. I shared my material with anyone, whether they wanted to pay for it or not. I did several interviews, too. The journalists who were on that junket with me particularly appreciated my feeds. I never had to pay for a drink at the Press pub. I was almost drowned in free grog.

So, there I was in the vast press stand, a typewriter, telephone and enough paper info to save the ozone layer and enough journalists to start a nation of their own. Suddenly I found myself redundant. As I sat there half watching a procession of the early heats, I was taken in by the sheer beauty of the games, the German one-way precision, change no lanes, do not adapt, and follow the plan like a train timetable. It all looked so good. The only thing out of place I noticed was that the inside stadium perimeter wall was lined up with folks in their wheelchairs. That gave me an idea.

At last I had struck gold. I got a couple of my buddies to virtually carry me into the Games Medical Emergency Room. I faked severe pain in my legs. After various scans and tests, the doctors said I should be hospitalized. 'No, no,' I pleaded. 'I am a journalist and have to cover the track and field events.'

'What else can we do?' the doctor asked.

'Fill my butt with pain killing injections and give me a pair of crutches,' I cried. 'And give me a letter saying that I am in great pain.' That did the trick. I walked out of there with those wonderful crutches and sports journalism history: the first journalist in the world to interview medal winners and commentate on the track. Nobody stopped me as I stepped inside the Olympic arena.

When Ugandan John Aki Bua won the 400 metres Gold Medal I ran halfway around the track interviewing him. He just could not stop running. I will never forget the broadest smile in the Games, which belonged to Australia's Raelene Boyle after she won silver in the sprints, and which epitomised the beauty of the joy of climbing her own personal Everest. American Frank Shorter, who could barely speak after winning the marathon, said, 'I am not sure I am alive. I hit a wall some kilometres back and I am sure I died there.'

I sat for three hours with the great Kenyan long distance champion Kipchoge Keino in the medical testing room. He just could not provide a urine sample: it took him an eternity to do so.

After the closing ceremony, I went to the Press bar and my last unforgettable moment came with a tap on my shoulder and turned around to see the beaming face of Wolfgang, the chief press officer. He continued to shake my hand and tap my shoulder with his other hand. 'Wunderbar unt danke,' he said, 'you no pay for anything,' or something that sounded like that as he walked away, waving his hand in farewell. I sent some money home and took off for some much needed R&R in Scandinavia: lots of Aquavit, Courvoisier and caviar, not necessarily in that order.

CHAPTER 10

THE INTERROGATION

In the 1960s and 1970s it was not uncommon for editors and reporters to be hauled up in front of government ministers or senior officials to be harangued, threatened or interrogated about a particular story or editorial: all done secretly, of course.

The Minister of Information, the late Zachary Onyonka, ordered me and *Sunday Nation* Editor Jim Glencross to his office to discuss a no-holds-barred editorial criticising the official Kenya TV and radio broadcaster Voice of Kenya, then under the steerage of George Githii.

The Minister asked, 'Fernandes what kind of a fool are you? Are you begging to be put in jail? Or should we send you to Maralal (a Kenyan Northern Frontier District detention centre during the Mau Mau era)? Why are you so stupid to write these things about Githii? You journalists are all the same. You think you are the president of Kenya and you can write any kind of rubbish you want. You are not the president. You are a simple person who is stupid. You are not a clever man, if you were you would not write such gaasia (rubbish). Would you, would you, could you?'

I responded, 'Minister, what rubbish are you referring to exactly? Please point it out to me.'

'You imperialist stooge who is a Kenyan,' he replied, 'you who are less than a donkey, a complete *kumbafu* (idiot), you want me to explain to you exactly what is rubbish? Haven't you got the slightest intelligence to recognise it for yourself?'

'I am trying to get it clear in my own mind what is in your mind because I cannot understand what you saying,' I responded. 'For example, is there any passage in the editorial concerned that has broken any law in Kenya, has committed any kind of libel or defamation or crossed any social or political mores? Has the editorial wrongly accused the Kenya Government in any way possible? Why has it caused you so much heartache that you should choose to abuse my innocent profession and my person? What is the mistake, what is the law?'

'You, white person,' he said, addressing Jim Glencross, 'are you just going to sit there and let this stupid *mhindi* make an even bigger fool of both of us? Can't you see that he is a mad man, why are you supporting him?'

'It is not a matter of supporting Fernandes or not supporting him,' Glencross responded. 'We do not know why we were summoned to come to your office. We don't know what legal authority you have to summon us, no order us, to be at your office. If it is a matter of crossing legal boundaries then the Attorney General and the *Nation*'s lawyers can sort it out. Or, if you like, you could calm down and tell us what we have done wrong.'

I broke in. 'Minister you are treating us just like the British treated Kenya's Africans. What you are doing is imperialism in reverse.'

'I am an imperialist, am I? Do I look white to you? You see, you see, you are a stupid man!' the Minister exclaimed.

'I must have become stupid over the weekend', I responded. 'I was not stupid over the past four years when we spoke often and you commented regularly on various stories about one political issue or another, when I used your photograph and you used to call the next day and tell me what a great job I was doing to build a great Kenya. I wonder why Kenyatta, Mungai, Moi, Njonjo, Kibaki, and the rest of the leading political lights in Kenya don't think I am stupid. If I am so stupid than why has

Kenyatta appointed me secretary to the Kenya delegation to the Congo Independence celebrations?'

'Minister,' Glencross broke in, 'all we are saying is that unfounded personal attacks are not the way to solve anything. Instead we should apply quiet, considered reasoning to understand what is wrong, what we can learn from it and how we can fix it.'

The Minister was in a rage. 'I can have you killed in five minutes! How can you talk to me like that? Don't you know I am a Minister in President Jomo Kenyatta's Cabinet and a Minister of the independent state of Kenya? How can you look down your nose at me, as if you are so superior? You *pundas*, don't you know that I have the power to cancel Fernandes' citizenship and deport you to Britain? In one minute you can be heading off to Embakasi Airport!'

There was a long silence.

The Minister, as if talking to himself, said, 'We let these imperialists into our country, give them the benefit of enjoying lots of money, the wonderful facilities Kenya has to offer, especially the wonderful sunny and warm environment instead of their dark, grey, rainy and snowy climate in Britain, and this is how they repay us. I should really get rid of them. We cannot allow a Minister of the Government to be treated in such a way. And this is a *bunyani* (shopkeeper) whose ancestors have robbed and robbed our poor ancestors for nearly 100 years. Why should we give them citizenship? This is like Israel welcoming the Nazis and giving them citizenship, even Hitler.'

After glancing out of the window for a few minutes, he turned to us. 'This is what I want you to do. You must write an editorial praising Githii and VoK and you must say you were misinformed. You must say how sorry you are for having written such rubbish about Mr Githii. Is that clear?'

Glencross replied, 'We cannot do that, Minister. You have not shown us what is not true, or what is wrong, or what is untrue. We do not know what there is to correct. If you show us and it is in fact true, we will do the honourable thing. We don't have any hidden agendas.'

The Minister said to Glencross, 'There you go again, you are being stupid. Fernandes, you see the sense; explain it to this idiot imperialist.'

'Minister, I have been desperately trying to make sense of a fragment of your vitriol, but I can't,' I said.

'Get out, get out!' he demanded.

Jim Glencross and I walked out and we looked at each other in utter bewilderment. We stood outside the Minister's offices behind the Nairobi Law Courts and asked ourselves what that was all about. Jim looked at me and said, 'amber?' My wife and I had used the traffic lights system to judge the gravity of the situation: green was all clear, amber was go home and get the children ready, red was head out to Embakasi Airport and head for London. I told Jim we were still in Green mode. I still had a few strings to pull. I called Dr Njoroge Mungai and explained to him what had happened. He said that nothing had been raised at the weekly cabinet meeting in State House Gatundu but he had heard a few sniggers about the editorial. As I said, Githii was Kenyatta's private secretary and he had a lot of pull. But Mungai's attitude was that it was not a serious matter and that Githii was old enough to look after himself and did not need the Minister for Information to bend any elbows. He told me not to worry about it. A few days later I met Charles Njonjo in Parliament and after I raised the subject with him, he did not see any issues but, as usual, he ended our conversation with the words, 'be careful'.

There were many occasions when Dr Mungai pulled me out of sticky situations, even defended me in Cabinet on very sticky subjects, such as accusing Paul Ngei of pilfering famine relief maize for his personal and tribal benefit, or accusing Dr Kiano of being Mr 10 per cent (he allegedly charged 10 per cent of the total invoice for import/export licences). There were several instances when the Special Branch escorted me to Gatundu and, after hours of waiting and wondering if was I was going to live or die, I would be released, thanks to Dr Mungai, Charles Njonjo, Mwai Kibaki, or arap Moi standing up for me. There were many others also who did not see me as a threat including the Opposition Kenya People's Union leader Jaramogi Oginga Odinga. I used to have some chilli-infested debates with him in his office in Nairobi, but he was kind.

Nairobi 2016: Lots of beauty, murder and mayhem and where corruption is almost a way of life. *Photo Brian McMorrow*

CHAPTER 11

A BULLET WITH MY NAME

Death threats aimed at journalists and other prominent people were fairly standard in Nairobi during the late 1960s and until my departure in 1974. Political journalists in Kenya had to walk the political tightrope with the precision of a brain surgeon. It was common to be picked up by the Special Branch for interrogation. We lived with fear of deportation every day. To survive, we placed our faith in the truth, as proclaimed by the masthead of the *Daily Nation*: *'The Truth Shall Make You Free'.*

The truth made prisoners of us rather than set us free. There were not too many editors who were brave enough to publish. If one story fell through the cracks, watch out. For example, if a journalist exposed President Jomo Kenyatta and his Kikuyu cronies for exploiting a loophole in the Constitution, such as freely sharing out Crown Land, she or he would be deported. If the journalist were a black Kenyan, though, she or he would probably be dead. In later years, the wailing was, 'but it is Kenyatta who set up the system. We are only following in his footsteps.'

Kenyatta could do almost whatever he pleased; he reigned in an era when the democratisation principle was not so compelling. He stamped out any opposition in the media and in Parliament, especially probes into land grabbing and wealth exploitation by his ministers and Kikuyu associates. As a dictator, he was much loved and much respected. Those who knew better were forced into silence. So, the message was: don't mess with Jomo Kenyatta if you value your life. The bottom line was that if you were foolish enough to challenge Kenyatta or his Ministers, you would most likely be on the next plane out or a corpse.

The Crown Land freebies have been spoken of and written about sparsely, but only after Jomo Kenyatta's death in 1978. Before his death, however, publication of the story would have surely resulted in death both for the writer and publisher. The publication would have been banned for life and its non-Kenyan employees would be deported on the spot.

In the absence of a story of that magnitude, I cannot recall any journalists being killed, but plenty were deported for revealing the truth or being associated with digging up the truth, such as about the Mau Mau oathing ceremonies post-independence. On the other hand, thanks to friendly nations with interests such as Britain and the U.S., Kenya was great example of an emerging African country, as far as the world knew. It was to a large extent at peace with itself, even though in the broadest of terms. A single party administration is no substitute for democracy. However, multiracialism of sorts was on view, tourists thronged in the thousands as did billions in foreign aid. To the outside world, mainly by the tourist telegraph, Kenya was idyllic. The reality was that Kenyatta was an autocrat, even a demi-god. His will was always done, whether it was constitutional or not. I must confess I could not even talk about my best stories with my fellow journalists, let alone get them published.

The white journalists, too, knew to push political stories only so far but moaned about it like hell, surely in denigration of a black system. Kenyatta knew no fear. He verbally flogged errant ministers with a torrent of four letter words in Swahili in front of thousands of Kenyans and visitors alike at rallies such as those that marked Independence in December 1963. In front of Kenyatta, ministers and members of parliament all cowered, all except his eternal nemesis, Odinga, who vied for the presidency. The token Vice-Presidency at Independence was never to his liking, he was always uncomfortable in the job. If Cabinet Ministers and Members of Parliament cowered in the presence of Kenyatta, what hope was there for humble journalists or anyone else for that matter?

Kenyatta was not a very tall or large man but he exuded charm and power in equal quantities. White settler elderly women swooned as he passed by, like teenagers at an Elvis Presley or Beatles concert. He was always impeccably elegant, a rosebud the standout decoration in his lapel. This also underscored his love of roses. Consider the political scenery: the North Western Kenya leader, Odinga, had come in as Vice President at independence in 1963 and was gone by May 1966. He would go to his grave opposed to Kenyatta and all things Kikuyu.

The Goan-Maasai Joseph Murumbi held the Vice Presidency for a few months in 1966 and left later, disillusioned and fearing that his political best friend Pio Gama Pinto had been murdered by the Kiambu Kikuyu mafia ruling. Murumbi was in a dark place because he was said to have coerced his life-long friend Pinto out of hiding.

Ronald Ngala, the leader of Kenya's coastal people, and the king of the Kalenjin, arap Moi, split the African representation into Kenya African Democratic Union (KADU) on one side, and the Kenya African National Union (KANU), which included Mboya and members of the Kiambu mafia on the other. Ronald Ngala was to die in a tragic road accident in 1978, but he was a spent political force on the national landscape, although he continued to hold sway in his constituency of the Kenyan coast. In 1966, Odinga formed the Kenya People's Union, signalling a head-on clash with Kenyatta and the Kikuyu.

Pinto was one of two Kenyan Goans who were true African nationalists. The other was barrister Fitz De Souza. Joe Murumbi was neither Goan nor Maasai; he hovered somewhere in between, the twilight of the half-caste. While he was a nationalist, I was never convinced that his whole heart was in it. Perhaps by the time I met him he was so disillusioned that he would have rather forgotten about his political past. He spoke very little about himself anyway. He was happiest talking art and music, especially African art. He quietly removed himself from the political scene and found solace in the beauty and comfort of the arts instead.

Mboya, who continued to grow in stature and popularity since independence, was not a Kikuyu favourite. He was out of favour with

Kenyatta, who had sent him to negotiate independence in October 1963; instead, Mboya was suspected of 'conspiring' with the British and settling on the Colonial Office-preferred December 1963. Even before that, Mboya was on the outs because he would not give up his parliamentary seat for Kenyatta. He was tolerated for his immense popularity, not only at home but also in the West. More importantly he was a sworn enemy of his fellow Luo, Odinga. That left Kenyatta, who was going to die any day now, arap Moi (who was going to succeed him), Njoroge Mungai (who was going to try and stop arap Moi) and Charles Njonjo (who was going to stop Mungai). Not in the inner sanctum, but with considerable political clout, were the very likeable Mwai Kibaki and Jeremiah Nyagah.

Mboya was cruelly gunned down in the doorway of his chemist's shop in broad daylight on a Saturday morning, July 5, 1969. His passing shocked the country. Odinga was not a threat either, but he continued making political noises of sorts on the outer fringes of the political spectrum, without any real muscle. He was the resident communist (a capitalist at heart, really) with purported strong leanings to the Soviet Union and China. There was a supposed friendship with Tanzania's President Julius Nyerere, a self-confessed socialist and a China-fancier; after all, they had built him a railway to Zambia. However, the West was encouraged to accept Odinga as the face of the threat of communism in Kenya. Nobody except Odinga argued. Odinga did not pose a threat because the reasonably strong Kenyan Army, backed by unlimited military support from the UK, made sure there was no threat to the security of the country, nor a coup. J.M. Kariuki, a fast-rising Kikuyu star who claimed alliance with Mboya and who was the only Kikuyu on Rusinga Island for Tom's funeral, once said that Kenya did not want 10 millionaires and 10 million beggars. He was assassinated in March 1975. J.M.'s public persona was exaggerated. He promised lots of money to self-help groups and delivered little. Robert Ouko, another Luo and former foreign minister who had better entrées than most presidents in the US Oval Office, was murdered in 1990. There are others, like Agriculture Minister Bruce McKenzie, whose passing has been documented elsewhere.

I first met Mboya in 1960 at a Luo soccer club match at the Nairobi Stadium. From that day on, I was in regular contact with him. He introduced me to his top specialists in the Planning and Development Ministry and told them I had carte blanche on free-to-air information. He was definitely Africa's answer to John F. Kennedy, if Africa had allowed him the miracle. It never did. If I was star struck, it was with due credibility. U.S. educated with intellect, charisma and friendly persuasion galore, he had access to the inner sanctums of the U.S., Britain, Germany, the UN and a bunch of other European and African power brokers. China and the Soviet Union considered him a black capitalist.

Ironically, Mboya's resume mirrors that of Foreign Minister Dr Njoroge Mungai, another presidential aspirant and more importantly a Kikuyu. Like Mboya, Mungai was another brilliant contact. My wife and I were the only Goans invited to a private party for the then Prince Charles and Princess Anne hosted by Mungai. Naturally, we were the only Goans invited to his wedding. Mungai opened doors to every president and prime minister in Africa. I did not spare him any tough questioning at press conferences, but I also got the inside running on major scoops. I travelled the world with him; our visits to the world's capitals usually ended with R&R at the nearest sauna with Aquavit, champagne and caviar. Naturally it led to many people associating me with Mungai and I am not ashamed to admit he was a great source. I would even call him a friend if pure journalism permitted it. Both Mungai and Mboya were handsome devils: suave and polished, they attracted women like bees to honeysuckle. Both married beautiful women. Both were U.S. educated. Mboya facilitated the transportation of hundreds of young Kenyans to the U.S. where they were granted scholarships.

Then there was Attorney General Charles Njonjo, the black Englishman and man most likely to influence Jomo Kenyatta. Njoroge Mungai may argue the toss on that one. Njonjo was Kenya's front door key to the British cabinets of both Labour and Liberal. And finally the charming arap Moi, with all the caring, poise and understanding of the teacher that he was. He never said much but he was always a president-in-waiting. I went on a few overseas trips with him, especially in Africa. I found him an easily likeable man, though always a wary one. Most analysts reckon his presidency from 1978-2002 was the worst in Kenya's history. In cahoots with members of his family and associates he is alleged to have looted and plundered billions from the country's coffers. It was a period when Kenya suffered a foreign investment drought as well as a foreign aid drought. Many were killed in political skirmishes and many more went into hiding or created new underground movements.

I had established my credibility with all the top players and I thought I enjoyed their confidence. So why, then, was there a bullet with my name? I pored over every nook and cranny of my own brain and never found the answer. In response to the growing death threats, Police Commissioner Bernard Hinga tried to look into one or two with no mention in the *Daily Nation* or to its editor. There were also the crank calls that poured abuse over the phone lines. More often than not, these ended with my putting the phone down. The first time I received a death threat, I must admit I was shaken a bit, but these were the days of the sweet bird of youth, the wind in your hair and an unshakeable belief in your mission in life. Besides, they don't shoot journalists in Kenya, I told myself. Did the death threats impinge on my freedom? No. I continued to proceed with as much caution as intuition would allow me. Foolishly, I convinced myself that I had friends in high places.

Some nameless folks have suggested that I was forced to leave Kenya because I 'knew too much'. Perhaps there is some truth in that. For example, as early as January 1974, I feared for the life of the enigmatic Assistant Minister, Josiah Mwangi (affectionately known as JM) Kariuki and I told him so. The ever smiling former Mau Mau liaison officer just laughed it off and told me I 'must be joking.'

After the murders of Mboya (15 August 1930 - 5 July 1969) and Pinto, JM was the man most likely to succeed Jomo Kenyatta. He was handsome, clever, articulate and generous. He made the poor people of Kenya his electorate and they celebrated him as their hero. He was one of the few, if not the only, Kikuyu to challenge Jomo Kenyatta on the issue of land redistribution (or land grabbing), Government corruption (which today is a way of life in virtually every aspect of Kenya) and the widening gap between the rich and poor. He was popular throughout the Kikuyus' Central Province but he was equally welcome almost everywhere else in Kenya. I had told him if Pinto, the hero of the Mau Mau, could not get away with challenging Kenyatta there is no way that he would. His argument was that there wasn't a chance in hell that Kenyatta would allow another Kikuyu to be killed. I had written one or two stories about JM and people had said in conversation that he had 'better be careful'. JM endeared himself to Kenya's poor people by attending hundreds of self-help (*Harambee*) rallies and promising large sums of money which did not always materialise but for which he got credit anyway. There were other skeletons in his cupboard: there was a story going around that he had received Chinese money for a project but that the money had somehow vanished (as money used to then, and still does in 2016). I left Kenya in June 1974; JM was murdered on March 5, 1975. His killers were never found.

If anyone had pots and pots of money and they wanted to shake hands with the first President of Kenya, Jomo Kenyatta, they made a pilgrimage to State House Gatundu (Kenyatta would not live in the palatial colonial relic, State House Nairobi, because he was afraid of the ghosts of white people who allegedly roamed the halls). There, foreign dignitaries, heads of multinationals, industrialists, corporate head-honchos, community leaders (the Sikhs and Aga Khan were amongst the biggest Asian givers), tribal leaders and anyone else would shake the President's hand, give him a cheque and enjoy the tribal dancing and African traditional music. Within 10 years of independence, the money donated must have amounted to billions. I was trying to find out how much had been donated and where it had all gone. I ran into wall after wall but I was certain I would eventually find out.

In 2016, Kenya's No.1 investigative journalist, John Kamau of the *Daily Nation*, wrote, 'Cash and donations flew from all over the country as visiting dignitaries and politicians lined up to express their "love" for Kenyatta. What became of the funds for Gatundu has been anybody's guess. While millions of shillings were raised for the project, there was little to show for the hospital and for years it remained a decrepit compound of long grass, unmotivated staff and unattended flower gardens with buildings long devoid of paint.'

Finally, in 2016, Jomo's son President Uhuru Kenyatta finally achieved what his father could not with the Gatundu Self-Help Hospital. Uhuru officially opened what is now 'a splendid architectural five-story masterpiece that dwarfs the former hospital'.

John Kamau has also written about the other story that could have landed me in hot water: how Jomo Kenyatta and his chosen few bought some of the most treasured coastal, beachfront and urban land in Mombasa and Malindi. I first got wind of the story at the Sikh Union Club in Nairobi where friends pointed out the Sikhs who were personal building contractors of some of the highest placed Africans in Kenya. I had asked Dr Njoroge Mungai if I would live if I wrote the story. His response was, 'who is going to publish it?' Even in the 1970s, exposing Jomo Kenyatta and the Kikuyu scams would result in the same fate that befell Tom, JM, Pinto and Robert Ouko: death.

You develop a thick skin and eventually the threats are reduced to empty words although, as I said, one really should not take a death threat lightly anywhere in Africa. My only crime would have been that I gave each of the top players the exposure they deserved in a balanced story. There was no bias. I was not the news: they were. I was merely the humble scribe, the messenger.

The crunch came one day in May 1974. After dinner that night, my wife said, 'Cyprian, we need to talk.'

'What's wrong?' I asked, somewhat nonchalantly.

She explained, 'You have always said that I was the perfect journalist's wife. Before we married you took me to the *Nation* offices and pointed to your blue Olivetti portable typewriter and said: there's my first wife. I have never argued this point. I have watched you absolutely immersed in one crisis after another. I have shared with you the agonies and ecstasies of journalism. We made new friends and travelled far and wide. It has been a heck of a ride. But I have to say stop now.'

I held her and comforted her as she sobbed and tears ran down her cheeks. 'Why?' I asked.

'Because they are going to kill you,' she sobbed.

'Who? Who is going to kill me?' I asked.

'I don't know. But I was told today, they are going to kill you,' she said.

'Who told you?' I wondered.

'This insurance salesman came to see my boss. He asked me for my name and when I told him he said he had a friend called Fernandes. "Does your husband write for the *Nation*?" he asked and I said yes,' she explained. 'Suddenly his smiling, happy face was ashen. He ran to the door, checked the corridor, shut the door quietly, and said, "dear lady, dear lady, get him out of this country today. They are going to kill him. They have a bullet with his name on it." I asked him, "Who is going to kill him?" He said, "I can't tell you. I must not say".'

She explained, 'before I could say anything else he had bolted out of the door. I was shattered. I told my boss. I told my sister Delfine.'

I said, 'He must have been another nut.'

'Nut or not, we are leaving Kenya. If you don't want to come, I am taking the children and going to Canada or England.' She was adamant and she was still sobbing uncontrollably.

'When do you want to leave?' I asked.

'Tomorrow, the day after, as soon as we can,' she begged.

I said, 'how about in four weeks?'

She replied, 'do it as quickly as possible.'

There was only one decision. Within four weeks we were out of Nairobi. Earlier in the year, I had been to Canada for an interview with the *Toronto Globe and Mail*. I secured an understanding that I would be in-waiting for the Foreign Editor's chair when I migrated. We had planned to stop over in England for a week but ended up staying five years and moved to Australia instead at the first opportunity.

In 2014 I finally wrote the stories that could have got me killed in 1974.

CHAPTER 12

BAD OMENS

I always feared for Kenya's future because I was convinced that it held nothing but danger and destruction since independence had come at a price. Harry Thuku took the first steps towards political agitation by forming the Young Kikuyu Association in 1921. The colonial government promptly banned it. Thuku reformed the organisation as the East African Association (EAA), fighting for the rights of labourers - especially women - and land. They were originally concerned with Kikuyu affairs but broadened their interests to a much wider political umbrella. The EAA became the Kikuyu Central Association with Johnston Kenyatta as its secretary general. In 1929, the association sent Kenyatta to London to put the land case and other issues directly to the British government and people. Kenyatta did not return until 1946. Thuku was eventually arrested and deported to Kismayu Island. In 1944, Thuku formed the multi-tribal Kenya African Students Union, which in turn became the Kenya African Union in 1946. Kenyatta became its president in 1947.

The Kikuyu were the first to see the potential of political agitation. They began with fighting for Kikuyu land rights and moved to taking the whole country. This will to dominate has led Kenya into crisis after crisis. The first instincts were to form regional assemblies or governments, which was just as doomed as the central government. Even before independence, Odinga and Mboya were locked in a mighty struggle. The young, handsome, articulate and self-assured Mboya was the darling of the West, especially the USA. It was not long before Mboya was sending plane loads of Kenyans for an America education. The socialist, Odinga, made his leanings to the East public. He also began sending Kenyans overseas for an education, but to Moscow. Odinga openly disliked Mboya but the latter was often too clever for the senior politician. Odinga was old school, Mboya was definitely new school. Both served under Kenyatta with their dislike for each other continuing to fester.

In-fighting among the Kikuyu was cancerous too. Attorney-General Charles Njonjo had a life long battle with Njoroge Mungai. Njonjo opposed Mungai who opposed arap Moi succeeding Kenyatta. This time Njonjo won and arap Moi became president. But it was not long after that Moi and Njonjo fell out, and that was the end of the Kenyan African Englishman. Perhaps the biggest pointer to the future futility of Kenyan politics was found in the Kapenguria six (Jomo Kenyatta, Bildad Kaggia, Achieng Oneko, Kungu Karumba, Paul Ngei and Fred Kubai), who were jailed on trumped-up charges of managing the Mau Mau. Achieng Oneko left Kanu with Odinga to form the ill-fated Kenya People's Union. Paul Ngei, a Wakamba tribesman, was a founding member of the Kenya African Democratic Union. The Kikuyu never trusted him although he served in government for a long time. Kaggia, disillusioned with the corruption around him, also left to join the KPU. Kaggia drifted further away when his best friend and socialist colleague Pinto was allegedly murdered by the Kiambu mafia. Fred Kubai retired from politics after serving several terms in parliament. Kungu Karumba was also disillusioned with the Kikuyu land grab and became a communist sympathiser. He disappeared in 1975. These were supposedly the founding fathers of an Independent Kenya.

Where did the unity go? In May 1960, James Gichuru was the stand-in president of the Kenya African National Union (KANU), with Odinga, Ronald Ngala, arap Moi and Mboya as the other key officers. However, Ngala and arap Moi declined the positions because they felt that KANU was Kikuyu and Luo-centric. They went on to form the Kenya African Democratic Party (KADU) to represent the Kalenjin, Masai, Abaluhya and the Coast. Ngala died in a car crash not long after. Everybody, it seemed, was watching everyone else.

KADU was eventually disbanded and merged with KANU. Daniel arap Moi became Vice President in 1967 after Joe Murumbi had held the post for a brief time. Odinga left the party in 1966 to form the Kenya People's Union. I cannot honestly say that I met a single politician who was there purely for Kenya and its people. Everyone, it seems, had a hand turned out or sticking behind his back. Greed, corruption and crime were already taking its toll in 1974. There would be much more to come: of that, I was sure.

While I had loved the Mathare Valley slum village as a child, I feared for its future. With independence gained, it was each man or woman for himself or herself. It would not be long before - like in the favelas of Rio de Janeiro - crime would come to live there. Crime cartels with the conspiratorial help of the police, politicians and other interested parties would soon rule the roost. It was always going to happen, and now it was just a matter of time.

STOP PRESS: September 2016, a survey of young people in Kenya has indicated that they are "OK" with bribery. Both India and Kenya have made bribery (*Toa kitu Kidogo*, give me (take out) something small) a way of life. Some folks say it is nothing more than GST (general service tax) or VAT (value added tax) Hand in hand with the continued construction of skyscrapers and infrastructure, Kenya now has a middle class. A recent report said that 10 per cent of Kenyans who live in the major urban centres are officially middle class.

CHAPTER 13

DR MAGANA NJOROGE MUNGAI 1926-2014

I often wondered how peasants with little or no education had the foresight to send their sons to some of the greatest educational institutions in the world. The answer probably lies in an article Jomo Kenyatta wrote for the Kikuyu newspapers, urging all parents to ensure they sent their children to school. By the time independence arrived, so many Kikuyu were well educated, highly qualified and ready to receive the reins of government. One example, Dr Magana Njoroge Mungai, was born on January 7, 1926 at Gicungo village, Kikuyu, Kiambu County. His parents were George Njoroge Kimotho Sengeni ole Mbuchucha ole Ngori from Kilgoris, Narok in Kenya's north and Leah Gathoni Kungu was Magana from Gatundu. The Church of Scotland Mission Elementary School at Thogoto was his first school. In 1942, he went to Nabumali High School in Uganda, which was founded by the Church Missionary Society. Bouts of black water fever and malaria forced him to move to the sought-after Alliance High School near his home in Kikuyu. Six of the 14 students in his graduating class served as Kenyan Cabinet Ministers: Robert Matano, Kyale Mwendwa, Mbiti Mati, Dr Gikonyo Kiano, Dr Munyua Waiyaki and Dr Mungai.

Dr Mungai had a great love for his siblings and his children, but was particularly proud of his mother. He said, 'my mother was among the first women in Thogoto to go to school and learn how to read and write.

She and my father were members of the Church of Torch, Kikuyu where the records of my birth were preserved. The records are still intact at the Church and they show my birth attendant as one Dr John William Arthur.'

While waiting for an opportunity to further his education, Dr Mungai worked as a farm clerk at Redhill, Limuru and East African Airways in Nairobi. In 1946, he got his Public Service Vehicle licence and began driving his father's 60-seater Chevrolet bus affectionately known as 'Guthera' between Nairobi and Limuru. It was also the year he first met Jomo Kenyatta who had just returned from the United Kingdom.

Soon, Dr Mungai was admitted to the University of Fort Hare where he graduated with a Bachelor's degree in Science in 1950. Fort Hare educated hundreds of other Kenyans, even though South Africa was a full-blown apartheid country. His roommate at Fort Hare was Mangosuthu Buthelezi who later became a leader of the powerful Zulus in South Africa. The Zimbabwean president Robert Mugabe was another schoolmate.

He applied to both the University of London School of Medicine and Stanford University in California. He raised money by selling Avon cosmetics on the streets of Cape Town before travelling to London by sea. In London he washed dishes at a restaurant while waiting to join the University of London, but he received admission to Stanford with a full scholarship. While in London he chanced to meet his brother Ng'ethe and the two prepared to leave for the US. While staying at the YMCA in London, he met Tom Kay, a Presbyterian Church member, who had been stationed in Nairobi and knew Mungai's father. Tom lent him the fare and he sailed from Southampton on the Queen Mary, arriving in New York on October 4, 1951. Ruth Porter from the Committee of Friendly Relations for Foreign Students met him. He had three cents on him. She loaned him $70 for the bus ride to Stanford. When he arrived he had 25 cents in his pocket. He got a job delivering food around the campus.

Dr Mungai obtained a Bachelor of Arts degree and began his Masters in Arts when he was admitted to the Stanford Medical School, and earned his doctorate in 1957. He did his internship at Kings County Hospital in New York and his residency at the prestigious Presbyterian Medical Centre where he specialised in internal medicine from 1958 to 1959. On his return to Kenya, having arranged for the provision of materials, professional advice and management services from doctors and nurses in the United States, he established a chain of medical clinics. These clinics throughout Central Kenya brought affordable medicine to poorer people who were often ignored by the Asian or European doctors.

Dr Mungai, who had made a name for himself in the fight for freedom by organising a delegation that went to London to press for Jomo Kenyatta's release, was also concerned with Kenyatta's health while in detention. He pressured the colonial government to allow African doctors to independently verify Kenyatta's health. He led a medical delegation consisting of Dr Munyua Waiyaki, Dr James Nesbitt and Dr Jason Likimani. This visit established Dr Mungai as Kenyatta's personal physician and served him in this capacity until his death in 1978.

He was appointed Kenya's first Minister for Health and Housing after independence in 1963. He founded the Kenya Medical Association, dismantled existing racist bodies and played a leading role in setting up the first medical school in Nairobi. He managed to get sizeable medical aid including 50 faculty members from McGill University in Montreal, Canada, who taught at the school when it opened in 1967.

In 1967 he was appointed Minister for Defence and Internal Security at time when the Shifta war was a Somali secessionist attempt on Kenya's Northern Frontier District. His diplomatic and military offensive resulted in the restoration of Kenya's territorial integrity and the end of the Somali offensive.

In 1969 he was appointed Foreign Minister. It was the era that produced truly outstanding people, men like Malcolm X, Martin Luther King, John F Kennedy and his brother, Robert Kennedy. These were gods of the 1960s. They were young, handsome, bold, brave, and with the ability to mould young minds beyond belief. To say that they were inspirational is the greatest understatement. Also in the cauldron of genius was a young boxer who, first as Cassius Clay and then as Muhammad Ali, turned the world on its head. Young people loved him with a fervour reserved for saints and they still do today, even though they are in their 70s or 80s. Through radio, television and newspapers, young Kenyans knew these super heroes just as well as anybody else. In 1960, our own home-grown heroes were also beginning to make their mark, albeit slowly and mostly in African circles, particularly via tribal partisanship: the Kikuyu in Central Kenya and the Luo in Nyanza.

Dr Mungai has probably gone down in history as the most polished, though sometimes flawed, freedom fighter never to have become President of Kenya, a role he would have cherished and excelled in. His opponents will applaud that he never made it. My eyes fill as I remember the years I spent with the dashing foreign minister. He was 18 years older than I but my peers often told me that I was much older than my years. So who was Dr Njoroge Mungai really? He was the Kikuyu young gun who was making waves wherever he went. Blessed with lady killer looks, dressed in some of the best tailored suits seen in Kenya, he was then a pin-up for any modern women's magazine. Any time you ran into him overseas, and in Africa too, a pretty girl, either black or white, was never too far away. He was not a show-off nor did he throw his money around. As I said, he was easily loveable. He was a young man who was way ahead of his time, especially in Kenya, which was only just beginning to shed its colonialist skin. Having lived in South Africa, England, the US and various other places, he was as cosmopolitan as the brilliant young men and women he met at university and in the early days of his medical career.

He also had a somewhat gentle tone of voice but it was precise as a laser and sharp as a samurai sword. He chose his words and delivered them while looking at you dead in the eye. If he was a sophisticate in politics, he was no less sophisticated in his social life. I had the privilege of dancing with Princess Anne and my late wife danced with Prince Charles when Doc threw a party for the royal couple at the Hilton Hotel in central Nairobi. I would often meet him in the sauna at the Norfolk Hotel and we would spend hours solving the world's problems while supping on elegant quantities of Aquavit and champagne. Not many black guys knew of Aquavit, champagne or white women in those wonderful, carefree days of the blissful 1960s. The great thing about Doc was that he did not see the colour in people, he saw only human beings.

I was told by wannabe experts in those days that if Charles Njonjo was the British colonial governor in residence, and Mboya was really a CIA spy, then Mungai was a Kikuyu first and a Kenyan second, third or fourth. But in the very early days no one could explain why. When I raised it with him once, he shook his head and said, 'don't waste your time by stooping to that level in the gutter.'

I would raise that issue with him again in 1972 with an eye on his future as the Member for Dagoretti. Some of his critics correctly pointed out that he was a great foreign minister but an absent Member for Dagoretti. Some called him the Member for Addis Ababa or the Member for Foreign Affairs. He was unconcerned about Foreign Affairs taking him away from Dagoretti for long periods. He was confident that his people on the ground had everything in hand and he was almost too confident that he would win easily.

I left Kenya in June 1974 and was headed for Toronto but stopped off in London. At a reception at the High Commission in London, he came to me and whispered, 'I can't talk to you here, and the Special Branch has been following me.' We never spoke on that visit. I learnt later that the Special Branch had kept a close watch on him for months. Some folks close to him thought he was planning on asking me to come and help with his election campaign but never got around to it. He lost the election mainly because certain people campaigned against him. Doc denounced 'the campaign to distort the truth, to vilify my person and discredit my achievements.' I thought that that was darkest period of his life. I know he moved on and went on to achieve great things in commerce but that period was a permanent heartache.

Looking back I must have been pretty naïve. Many people have told me that Mungai and Mboya did not get along at all and, as part of the Kiambu mafia, Mungai was partly responsible for his assassination or was aware of who was responsible. I knew both men but neither mentioned the other derogatively. Similarly, I had admired both Charles Njonjo and arap Moi.

Somewhat immune to all these political viruses, Mwai Kibaki went about the business of looking after Kenya's *pesa* (Swahili for money) unperturbed. He went on to become a much lauded President. Above everything else, Doc was a family man. You did not see any public bravado between him and his brothers Ng'ethe and Nyoike or sister Jemima. All I saw was a pretty close family. He was proud of all his children, his nephews, nieces, in-laws and the extended Mungai family. And, of course, some of his best friends were some of the best medical brains. To the end, while his heart turned to growing roses for export, his soul was firmly fixed in medicine.

I was also saddened when his marriage to Lillian Njeri ended in divorce. They married in May 1972 in the society wedding of the year after a fairly long courtship. Lillian was a real beauty and they had a boy and three daughters. They looked like they were made for each other. Sadly not.

During 1969 and 1970, as Kenya's Foreign Minister, Mungai had spearheaded the campaign against arms sales to South Africa. The British were the arms merchants and the South Africans contended that the arms were needed to make the Indian Ocean shipping lanes safe from the land. They were not intended for use against black South Africans or African nationalists or against neighbouring African countries. I travelled with Mungai to most African forums, especially the Organisation of African Unity in Addis Ababa, and individually to various countries in Africa, and to India and the Far East.

At other national forums we met up with leaders of the Caribbean countries. The OAU unreservedly supported the campaign. Milton Obote of Uganda, Julius Nyerere of Tanzania and Kenneth Kaunda of Zambia were strongly vocal in their support. Kamuzu Banda of Malawi did not care one way or another. In the corridors of the OAU, while lobbying OAU support for independence of what is now Zimbabwe, Robert Mugabe was more despondent because he was afraid the arms would be used against his country. In those days, Robert Mugabe was a very likeable man, quietly spoken, dapper in dress with a ready greeting.

Most leaders and governments agreed that the South African plans for safeguarding the Indian Ocean sea routes were nothing but a pack of lies. By the time the Kenya delegation reached Singapore in January 1971 for the Commonwealth Heads of Government summit CHOGM, there had been substantial weeping and gnashing of teeth, fearing that the arms issue would split the Commonwealth (with Britain, Canada, New Zealand and Australia on one side) or would result in the demise of the Commonwealth. Similar fears had been held at previous summits and the organisation (the so-called family of the British Commonwealth) had remained unbruised, unscarred, supposedly united with a single voice. The British aid that subsidised so many former colonial countries was probably a factor as to why so many of them had toed the line. This time around, however, Mungai had managed to capture the imagination of a lot of people, not necessarily that of their elected leaders. But the air was filled with anticipation that on this one occasion, at least, Africa and humanity would be the victors.

On the eve of the conference I went for drinks at the US Embassy. The talk was all about the arms campaign. The US had kept out of the argument, saying it was really a matter for the Commonwealth. That night, one of my American military contacts who I usually ran into at various conferences, especially at the UN Security Council, said to me, 'forget it, Skip, it is not going to happen. And you did not hear it from me.'

'This time it will,' I said stubbornly.

After the conference opened, there was a fairly short debate on the subject. The clever British Foreign Secretary, Sir Alec Douglas-Hume, nuked the arms campaign. I had great admiration for Douglas-Hume as a political strategist. He had refined his skills while working in the back rooms of the British House of Commons. The nuking was a simple slingshot. He told the summit that the arms issue should be decided by the heads of government or leaders of delegations: i.e. the elders of the British Commonwealth. This move extinguished any of the fire that had been displayed earlier by respective foreign and defence ministers. Heads of government or heads of delegations were not well versed on the subject, nor aware of the tricks of the arms trade. This also meant that the final discussion on the subject would go ahead without the chief architect of the anti-arms sales campaign, Mungai.

On the eve of the Big Chiefs' meeting, the senior members of the Kenya delegation decided that the campaign could not succeed without Mungai in attendance. With that, a whole bunch of Mungai's support crew, analysts, speechwriters and researchers, headed for the makeshift office to update the presentation for the meeting.

Later that night, I went to dinner with arap Moi and Charles Njonjo. Everyone seemed in an elated mood. Arap Moi could not stop laughing as Njonjo and I got stuck into our escargot. 'You guys are eating insects', he said. Naturally, everyone else tucked into beef steaks. When we returned to our hotel, I popped into Mungai's room and played the devil's advocate on some parts of his presentation. Before I left, he said, 'this is what we have been working for the past two years and the moment has arrived.'

The next morning most of the team was up by 7 and at breakfast. Everyone, except Mungai. I later found out that arap Moi had called Mungai very late in the night and had told him that he, not Mungai, would be going to the Big Chiefs' meeting. The Yank had been right on the button.

CHAPTER 14

IDI AMIN, MILTON OBOTE

At the end of the Singapore summit conference, there were a number of kerbside press conferences. I happened upon Milton Obote and a group of other African leaders and asked the first question: 'Dr Obote how could you and your fellow African leaders allow yourselves to be bamboozled by a simple procedural motion?'

Obote said, 'That is Cyprian Fernandes, a colonial stooge and I will not answer such a stupid question.'

Among the group of journalists were some of Fleet Street's best and a chorus went up, 'Answer the question! Answer the question!' Obote and the Ugandans turned and left in disgust. That was the last time I saw him as President of Uganda.

While I was walking with this group of journalists, deep in conversation, we stopped at a traffic light. Instinctively we all took a step forward when the pedestrian light turned green. Unfortunately, my foot was the only one still on the road when a car raced past, over my foot. I did not really feel the impact and we walked across the road as if nothing had happened. My foot only began to throb with pain when I arrived in Hong Kong many hours later. I had dinner with Joe Rodrigues' brother and his wife and later went to a casino in Macau returning at around 4 am. The hotel I was staying in had cubby-hole bars at every lift. The silly thing about it was that there was a mini-bar in every suite. As I approached the lift, there was a fairly large Dutch type with an even larger voice and there were four Chinese grinning and nodding, not understanding a word he was saying.

'Come here you black bastard. I want to buy you a drink. I am celebrating, another black gorilla has come to power in Africa,' he said.

'No thanks, I buy my own drinks. By the way, who is the gorilla?' I asked.

'Someone called Idi Amin,' he answered.

The Dutchman turned out to be a South African seaman and had heard on the ship's radio that there had been a coup in Uganda. I knocked back a double 18-year-old Glenmorangie and hobbled to the lift and to my room. I rang the airport and said that I held a first class open ticket and needed to catch the first plane to Nairobi. I was told there were three flights. 'Is any flight being diverted to Singapore?' I asked.

'Yes, East African Airways,' was the answer.

'Can I have a first class seat, please?'

'No, you cannot. First Class has been reserved for VIP guests.'

'Can I have the first seat, just behind the curtain separating First from Economy?' I asked.

'Sir, you can have the rest of the aircraft, it is completely empty.'

I grabbed my stuff and headed for the airport. At the check-in, the pain in my foot was excruciating and the check-in lady noticed.

'Have you got a medical certificate allowing you to fly?' she asked me.

'Why do I need one?'

'You might have a medical emergency on the aircraft,' she explained.

'Where do I get a medical certificate?'

'The best place would be the new Princess Margaret Hospital.'

I hobbled into a cab and when I arrived at the hospital, I flashed my Press Card and was seen immediately. They began by taking my temperature, measuring my blood pressure, and going through the motions of a full examination.

I said, 'Please stop. It is my foot.'

'It will need X-rays,' someone said.

'Just give me some pain killing injections and a large box of painkillers to last me 17 hours of flying,' I pleaded. They obliged, including the certificate that enabled me to fly. I was on that East African Airways flight faster than anything the world had seen. When we stopped off in Singapore, I was at the top of the stairway in First Class as Milton Obote and his entourage came aboard. We nodded in greeting. It was a very sombre Obote, his face in grim concentration. Gone was the dismissive arrogance he had displayed the previous day at the press conference. It would be wrong to say he looked a broken man, but the spark of his previous life was missing. Where once there might have been cheery banter as the delegation seated itself, now there was nothing but an eerie silence

I was not surprised by the coup d'état. Before I had left Nairobi, Ugandan contacts had warned me that something was in the wind. I had called Editor-in-Chief Boaz Omori in Nairobi to find out if there was any news. There was none and, according to him, a coup was nothing more than political mischief. As it turned out, Obote had made arrangements to sack Idi Amin while Obote was in Singapore. Such was the man's confidence. Idi Amin beat him to the draw. On the other hand, there were rumours that Obote intended to sack Idi Amin on his return to Uganda. The tears finally came streaming down Obote's face after he listened to a BBC broadcast on the aircraft's radio. The BBC report confirmed the coup.

I tried several times to attempt an interview with Obote but with little success. In the First Class aisle he said to me, 'leave me alone, I am going through a private hell of my own.' So I sat there noting his every move, gesture, facial expression, as he rubbed his face with his hands, talking in quiet tones to his confidantes. As I sat down at my typewriter in Nairobi that night the intro to my story was quite simple: as Obote sped home not knowing whether he was still President of Uganda or just another man in the street, his only comment to me was, 'leave me alone, I am going through a private hell of my own.' Whatever the truth, Idi Amin took charge of Uganda with Israeli help and the blessing of the British. The Israeli motives have been well documented elsewhere: Israel wanted the war in Southern Sudan to simmer on and keep the Arabs in the Sudan preoccupied.

Back in Nairobi, while I digging into background information, I chanced upon this note (purportedly officially British):

AMIN DADA, GENERAL IDI, President of Uganda

'Born about 1925. Tribe: Kakwa (West Nile). Joined Kings African Rifles about 1945 as a private soldier and worked his way up through the ranks. One of the first Ugandans to be commissioned Army and Air Force Commander 1967. Major-General 1968. After coup promoted himself to General. Popular and a natural leader of men, but simple and practically illiterate; a man of the people. An imposing presence, 6'3" in height; once a good heavyweight boxer and rugby player. As Head of State, has shown an engaging lack of formality and a disregard for his personal safety. Benevolent but tough. Well-disposed to Britain; perhaps to an extent damaging to him in the African context. Speaks passable English. God fearing and deeply religious. A Muslim with four wives and seven children.'

Kenya was not exactly jubilant with Idi Amin, but there was some celebration that Tanzania's chief collaborator Obote was out. The extremely left-leaning Julius Nyerere and Milton Obote had no time for British/US capitalist ally Kenya. The British, on the other hand, were 'blinded by Amin's expressed love for England and his intentions to build a pro-Western Government'. He needed help and the British were happy to provide arms and other assistance. Obote and 20,000 Ugandans took refuge in Tanzania, which had been offered by President Julius Nyerere. Around 1964 a rumour claimed that Amin and Obote had been involved in smuggling gold. Some said this went as far back as 1960, with the fall of the Belgian Congo when Belgians sought out Obote's help to transport their valuables to safety. There was an unconfirmed report that Obote had double crossed Amin, keeping the larger share for himself.

Who the heck was this guy Idi Amin? Kenyans were glad that he had gotten rid of that arch black communist Obote. The challenge was to interview Idi Amin. The problem was the borders were shut and to enter illegally was virtual suicide. On Friday, February 12, still hobbling about in pain, I rented a car from the Eboo's where the Nation had a hire-deal, told the driver to lie down in the back seat when we got to the border, and calmly drove into Uganda several hours later, entering illegally and breaking the curfew. I stopped at Entebbe and went to the shores of Lake Victoria and saw the corpses of Amin's victims bobbing about. I then drove to Kampala and visited this huge, mushroom-like tree where Idi Amin claimed God had come to him and told him to save Uganda. I took a photo of a four-year-old pissing on the tree, but I never got it published because it was too insulting to Ugandans.

Next, I drove north to the Apac District, the Lengo and Acholi village areas of Milton Obote and his wife, Miria, who was a beautiful and gentle soul. I visited his parents and checked out that all was well in the northern areas. The coup had not reached them. Driving non-stop, with breaks only for meals and nature calls, I headed south until I reached the border with Tanzania. I drove several hundred kilometres along the border until, on the southern side, I saw Tanzanian soldiers digging in. I went across nonchalantly and had a chat with a senior officer who gave me a drink of water and told me they were conducting normal training exercises. I was not able to take any photographs.

Along that border, people were fleeing from either side of it not knowing whether they were Tanzanian or Ugandan. On my way back to Kampala,

I saw a Ugandan Military convoy and followed them to their camp where they, too, were digging in. I flashed my Press Card and told them I was in Uganda to celebrate the army's great victory. I got a couple of beers for my trouble. The bottom line was that Tanzania and Uganda were readying for war. I had to rush back to Kampala and file my story in time for the Sunday Nation. I had just sat at the telex machine and typed 'Mutukula, Saturday by Cyprian Fernandes.'

The door burst open and four armed soldiers rushed in. One of them said, 'you must come with us.'

I typed 'They've got me' and hit the *send* button.

The four soldiers frog-marched me into a waiting Jeep. They sat two astride me while I sat on an army tool box in the middle. A fifth soldier sat in front with the driver. Once I got into the Jeep, I knew I was a dead man. How do you face death? Is it like Philippe Petit, who said once he was on that tightrope high above there was no turning back from one twin tower to the other? Or did you face it with great courage epitomised by martyrdom? Or without a moment for reflection?

I had time to think. I said a prayer as we drove and silently told my wife and daughter how much I loved them both. Their faces kept flashing in front of my eyes. A million thoughts entered my mind, but the most harrowing one was that soon I would be dead. I was too numb to be afraid. Instead I gave in to my coming death fairly easily; after all, I had only myself to blame. That's it, I can't fix yesterday, and I will take the now as it unfolds.

I was quite amazed at how much detail in the Kampala streets came to life in that brilliant sunshine. The smiles seemed much larger and the colours much more vibrant. There were more than a few times that I begged God for my life and in the end I commended into His hands my life. The Jeep stopped at the Ugandan Parliament House and I was very surprised when I saw a friendly face apparently waiting greet us. He was an army captain I had known. When he saw me sitting with my hands on my head, he said, 'Mr. Fernandes, what are you doing with your hands on your head? Don't you know you are the guest of his Excellency, President Field Marshall, Idi Amin Dada?' My immediate thought was: why hadn't someone told these four idiots who had arrested me?

'You are very welcome to a free Uganda and the President is very much looking forward to meeting you,' the captain said. I wondered how he had known I was in the country.

I was ushered into the Cabinet Room where Idi Amin and his ministers were seated around a large ebony table. Amin was fairly dark but you could see a reflection of his face in that black ebony table. He got up and came to greet me with his hand thrust forward. 'Welcome to a free Uganda, Mr. Fernandes,' he said.

'I understand you have been across our border into Tanzania,' he said as we walked towards a large map.

'Yes,' I said, 'I have seen some Tanzanian soldiers digging in.'

'Don't worry about them, my sums will blow them to little pieces,' he boasted.

'What are sums, Mr. President?' I asked.

'Surface to Air Missiles,' he said.

'May I quote you on that?' I asked in a matter of fact way.

'I think that is why you are here,' he answered in the same manner.

He invited me to sit. That is when I made a horrible mistake. Having driven for nearly 24 hours, my body was covered in dust, some of it was red ochre, and I was thirsty as hell. So I asked him for a drink. He gestured to his Foreign Minister Wanume Kibedi to oblige me. He returned with a wooden crate of Fanta orange thick with dust.

'Mr. President, could you oblige me with something stronger, please?' I asked. Again Wanume Kibedi set off and returned with a crate of beer, which was also covered in an inch of dust. As I desperately quaffed the beer, I suddenly remembered Idi was a Muslim and immediately stopped drinking.

I sat there for nearly two and half hours and listened to a pack of lies. He told me he was out hunting when soldiers came to him armed with tanks and told him they had made a coup and wanted him to lead Uganda. He denied he had masterminded or led the coup. 'I am a simple soldier,' he told me. There was no mention of Israeli help. But he did give me a quote I have never forgotten: 'Uganda is corrupt. The Ministers are corrupt. The civil servants are corrupt. Everybody is corrupt. I want to clean up Uganda and give it back to our people as innocent as a baby that has just come out of its mother's womb.'

I liked the guy. He was simple but sincere, and he appeared genuine about cleaning up Uganda. He also said he wanted to get rid of communism, socialism, and all these anti-West ideas. I went back to my Kampala office and called the *Sunday Nation* editor Peter Darling and said those immortal words every journalist dreams of: 'Hold the front page, I got the interview.' I died a thousand deaths in that Jeep but soon I would be flying back to Nairobi, thank God.

I wrote:

'Amin tells his lies

'The Military Head of Uganda, Major General Idi Amin Dada, was to have been shot at 3:40 on the morning of Monday, January 25, 1971. Acholi and Lengo in the Ugandan Army and Air Force were given the go-ahead to assassinate Amin and arrest and disarm all non-Acholi, Lengo officers on the afternoon of Saturday, January 24.

'The former President, Dr Milton Obote, chairing a meeting by telephone from Singapore where he was attending the Commonwealth Heads of Government meeting, ordered that Amin be killed. Two of those who participated in the ill-fated plot series of meetings, Basil Bataringaya the former Minister for Internal Affairs and the former Inspector General of Police E.W. Oryema have admitted the plot to kill Amin.

'The fantastic plot by the former leader to control Uganda by placing armed control in the hands of Acholi and Lengo people was revealed to me by the man who, by an equally fantastic piece of luck, lived to tell the tale... Major General Idi Amin. The 'Obote Plot' was to have been revealed but the new Cabinet decided to withhold the information. However, in a 2.5-hour interview with me, Amin revealed the fateful events that brought him to power.

'Amin said, "One man saved Uganda from the terrible thing that Obote had planned for us all." His name was Sergeant-Major Mussa of the Mechanical Battalion. If it had not been for him, Amin would not have been alive that day.

'According to Amin, "That fateful day started most deceptively. It was a bright and sunny morning. Unsuspecting, I went hunting in the Karuma area. While I was hunting and doing my duty for my country, my people and my President, my death and the annihilation of Uganda was being plotted. I learned this later. Ask them and they will tell you it is all true.

'On the 24th there were several meetings. All of them were attended and chaired by Basil Bataringaya. Also present at the meeting were E.W. Oryema, Mr. Okware, Commissioner of Prisons, Senior Assistant Commissioner Dusman and Mr. Hassan, chief of the CID. There were also others.

'On the afternoon, after the meeting had been held at police headquarters, Parliament Building, this very building where you and I sit today, with thanks to the Almighty God and at the Office of the Inspector General, it was decided. Obote ordered my death. Oryema and Batangariya have confessed to this.

'At that precise moment I was probably shooting my third Uganda Kobi, an antelope. And so it happened. I returned home at six that evening. I did nothing special and did not sense anything at all. At 7.30 the world seemed to erupt on my front door step. There was a tank and the men on it were shouting almost hysterically and like a tall giant Sergeant-Major Mussa stepped off and told me there had been a coup but he had executed a counter coup.

'Make one thing clear. The soldiers and I did not plan a coup. It happened spontaneously. The Acholi and Lengo officers were half way to victory when the ordinary soldier, seeing the danger, took the initiative. One man, Sergeant Major Mussa did it. By six o'clock, the Acholi and Lengo officers had acted efficiently and precisely. All non-Acholi, Lengo officers had been disarmed or arrested. Then it came to the all-important Mechanical Battalion on Lubiri Hill, ironically situated where once the Kabaka's (king of the Bugandan tribe) palace used to be. It was here that Mussa acted with precision, seeing what was happening all around him.

'He made a beeline for the armory and at the same time warned the other soldiers in the battalion. Single-handedly he overpowered the guard and thus armed his fellow soldiers. He took charge of the situation and commanded the counter-coup for those few minutes. Then he made another beeline... for my residence atop a tank and asked me to do my duty and take command of the situation. I acted with hesitation. Then I took charge. Meanwhile, another hero was being born to Uganda. I was left without a single officer, only NCOs and soldiers. Another brave man was in the process of putting his life in danger. He was Second-Lieutenant Maliamungu, Swahili for God's property. Atop a tank, he raced to Entebbe airport, where the Air Force was all set to follow Obote's orders. Maliamungu stopped the planes with his tanks. Later, other tanks assisted him.

'Otherwise, Uganda might have seen genocide. If not for Mussa, Uganda might have suffered annihilation. Maliamungu was shot in the leg, but he refused treatment. He still refuses treatment. He is still in charge of Entebbe and is doing a fine job. There was another man, Sergeant Yekka. He, too, had a very honourable part to play in the salvation of Uganda.' (Amin never told me Yekka's role.) 'Then I stepped in. I ordered all soldiers to stop fighting. I ordered them to stop killing each other. Immediately there was a response. In some cases rebel officers decided to run away. They did. They are now coming back.

'I was on radio communications throughout the night until the morning. I was ready and willing to die for my country. I had fear of nothing. I felt no remorse. Only one thought nagged my mind: Save Uganda. Save Uganda. I had a small part to play. Ugandans, true national Ugandans, saved themselves and their country. That was what happened. Now, Uganda is in the process of putting the final touches on its second chance to save itself.'

Idi Amin's grasp of the English language was not the greatest and I tried to tell the story in his own words. Was his story a total lie? Was there ever a Mussa, Yekka and Maliamungu? Over the next two years, I was never able to find them. It is generally accepted that the Israelis neutralised the Air Force by sabotaging the aircraft.

Idi used to call me regularly on the phone for a chat or tip me off on a story. I made several trips to Uganda until one near-fatal day. During one of my many forays into Kampala, I had heard about Amin's death squads shooting innocent people and throwing the bodies over the railings of a bridge to be devoured by waiting crocodiles. I decided to chase this up and after a lot of help from sympathetic Ugandans I arrived at the bridge and was met by several men. They showed me blood caked at the railings, almost as thick as cow dung. I was told the killings took place around 6 pm. There was some natural light left by the setting sun. I was at the bridge, hidden in the bushes, and a little after 6 pm a military truck pulled over and a number of men were lined up then shot in a blaze of automatic gunfire. The corpses were thrown into the river below. I raced to my hotel and as I picked up the keys to my room, the receptionist handed me a folded piece of paper. It said, 'Get out quickly.'

I raced to Entebbe airport and headed for Nairobi. I had gotten the photographs but they were a little grainy, yet I thought there was enough to show people being shot, with gunfire flashes most prominent. I took the story, the pictures and negatives to my editor Boaz Omori. He asked me to wait outside his office while he reached for the phone. When he called me back, he said, 'I can't publish this. It is too sensitive and controversial and the photos are not clear enough as evidence.' He tore up the pictures and negatives and threw them into a waste basket.

Weeks earlier Idi Amin had visited Nairobi and walked the streets with throngs of Kenyans celebrating his success. He met Jomo Kenyatta and his ministers and was recognised as a friend of Kenya. Boaz Omori could not jeopardise that. The Kenyan government had already warned him. Many weeks later the story flooded the British papers, thankfully. That was the last time I went to Uganda, a country whose president and ministers once welcomed me and where I did not need a passport. That was also the second and last time I had faced possible death in Uganda.

Idi Amin has gone down in history as the most murderous despot in African history. He is reputed to have killed more than 300,000 of his countrymen. He also expelled the whole of the Asian community in Uganda, around 50,000 people.

With the help of Tanzanian soldiers, Obote deposed Idi Amin who went into exile and eventually died in Jeddah, Saudi Arabia, in 2003. Obote was overthrown by his right-hand man and friend Tom Okello in 1985. Obote died in Zambia in 2005.

CHAPTER 15

JOE RODRIGUES

I am indebted to Gerard Loughran author of *Birth of a Nation: The Story of a Newspaper* in Kenya for considerable help in research. *Birth of a Nation* celebrated the *Nation*'s 50 years of publication. Loughran spent a dozen years at the *Nation* in senior editorial capacities. He has a high-level standing in international journalism. I am also indebted to Cyrilla, Joe Rodrigues' widow, for recalling some of the traumatic as well as the happy milestones of her husband's life and career.

The finest South Asian journalist in Kenya, Jawaharlal Joel Joachim Joe, was nearly lost to medicine in Bombay where he grew up. His father, Francis, was an Indian nationalist and a senior executive with the *Times of India* and the *Indian Express*. He wanted his son to become a doctor rather than follow in his journalism footsteps. For two years young Joe remained chained to science against his will. It took a considerable amount of courage for the young man to tell his mother that his heart was in the arts and journalism and not in science or medicine. It was left to his mother to convince his autocratic father. Needless to say he did do his father proud.

Joe was one of seven children, five brothers and two sisters. His eldest brother Sunith was a General in the Indian Army. He progressed to Army Chief of Staff and later Governor of the Punjab. The family lived in Bombay but had their ancestral home in Cortorim, Salcette, Goa. The oldest frontline newspaper in Kenya, the *East African Standard*, was the exclusive domain of Her Britannic Majesty's colonial government and the white British settler community. It employed only white journalists. Asians and Africans did not get a look in.

With the birth of the Aga Khan-owned *Daily* and *Sunday* newspapers, Africans and Asians finally found a medium for their stories, hopes and aspirations. These were real newspapers produced in the vein of Fleet Street journalism, unlike any others in East Africa. Through its South Asian journalists, the *Nation* was able to attract a dormant Asian readership as well as tell their stories. *The Standard*, devoid of any Asian journalists, was not.

In 1960, the Aga Khan, through his right hand man the late Michael Curtis (a former Fleet Street editor), aspired to freedom of the press in Kenya and pushed the boundaries as far as the colonial government would allow them. John Bierman (now deceased), the fearless founding editor of the *Daily Nation,* gave Kenyans a taste of what real press freedom was about as the *Daily Nation* totally supported black Kenyans' push for independence. With Jack Beverley the *Sunday Nation* Editor, they brought to Kenya the best of what Fleet Street could offer Kenyan journalism. This was a new experience for its readers. The *Nation* papers were no one's mouthpiece; they were fair, balanced and sought the truth. From 1960-1963, Kenya enjoyed a freedom of the press in the *Nation* papers that came close to the Fleet Street ideal.

Without a doubt, the South Asian journalist who excelled in most aspects of newspaper journalism was one Jawaharlal Joel Joachim. Joe was a journos' journo. The consummate professional, he was an exquisite technician: layout specialist, editorial writer, and one of the tightest copywriters in the country. His colleagues joked that Joe could rewrite the Bible on the back of a box of matches. They might have stretched that a bit but he certainly was a master in the word game. In effect, he was capable of putting together the whole paper on his own: he had all the skills and the capacity to do so. He seemed to spend almost every waking moment at his desk in Nation House. He was the first in and among the very last to leave. His wife Cyrilla from Porvorim, Bardez, Goa, a Mombasa-born girl he married in 1953, often said he spent 16 hours a day at the *Nation*.

He rested a bit on Saturdays and was back at work on Sunday. Cyrilla was a newspaper widow from the very start. Joe enjoyed a good laugh and regaled his close Goan friends with some real howlers but their soirees at the Nairobi Goan Gymkhana were rare, much to Cyrilla's chagrin. Some said newspaper production for Joe was an addiction he simply loved and thrived upon. Cyrilla often complained the newspaper came first and then his family. Above everything else, Joe was a very private person, even at home. Some wrongly interpreted this privacy for aloofness. He hid his emotions well at all times, even with Cyrilla. He was blessed with ice-cool calm that not even a bomb could disturb. His quiet manner was both soothing and corrective when it needed to be. He was generous in more ways than one. He was 'St Vincent de Paul' to many of his colleagues and an easy touch for a short-term loan. You could trust him impeccably. The bottom line was: if Joe said it, it was true.

He did not have too many vices. He enjoyed du Maurier cigarettes, a glass of imported beer or a scotch and soda. Other than that he was Mr. Clean. Joe did not like and did not court the limelight. Joe and Cyrilla had many Goan admirers, among them, a special group of seven couples. Joe had an absolute ball with this group of people every time they met. Unlike most other Goans, they were not club-oholics and infrequently visited the Goan Gymkhana. Instead, their social life revolved around those infernal diplomatic cocktail parties Joe used to drag Cyrilla to. I suspect I was probably the only Goan who spent a lot of time with him away from work. I only went to his home for dinner once when he was down in the dumps. He was madly in love with Cyrilla but Cyrilla says he was not a romantic and did not tell her he loved her as was the want of autocratic men of that time. Cyrilla was the stronger of the two and she spoke her mind without hesitation, the very opposite of Joe. She voiced the things that the very private Joe would not. His only other cares in the world were their two children, Joy and Allan John.

Gerard Loughran provides a glimpse of Joe away from work: 'He invited me to a Saturday curry lunch at his house. Out on the lawn was a table groaning with food. Joe took me around it saying, "This is so-and-so, it is very hot, this is something or other and it is quite mild, this is not hot at all", and so on and so on. I was flabbergasted and said something like, "Joe, what a spread!" He replied, "That's why we Goans are so poor, we spend all our money on food!" Later, there was a minor crisis when his children managed to lock themselves in the house. Cyrilla was frantic; Joe was as cool as a cucumber. The children were released after a while, I forget how, and normality returned. Joe was not a coward nor did he go out of his way to seek out trouble or incur the wrath of the Kenyan government or opposition politicians. He served the public interest. Everything Joe did or wrote was the end result of his own considered legal scrutiny: was it true? Was it fact? Was it legal? Was it balanced? Was it in the public interest? Legal vetting is second skin to most good journalists. Joe was also probably born immune to bias, prejudice, partisanship and taking sides. He was super clean and no one, not even his family, the Aga Khan's Ismaili community, his own Goan community or other South Indians were allowed to taint his integrity. He did not do anyone any favours. On the other hand, the *Nation* had iron-clad guidelines concerning religious/ ethnic sensitivities and these were breached at an editor's peril.'

John Bierman is also credited with a little sub-editing on his new sub-editor's name. The story goes that John told Joe no way was he going to get his Queen's English Pommy tongue around "Jawaharlal". Bierman asked if he had another name.

'Yes, Joel.'

'That will do, Joe,' said Bierman at that impromptu christening.

By the time Joe reached Uganda in 1956 to join the *Uganda Mail*, he was already a pretty seasoned journalist. With a great command and love of the English language, he cut his journalistic teeth on the *Times of India*, one of India's greatest newspapers. He always had journalism in his DNA as he walked in his father's footsteps. He also spoke English without that lilting Bombay twang; it made him sound more East African or a London Asian, not quite that irritating upper class English nasal delivery. It was Cyrilla's late uncle Louis Mascarenhas who got Joe a job on the Patwa brothers' *Uganda Mail*. It was a short-lived association. The colonial government found the *Uganda Mail* a tough customer and promptly shut it down on the grounds the premises were unsafe. Joe and Cyrilla moved to Nairobi and found an opportunity with the *News Chronicle* whose then editor, Pinto, was in detention. Pinto was an extraordinary African socialist and freedom fighter. He would be assassinated on February 25, 1965. Joe and Pinto became good friends and, with the likes of Mboya, Bildad Kaggia and Joe Murumbi, attended many political meetings. Joe, unlike his father, was not a political animal. He was a journalist. While in Nairobi, Joe also briefly worked on a paper called the *Guardian* owned by a Mr. Desai. Joe had applied to the *Standard* for any journalistic position but received a reply that there were no suitable positions vacant.

When, in 1960, Joe was snapped up by John Bierman as a sub-editor for the *Daily Nation*, he was first offered three-month probation on the 5pm to 11pm shift and continued working on the *Chronicle* and the *Guardian* during the day.

After the first night, he told Cyrilla, 'It is pretty simple work.' After the second night: 'John Bierman stands over my shoulder all the time. That makes me a bit uncomfortable.' What Joe did not know was that John was full of admiration. He was amazed at Joe's sub-editing skills, his speed and his accuracy. After the third night he told her 'I have got the job full-time at 1900 shillings a month.' He didn't bargain for his wages and this would remain one of his hallmarks. Some would say it was an unwelcome one since he never asked for a raise or a particular reimbursement. He never argued over money when he really should have.

The first four years, 1960-1964, were amongst the happiest for both Joe and I. Joe progressed from sub-editor to night editor, then to Chief Sub-editor. In 1966 he was Editor of the *Daily Nation* and in 1968 became Managing Editor. With the exception of Joe and Pinto, both of whom became Kenyan citizens, most South Asian journalists did not have a permanent stake in Kenya. I knew that one day I would have to move on. More importantly we were not aligned with any tribe, any party, or the dying embers of the colonial government.

When Joe and I joined the *Daily Nation* in 1960, it was an era of great hope: surely independence would come sooner rather than later. From day one the *Nation* supported African independence, which until then was unprecedented in frontline newspapers. The Mau Mau rebellion had ended and, along with it, the state of emergency that had been declared in 1954. Now the likes of Odinga, Tom Mboya, James Gichuru, Mbiyu Koinange, and the rest of Kenya were agitating for the release of Jomo Kenyatta from detention while also pushing for independence. For the time being there was a kind of peace among all those politicians scrambling for their piece of the independence pie. Lurking in the political shadows was a huge struggle for power between Odinga's Luos and Kenyatta's Kikuyu.

We would meet regularly just off Victoria Street at the Lobster Pot restaurant for a beer after the first edition had been put to bed. This was the only time Joe allowed himself a moment or two of self-indulgence about his career. He felt a sliver of disappointment when Boaz Omori, Editor of the Swahili paper Taifa and a warm, gentle man with a beautiful smile, was made Editor in Chief. Joe accepted the Aga Khan's policy of having a black Kenyan as Editor in Chief. He was content with his lot as Managing Editor. When I suggested that he should be pushing harder for the top job, he asked 'Why? I am happy with what I am doing. I don't need the headaches and threats the top job brings.'

At home, he shielded Cyrilla from all the goings-on at the *Nation*. He rarely talked about anything that was troubling him; he kept a brave face and did not allow anything to worry his wife. However, when Cyrilla did press him, he told her, 'So what if they want a black man as the Editor-in-Chief? I have a good job and I am happy about it.' Many years later, he only eventually got the top job because the management team could not find a suitable black-skinned replacement after George Githii's acrimonious exit. Cyrilla tried hard to convince him to turn down the job. She had a strong sense of foreboding but Joe eventually took it on. A senior *Nation* personality discounted this reason for his appointment and insisted 'Joe was the right man for the job'.

Joe understood the limitations of any journalist working in Kenya: President Jomo Kenyatta was a dictator, almost a demi-god, and those closest to him ensured that nothing threatened the 'good name' of the President. There was no public criticism of him in print, on radio or television, or even in private. You could not even be satirical about Kenyatta as you freely would about prime ministers in the UK or Europe or presidents in the US. You could not take the mickey out of Kenyatta or any senior politician if you valued your life. Even if you were right, you could not challenge a government policy; that could be interpreted as challenging Kenyatta and later President Daniel arap Moi himself. Any normal criticism was taken personally. Kenyatta was ruthless and brutal. He harangued erring ministers at public rallies and he did not spare the language either.

At a private farewell party with no *Nation* management present, Joe said he neither resigned nor retired: he was fired. His long *Nation* career ended on July 31, 1981. He was succeeded by Peter Mwaura. I have not been able to find any evidence that indicates why Joe was sacked. One source said that there was talk at high level in the company of incompetence by Joe, which seems highly unlikely after all those years and appears more a ploy to conceal the real reasons. These seem to boil down to either: Joe's independent stance angered the government and particularly Attorney General Charles Njonjo (in Moi's case 'king maker'); or, he was a victim to Ismaili/Islamic/Arab pressures, the theory favoured by Joe himself.

The following three events sealed his fate in 1981. The first incident came in the aftermath of a terrorist bomb that destroyed the magnificent Norfolk Hotel in Nairobi, killing 15 people and injuring 18 others. Gerard Loughran said in *Birth of a Nation*: 'It is widely assumed that the attack was the work of Palestinian terrorists in reprisal for Kenya's assistance to Israel in Uganda's hostage drama; also the Block family who owned the hotel was Jewish.' Joe Kadhi wrote one of his *Why?* columns, denouncing the Libyan-funded Nairobi newspaper *Voice of Africa* for claiming that the bomb was planted by Israel; he also attacked the Palestine Liberation Organisation for describing Kenya as 'a police station for US interventionism'. These comments were fair and in line with government policy, as Joe pointed out in a letter to the board, stating 'This country is moving closer to Israel in the intelligence and security fields and away from the Arab world. The promise of cheaper oil has not materialised and the machinations of Voice of Africa and its Libyan backers, particularly vis-à-vis the Norfolk bomb and its aftermath, have combined to harden the government's attitude.' The Kadhi column was felt in some circles to have a negative impression of Arabs generally and a barrage of complaints was directed to the Aga Khan. Since the Editor-in-Chief was responsible for all columns and commentaries, Joe came under fire for letting this one through.'

In any western democracy, the column would not have raised a single eyebrow.

The second incident was Joe's famous Bondo editorial on April 18. The ruling Kenya African National Union (KANU) electoral machine barred the late Odinga from standing in the seat of Bondo in the general elections. Joe defended Odinga's constitutional rights in an editorial headed 'A time for magnanimity.' The editorial said the decision to bar Odinga was 'unconstitutional, undemocratic and not conducive to the national compromise to which President Moi has been exhorting Kenyans'. Joe was arrested and interrogated and the *Nation* promptly published a back-down short of an official apology.

The third incident began with an angry President Moi calling Joe at home on the morning of Friday, May 22. 'Moi was angry about the use of the word "anonymous" in a *Nation* story about a national strike by doctors. The relevant sentence said "On Wednesday, the Kenya News Agency released an anonymous statement said to have been released by KANU, condemning the strike and calling on the government to deal with the strikers." The wording seemed to throw doubt on whether this was a genuine KANU statement, but that was not what offended Moi. A Kenya News Agency (KNA) statement quoted him as saying, "KANU is the ruling party. It is the government and therefore my voice. How can the publishers of *Nation* imagine the views of the party are anonymous? They also want to say Moi is anonymous."

'The word "anonymous" had been inserted into the story by Chief Sub-editor Philip Ochieng, whose English is impeccable. The statement bore no indication which KANU official or officials had issued it, and this was what Ochieng was trying to point out. In the conspiratorial world of Kenya, his semantic intervention was given a sinister connotation.

At about 4pm, Kadhi the *Daily Nation*'s Managing Editor and the acting News Editor John Esibi were picked up. Soon after Joe, Ochieng and reporters Gideon Mulaki and Pius Nyamora were also arrested. Joe was released 24 hours later and the others after three days.'

There was also Njonjo's outburst about the 'sensationalist' reporting of a case involving his cousin.

According to one observer, the 'internal' Kenyan issues of Bondo, the doctors' strike and Njonjo's outburst were par for the course in the running battle at that time between the Government and the media. Any support for Odinga, no matter how well argued and honourably based, was bound to infuriate the Kikuyu establishment; the 'anonymous' row seemed to be a mischievous dig by Ochieng whipped into a froth of dubious indignation; and as for 'sensationalism', in a Kenyan context this seemed to mean reporting what a politician did not want reported. The *Why?* column appeared to be different. The main objection was that it implied all Arabs were fanatics. The BBC correspondent Tim Llewellyn said there had been a concerted Arab and Muslim campaign pressuring the Aga Khan to get rid of Kadhi and/or presumably Joe as his superior. It is difficult to establish whether this was true or not, but it is notable that the Nation Newspapers Limited board meeting that backed Joe referred to 'complaints directed to the principal shareholder'.

Aiglemont (an estate at Gouvieux in the Picardie region of France that functions as the secretariat and residence of His Highness Prince Karīm Aga Khan) was always sensitive with regard to the Arab-Israel issue which Joe wrote about to Michael Curtis on February 21, 1981 clearly implying the *Nation* should be nudging its policies towards the Israelis. Philip Ochieng said in an interview with Loughran that, 'There was a perception Joe was siding too much with the Israelis, forgetting that his owner had certain affinities with the Palestinians. His argument was that to stay with the government, you had to favour the Israelis.'

Kadhi told Loughran, 'People (Aiglemont) were angry about a trip I made to Israel but Joe gave permission provided I came back via Cairo to ensure my stories were balanced and I did that. Aiglemont hit the roof.

I feared the *Nation* could never be impartial covering any Islamic issue, Pakistan or the Middle East, though I am a Muslim.' Kadhi recalled one time designing the foreign page with plans to use a story about Muslim terrorists in Afghanistan and Michael Curtis begged him to find a substitute.

Loughran adds: 'On July 22, in a farewell meeting with the Nation Newspapers Ltd board, Joe said his departure from the company was not connected with government pressures as he was led to believe, but with the *Why?* affair because the Editor-in-Chief approved all commentaries. He said the column was not a condemnation of Arabs but an expression of concern over the perpetuation of terrorism. The Board wished him well for the future.'

One aspect of the *Why?* debacle remains unclear: whether Joe did or did not see Kadhi's column before publication. According to one source, Joe said he had not seen the column. Joe also did not discipline Kadhi as requested. The company assumed he did not discipline Kadhi because he had in fact seen the column.

In a letter to Harry Evans, the brilliant editor of the *Sunday Times*, Joe said 'I now have good reason to believe that my departure has to do with the Arab League and local Muslim pressures.' It is not clear exactly when the decision was made to remove Joe, but Njonjo hosted a dinner party for the Aga Khan when he came to Nairobi in March for the International Press Institute (IPI) assembly and it can be presumed Joe was discussed.

Loughran again: 'Joe's letter to Evans claimed the company was negotiating with Peter Mwaura during the IPI assembly in early March. Cyrilla said Sir Eboo Pirbhai (the highest ranking non-royal Ismaili after the Aga Khan) summoned Joe and told him the message from Paris was that he had to resign for his own security. I do not know when this meeting took place. Joe himself said he was told he had to go by Michael Curtis in Nairobi at the end of May because a decision had been taken to revert to a black Kenyan as Editor-in-Chief. Both times he was told he was "in personal danger". Presumably this was a reference to the Kenya security authorities since Joe had been detained after the Bondo editorial. It is unclear whether there was ever any serious threat to Joe or whether this was an attempt to frighten him into quitting. He himself did not seem to take it seriously.'

The Bondo editorial was written within days of the IPI assembly at which Moi had stated, 'We in Kenya steadfastly uphold the freedom of the press' and Information Minister Oringo said the press should be seen as an ally of government, not an enemy. Of course, Joe was not so naïve as to take these statements at face value, but like the courageous and canny political animal that he was, perhaps he decided that then was a good time to test the sincerity of their claims and push the boundaries a bit, given that the Western editors were still motoring out to Jomo Kenyatta International Airport. Some thought the headline, "A Time for Magnanimity", was excellent.

The government, after having enjoyed almost complete control during George Githii's tenure as Editor-in-Chief, found it difficult to come to terms with the somewhat independent stance the *Nation* was taking under Joe.

In the aftermath, Joe took over a stable of three magazine titles and increased this to 12 but this was no challenge, more a step backwards. Joe was never the same man but he never showed it and bottled everything up.

The *Nation* dumped Joe with a pittance in severance pay. There was always a colour bar at the *Nation* as far as remuneration was concerned. The expatriate whites were on huge salaries and benefits. When Stan Denman retired as Chairman he had a pension for life as he had been hired on expatriate terms. Joe, being an Indian, was not considered an expatriate and was only given a small lump sum, most of which was gobbled up by income tax. This was a brutal time for Joe's family.

Within days, he had a job offer from the outstanding journalist of the modern era, Harold Evans, editor of the *Sunday Times*. *The New Statesman*, India, was also quick to offer Joe a senior editorial position. Joe turned down both as he did the two other times he was head-hunted: once by the *Standard* for the job of editor while he was still at the *Nation* and the other time by Moi, after Joe had been sacked by the *Nation*. Moi wanted him to edit a KANU newspaper. I would like to think that Joe represented the South Asian community and he did it with such brilliance that his star still shines today and people speak of him with respect and sadness at his early passing. With his IPI and UPI connections in the UK, US, and Australia, Joe could have migrated to a lucrative job overseas. On a visit to Australia, I tried to convince him of the great opportunities for him down under. He would have none of it. He had always said 'Kenya will get my bones', which was prophetic. Most journalists thought that the stress of the job eventually killed Joe, who suffered a massive heart attack at the age of 56 in 1987. The truth, however, is that the men in Joe's family were plagued with chronic heart disease. But it is still not drawing too long a bow that the *Nation* job somehow contributed to his death. It is a tragic irony that for a man who gave his all to journalism, journalism did not serve him well. There is no record of anyone asking why Joe was really sacked, why no one from *Nation* management officially wielded the axe, or why was it left to an outsider like Sir Eboo. We will never know.

CHAPTER 16

JOE ZUZARTE MURUMBI

Murumbi, Kenya's first Foreign Minister and later Vice President for a short while, was a rare African politician. Like his friend and mentor Pinto, Murumbi was an honest man. The man I knew was something of an introvert. Even while campaigning he did not seek the media limelight, he was happier talking to his voters. More often than not he was a difficult man to interview on politics. He found it difficult to talk about himself and even more difficult to talk about the various strands of politics prevailing in the country at the time. I even got the feeling sometimes that he was a reluctant politician. But he was a gentle man most of the time, even poetic, always in a far off world of his own, the world of art. He was born of a Goan father and a Maasai mother, the daughter of Chief Laibon Murumbi. He was Masaai, and nothing else. I would also say that his Maasai heritage did not sit too well with the small-minded Goans. He was not exactly a regular visitor to the Goan clubs.

Murumbi was educated in Bangalore and lived there for 16 years. However I have never been able to find any record of him visiting Goa. More importantly, on his return to Kenya he chose to live as a Maasai, his mother's people. He succeeded Odinga as Kenya's second vice president in May 1965. He resigned on August 31, 1966. Murumbi donated 8,000 rare books to the National Archives Library and stipulated that 'the collection would be preserved at his Muthaiga home, which would be expanded to become the Murumbi Institute of African Studies, with a library, hostel and kitchen'. Despite a huge demand from overseas he sold his vast art collection to the Kenyan government at a concessionary rate. Unfortunately, the government sub-divided the Muthaiga property and allocated it to developers. It is said that he never recovered from the shock he experienced when he visited the site, only to find developers turning it into private real estate.

The Murumbis spent most of their retirement between his Muthaiga residence in Nairobi and his 2,000-acre Intona Ranch in Transmara, Maasai country where he had built himself a 30-room home. The house fell into neglect after his wife Sheila died in 2000. From having been a luxurious retirement home with many servants and part of his famed art collection on the walls and hallways, the imposing house now does not even have doors and windows, thanks to vandals.

Roots had torn their way into what was once a beautiful swimming pool. It was reduced to a cracking brick mortar edifice, greenish with algae, and which would soon disappear without trace. In one of the rooms, a not-so-good graffiti artist listed the names of Kenya's past vice presidents and the incumbent Kalonzo Musyoka. The house is near the world-famous Maasai Mara game reserve and would form an additional tourist attraction or an exclusive lodge, as one observer put it (*Nation*).

Murumbi's elevation to the vice presidency was designed to drive a wedge between Murumbi's socialist leanings and the man he replaced, Odinga. It did not work and Murumbi resigned a frustrated man on August 31, 1966. He buttoned his lip, and simply moved out of political life to focus completely on his magnificent collection of art and books. His isolation led to mainstream Kenya 'forgetting' Murumbi, especially after Murumbi and Alan Donovan started the internationally-lauded art gallery *African Heritage*. This was reckoned to be a high-brow gallery which had nothing to do with the common man, and Murumbi was often dismissed sadly as a class conscious nouveau riche. They considered him the first African snob. He was none of those things really, just someone at peace with himself and his own world. He was labelled a left-leaning, West-bashing anti-capitalist. The fact that he left politics to enter into business cans that theory. He loved life too much to be a communist.

Goans have tried to make a big deal of the Goan half of his life. I think he shunned that. There could not have been more than a couple of times that he visited the Goan clubs and mostly in the company of Pinto. I remember reading a long time ago that when he was asked who he would like to live as, he told his father: a Maasai.

In his own words, this is Joe Murumbi's childhood as told to Anne Thurston, a researcher and archivist who worked in Kenya during the 1970s. Thurston recorded a series of conversations that were planned for an eventual memoir. Much of Thurston's material is the basis for *A Path Not Taken* compiled by Alan Donovan:

'My father, Peter Zuzarte, was from an old landed Goan family who lived in a place called Guirim. In his day, well-to-do families could afford to have a priest and a chapel in the house, which my father's family had. In the chapel there were jewels and ornaments worth a great deal of money, and the priest, who studied Latin and Greek, administered the household. My father, however, wanted to go abroad, and when he heard that clerks were being hired for work in East Africa, he applied for a job and was selected to come by Mackinnon Mackenzie, the recruiting agent in Bombay. From Bombay he travelled to Aden in a P&O boat and by a German boat to Zanzibar. From there he sailed by dhow to Mombasa, arriving in Africa for the first time in 1897. He then walked to Baringo Station, which was at the time in Uganda Province. In Baringo he served as a district clerk under Geoffrey Archer, the District Officer, who later became Governor-General of Sudan. Later, from Baringo he was posted to Naivasha which was also in Uganda Province, on the border, and from there he went to Eldama Ravine, a small town in the Rift Valley. He worked as a clerk, but he then gave up his job and started his own shop. It was in Eldama Ravine that he met my mother, I don't know the circumstances, and it was there that I was born, in 1911. Later we moved to Londiani where he again set up a shop.

'My mother grew up in the Eldama Ravine area. She was the daughter of Murumbi, the Laibon of the Uasin Gishu Maasai. My grandfather was not able to come to terms with the British. Sir Fredrick Jackson, in his book,

Early Days in East Africa, called him "the one-eyed Cyclops - an evil man". On one occasion my grandfather incited the Maasai warriors and the Sudanese, who had been stationed at Eldama Ravine by Lord Lugard to be moved to Uganda when needed, to rebel against the British. They nearly killed the District Commissioner and afterwards a nine-foot stone wall was built around the District Commissioner's house for protection. My grandfather was deported to Narok then and on two other occasions. The third time he died there.

'My father's shop was situated in an area reserved for European shops, away from the main Indian trade area. By some wangle he set it up on a plot which was in the name of an American lady, who she was I don't know. The only other shop in the European area was the post office. Nonetheless, my father maintained contact with the other Indian merchants in town. They used to come to my father's house and he used to visit theirs. The shop was a corrugated iron building, rather a big shop, and attached at one end was our residence; behind was a kitchen. It was the only shop in the area where one could buy drinks and a good range of supplies. I remember as a child seeing the Boer settlers, arriving in wagons pulled by teams of oxen, stop at my father's shop to buy their supplies. After Londiani, where there was a railhead, there was no other real source of supplies until Kitale or Eldoret. When there weren't many customers, I would sit in the shop with my father and he would teach me the alphabet.

'My father used to grow roses. He told me, although I don't remember the incident as I must have been very young, that Teddy Roosevelt (US President) once came to Londiani and, my father's shop being the only place where he could buy supplies, he called there and saw the roses. He and my father exchanged information about grafting roses. My father was a keen gardener; it was a skill he developed himself. There were several Indian shopkeepers, although as I've said, they were in another section of Londiani, and there were two children. However, I don't remember at all playing with anybody other than our dogs, my mother, and my father. The dogs, Jack Russells, were called Roddie and Spot and were very important to me as a child. My first reading book had a picture of a dog pulling a little cart, and my father made a cart for me to ride in which Roddie and

Spot used to pull. When my father went out he'd call the dogs to sit on either side of the front door and no one would be allowed to enter until he came back.

'My mother was a linguist, a self-taught one I think. I used to speak to her in English even though I could speak some Maasai. My mother spoke about eleven languages including Maasai, English, Hindustani, Lumba, Nandi and Kikuyu. She had a gift for languages; she picked them up from other people. My mother also used to wear Western clothing, but later on she went back to Maasai dress. Throughout her life with my father, I remember that now and then she used to take me off to a place called Kedawa, which is very close to Londiani, where she had friends. I've read references to these trips in my father's diaries, which unfortunately I lost, and I remember riding strapped to her back; I still remember its warmth and how I used to fall asleep. I remember, too, going through the Londiani forest and being impressed by some little red birds there, but I've never been able to determine what kind they were. At Kedawa there was a big Nandi and Maasai population and they held feasts there. I remember all the old people sitting down in a circle, in the centre of which was a big pot, which contained a brew. Each man had a long reed which he dipped in the pot to suck the brew. When they slaughtered a bull or other animal, all had a good feast and my mother used to give me roasted ribs. There I'd sit with my roasted rib, tugging at it and enjoying it very much.

'It was very cold there (in Londiani) and I used to sleep in front of the fireplace. Before I went to sleep my mother always brought me a cup of beaten egg: what they call zabaglione in Italian. It is egg white beaten up with some milk, brandy and sugar. Eggnog. Then my mother used to kiss me good night and lift my legs up and tuck the blankets under my feet. I'll never forget the way she used to do this.

'We lived in Londiani until I was six or seven years old and then my father decided that I should be educated in India. At first, mother was very, very angry and she took me away to Kedawa. My father then sent a friend of my mother's, the wife of the game warden at Eldama Ravine, Mrs. Ross, after her. Mrs. Ross explained why it would benefit me to go to India and finally my mother relented and let me go. I had clothes made for me and I remember particularly a suit I had. It was a sort of greenish woollen suit with braces and a belt, and I had a big collar with a black bow. The trousers were short and narrow and came below the knee, with buttons at the bottom, and I wore long socks. I had a tweed cap, too. My father had a wooden box made for me. My father took me to India to school, but I left my mother in Londiani. I can't actually remember our parting, but it must have been very painful because she didn't know where I was going... India was so far away. She had heard about India, but she didn't know where it was. I was not to see her again for many years.

'I don't remember the train journey from Londiani, but I remember going to Mombasa and travelling to Bombay on a ship. It was very hot on the ship because ships were coal-fired in those days. At night, as it was wartime, we were not supposed to show any lights. I still missed my mother, but it was all so very exciting, seeing new places, new people, and a new country. We landed at Bombay and stayed there for a week-or two, and then my father took me to Mysore in south India. A festival was in progress, and the whole town of Mysore was in a festive mood. I remember that the girls were all beautifully jewelled and the elephants decorated. My father took me to the Maharaja's stables where his magnificent horses, saddlery, and carriages were kept. From there we went to Bangalore. My father had arranged with the nuns of the school there that he would bring me. We sat in the parlour and he spoke to the nuns. Suddenly I realised that he had left, and I ran to find him. Of course I was brought back again. The nuns gave me a cricket bat to try to divert me, and in time I settled down at school.

'It was a very good school. As a matter of fact, at the time the best schools in India were run by Jesuits, because, you must remember, all Jesuit fathers had a training of about 12 years in which they were taught to be first class teachers. They ran the school very much along the lines of an English public school with an emphasis on leadership and sports. Most of the students were Anglo-Indian, but there were a few European boys as well.

'When I was about 12, I moved to a school in Bellary, another town in south India. Although I knew nothing about the outside world, this time I had to travel on my own. The day that I left I saw the other students get into a train, and I followed them, with little idea of where I was going. I thought that probably I'd land up in the right place eventually. After sitting on the train for about half an hour, the administrator of my school came in, red hot and puffing away. Apparently he had been looking for me through the whole train. As soon as he saw me he flew into a fit of temper. "Where are you going?" "I don't know, to my school, I suppose." "Have you got a ticket?" "No." "And how are you going to travel by train?" I did, however, eventually arrive at the school. Being an African I was rather a curiosity and the students all came around to examine me.

'This was also a Jesuit-run school but it was later taken over by the Mill Hill Fathers. It was a good school; it was a Catholic school. Discipline was humanitarian, but it was very tough, and sometimes we resented it. However, afterwards, I have realised that being subjected to discipline and to religious teachings gave me an anchor in life, a conscience to judge what is wrong and to try to do what is right. This school had a major effect on my life. Much of my character and many of my values were formed at Bellary. There were two who were tremendously important to me. Mother Elizabeth was a Portuguese nun, about 35 years old, who really looked after me when I went to Bellary. She loved me very much and I loved her. She was so kind, so affectionate and motherly; she looked after me like I was her own child. It was she who gave me my first pair of long trousers, and I was very proud of them. You see, I had to cling to something, I didn't know whether my mother was alive or dead, and she helped to fill the gap. As a boy, I worshipped Mother Elizabeth and I willingly did everything I could to help her. The other person was the principal. Father Callenberg. He was loved by people of all religious communities in Bellary because he never showed any discrimination between Catholics and Protestants, Hindus, or Moslems. Whenever a poor man came to him he helped him, no matter what his religion was. He was also dearly loved by the students, for he was so human in his attitudes toward the boys and their problems. This was certainly true in my case. When I was two years from finishing my secondary education, my father's shop was burnt down, and he had no money to pay for my education. I didn't know what was going to happen to me, but Father Callenberg took over paying for my education, and I was able to complete it. Later when I was working in Bellary, I did what I could to make a contribution to the school in gratitude for what Fr Callenberg had done for me. Yet, there is another major reason why I shall never forget Father Callenberg. From the age of seven until I left school at the age of 19, I had been cloistered between the four walls of a school; I had hardly any experience with the outside world. When I finished school I was shy, I couldn't mix with people, and I found the world outside a complete contradiction to what I had been used to at school. I got so confused that I lost my faith in religion. When Father Callenberg noticed that I was not coming to church, he asked me why, and in response I wrote him a long letter telling him how confused I was. We carried on a correspondence for about two years, and in the end he brought me back to the belief that God did exist and was all powerful. I'm not very religious in the sense that I go to church every Sunday, but I have maintained this firm belief in the power of God. I know that if one believes in God, one helps other human beings in need as Father Callenberg did, and that God returns this in some form.

'After leaving school Father Callenberg helped me to get a job as a clerk, first in a garage and later in a company called Burma Shell in Bellary. I lived with an extremely nice family called the O'Malleys. Old man O'Malley was an Anglo-Indian, and his wife was an Indian. As Mother Elizabeth had, Mrs O'Malley looked after me like a mother. Moreover, she was one of the best cooks in the world. She used to cook gorgeous food; we had a different dish every day. She encouraged me to learn to cook, and this was very important to me because when I left Burma Shell, I got a job doing famine relief work in the villages. Mrs. O'Malley used to send me all the necessary condiments every month. In south India there were areas where the rainfall was very scarce, and if the rain failed for one year, there was famine. The Government used to institute famine relief measures and make the villagers build roads for a pittance. I got a job as a clerk keeping the muster rolls and helping to plot the roads. The people in the villages were terribly kind and honest. Yet, it was in the villages that I first had contact with the caste system. I didn't really understand the system at all, but when I shook hands with the lower caste Hindus or brought them water from a well, I was told by the higher caste Hindus that this was wrong. This sort of thing annoyed me. It was very pathetic because the villagers were fine human beings and they worked harder than anybody else for it was they who tilled the fields. This was the beginning of my political conscience.

'When the famine relief work was over after nine months, I got a job in an ice factory making ice. The ice business was during the hot weather, but when the slack season came, my boss said he didn't want to sack me and sent me to the workshop. I used to work night shifts because I could handle the machinery. One Sunday morning I was waiting for my relief when I saw young O'Malley coming toward me with an elderly man. I thought the man had come to buy some ice and asked what I could do for him. He looked at me with a painful expression and said, "I don't think you'll remember me. I left here many years ago." Something instinctively told me that it was my father. When my relief came I went with my father to the railway station, because he had to catch a train, and he told me how it was that he had found me. He had been to Bombay to see my step-brother, then to Mangalore in south India to see my step-sister, and then he took a chance and came to Bellary where I had been at school. Arriving on a Sunday, he went to the church and asked whether the people knew me. Luckily I was still working in the same town and they directed him to my home where he met the O'Malleys.

'My first question to my father was: where is my mother? He wouldn't tell me, but he said he would write to me about her, and not long afterwards he wrote from Goa asking me if I could come back to Kenya as he was in difficulty and needed my help. I agreed. However, when he returned to Kenya he made enquiries about my mother, from whom he had separated, and he wrote again to tell me that she had been killed by a lion. When I heard this, I answered that I didn't think I'd come back. My father then made further enquiries and found that my mother was not dead. He wrote back to me and told me that he had made a mistake, that she was alive, and that she wanted me to come. When I got this letter, I wrote to Mrs O'Malley, who had gone to see her daughter in a town far away from

Bellary. I told her that my mother was alive, but that I didn't want to leave without seeing her. She wrote to me and said, "I've been like your mother, but now that you've found your real mother, don't keep her waiting, go as soon as possible". And so, in 1931, with my childhood passed, I left India to return home to Kenya and my parents.'

In Kenya he worked as a clerk in the colonial service and went to Somalia to work with the British Military administration. In 1952 he began dabbling in politics and soon became Secretary of the Kenya Africa Union after the union's key leaders, including Jomo Kenyatta, were placed in detention.

Those of us who knew Murumbi at the family level know that he exhibited reserved traits and a love for dogs to the end of his life, a sure heritage from his upbringing.

For everything he achieved in his life – as a freedom fighter, one of the architects of Kenya's constitution, the biggest player in the legal defence of the Kenyan leadership in detention during the Mau Mau emergency, setting up the network of the Kenyan diplomatic corps, Kenya's first Foreign Minister, Kenya's second Vice President - Murumbi died of a broken heart.

The National Archives department has set up a library containing some of the 6,000 'rare books', those published before 1900, entrusted to them upon Murumbi's death. He slipped away on June 22 1990, after suffering a heart attack. His wife, Sheila, died in October 2000.

A Ford Foundation grant worth $US50,000 assisted the Murumbi Trust to restore, interpret, preserve and label the unique, historic collection of political, artistic, textile, material and cultural artefacts displayed in permanent glass showcases at the Kenya National Archives 20 years later. It had been Murumbi's final wish to be buried near his old mentor and friend, Pio Gama Pinto, the victim of the country's first political assassination in 1965. As the cemetery was full, Murumbi was buried nearby in the City Park and the remains of Sheila Murumbi were interred next to her husband in 2000. Subsequently, their graves were vandalized and the plot was threatened to be taken over by private developers. After a public outcry, the graves were at last rehabilitated and some of Murumbi's favourite sculptures placed nearby the gravesites.

In 2009 the Murumbi Peace Memorial was unveiled in the park. In homage to Joe and Sheila Murumbi, it has been proposed to build a Murumbi Memorial Gallery in Central Park in central Nairobi, just near a site where Murumbi had proposed a National Art Gallery.

CHAPTER 17

PIO GAMA PINTO

On February 24, 2015, Goans joined people around the world in remembering one of their revered fallen heroes, the political martyr, Pinto. Kenya became independent in December 1963. In 1965 he became the first Kenyan politician to be assassinated.

Pinto was an ultra-national Goan Kenyan freedom fighter. The other, was Fitz de Souza, lawyer, constitutionalist, parliamentarian and deputy speaker. The much heralded 'Goan' Joe Zuzarte Murumbi opted for his mother's Maasai heritage. There was no political capital in shouting about the Goan in him, after all Goans did not exactly treat Africans as their equals and, instead, took the racially superior position of being Portuguese Goans. Many years later, after all the political mayhem had cost many lives, he joked, 'now I am an art lover.' The truth is that Joe Murumbi did much to help the Maasai, especially with scholarships for children.

The other Goan leading light, JM Nazareth, chose to side with India in its fight for independence from Britain. He divorced himself from the Portuguese. In 1960, perhaps the most famous Goan in African political history, Pinto, stopped being a Goan. This is what happened.

In Kenya, while quizzing cabinet ministers or Jomo Kenyatta and other African presidents, there was always a chance if I embarrassed any of them that I would be on the next plane home or even suffer the same fate that Pinto did. In the 1960s, the illustrious journalist Joe (Jawaharlal)

Rodrigues used to take me for an after-the-edition-has-been-put-to-bed beer at the Lobster Pot bar and restaurant. On one of these occasions, we bumped into Pinto who was meeting other people there.

A bit of background: Pinto had rescued Joe from Kampala, where he was floundering on a print-sheet of no consequence, to succeed Pinto as Editor of the *Daily Chronicle*. Joe was forever grateful. After the initial niceties, the talk turned to a trickle of Goans returning to Goa. Some were also leaving for Lisbon and I asked Pinto how the Goans were treating him these days.

'I have no time for them. After what happened in October 1960, they made it clear that they were not on my side when it came to supporting African aspirations for freedom. I stopped thinking about them and now concentrate on the challenges ahead for Kenya. I have nothing to do with them,' he said. Joe did not say anything. He did not even raise an eyebrow. He was that kind of guy. He did not chat about politics with anyone. Minutes later, after we'd finished our beers, we said our goodbyes and left. In a conversation with Luis de Assiss Correia (famously called 'Tom Mboya's travel agent' for helping the Kenyan leader airlift hundreds of students for further studies in the USA), he told me his impressions of those difficult days.

'Pio told the little-minded Goans that their halcyon days were soon to be over. After that he did not have time for the Goans. Pio then devoted all his energies to his mission, which had started as a 17-year-old, which was the liberation of the Portuguese colonies.'

Luis generally did not involve himself in local Goan politics but he was a friend of Pio's and they met regularly for lunch. On the day Pinto was killed, they were due to have lunch at Parliament House. It was not to be.

Tony Lopes, a former General Secretary of the East African Goan League was until recently perhaps the one person (died 2016) who could have thrown light on Pinto's shunning of the Goans in Kenya. With Pio, and the League's President Alex da Costa and Vice President Euclid De Souza, Tony was at the heart of the Goan war in 1960. Perhaps Pinto's staunchest supporter was Peter Carvalho. He was with Pinto at the Goan Institute demonstration and the League gang including Mboya regularly dined at his house. Peter was the quiet achiever of group.

There is little doubt that Pinto had separated from the Goan community long before Kenya's self-rule in 1963. In fact, in his early years he had already gained the wrath of the politically placid (naïve even) Goan club community. My friend and author Braz Menezes says Pinto was labelled a communist and a radical at a time when few Goans really understood what a communist was. In October 1960 he had set the divorce in motion with his plans to disrupt the visit to Kenya of the Vice Premier of Portugal, Pedro Teotinio Pereira, a sabotage mission that was opposed by the general Goan community. Pereira was visiting at the invitation of the colonial government. His main aim was to renew links with the Goans in Nairobi and Mombasa. His program would see him officially open the Fort Jesus Museum in Mombasa and visit the Vasco Da Gama (the first Portuguese to set foot in Kenya on his pioneering search for spices) memorial in Malindi.

Pereira arrived in Kenya on a six-day visit on October 27, 1960. His visit was pure Portuguese propaganda. Britain and Portugal colluded to prop up each other's claims to their respective patches in Africa. Pereira had arranged the financing of the Fort Jesus Museum through the Gulbenkian Foundation of which Pereira was the administrator. Some 30,000 pounds was made available. Fort Jesus was hijacked and forced into celebrations marking 500th anniversary of the death of Prince Henry the Navigator. At stake was Portugal's colonial identity.

In the media, the *Goan Voice* on the side of the loyalists and the *Goan Tribune* for the East African Goan League fought the war. There was also strong opposition to the visit by *The Colonial Times* and *The Daily Chronicle*. Pinto's links with the latter publication dated back to 1953 when he became editor. Indian merchants owned both the *Chronicle* and the *Times*. It was rich Indians who propped up Pinto's efforts, especially against the Portuguese and especially in Goa. In the weeks before the opening of Fort Jesus, Pinto made clear his opposition to the visit. He challenged the contention by the Goan Overseas Association that 'Goans look to Portugal as their Fatherland.' Letters in the *East African Standard* (then a paper strongly supporting colonial rule) stomped on the East African Goan League as being unrepresentative. The letters were like a knee into Pinto's groin.

Catholic priests, perhaps putting an unofficial spin on the subject, had vilified socialists and communists as being akin to devil worshippers and told the Goans that they should have nothing to do with them. My memories of these times are that religion wielded incredible influence. Worse still, Pinto was a Mau Mau. Goans could not be seen supporting a member of this 'evil and barbaric' guerrilla force, considered 'a murderous land army'. Photographs of the corpses of their victims were published in the local media. It was a horrific scene to say the least. How could anyone expect the Goans to support someone who associated with such wholesale murder? They did not know it at the time, but Pinto not only financed the Mau Mau chapter in the village of Mathare Valley in Eastleigh, metres away from the St. Teresa's boys and girls schools, but he also armed them. The worst legend that the church and Goan gossip gave birth to was that Pinto had taken the Mau Mau oath. This was frightening, terrifying, devilish. Goans could not afford to show any sympathy for the African cause, otherwise they would probably be on the next boat to Goa. On the other hand, the colonial government matched the Mau Mau atrocities on Mau Mau captives and sometimes on innocent detainees.

Pinto was one of the greatest African socialists of his era. He might have been a communist, but he was no devil worshipper. Most Goans did not know what a communist or a socialist was. But the church said they were evil monsters and in ignoring these warnings, Pinto seriously miscalculated the Kenyan Goans. Among his strongest supporters were Dr Euclid de Souza, Alex da Costa, Tony Lopes, Peter Carvalho and many others who did not show their support in public. Peter Carvalho's daughter Luisa Heaton, who remembers a little of the events of 1960, writes: 'My father was also part of the fight for Kenya's independence and he never missed an opportunity to take part in demonstrations outside the British Embassy. It caused my mother a lot of anxiety in case "anything happened to him".

However she was behind him all the way. We did spend a lot of time on our knees saying the rosary for his safe return home on those nights. Our family has recently discovered a very curious fact. On a number of occasions when my father was picketing the British High Commission in the 1950s, inside the High Commissioner's residence was my daughter-in-law's grandfather who was the Governor of Kenya - Sir Evelyn Baring's - Personal Assistant. Two men - Peter Carvalho and Geoffrey Ellerton - about the same age, divided not just by the imposing front door of the residence, but by their political beliefs and loyalties, culture and race. They were not to know then that 50 years later their grandchildren would marry each other! A form of Truth and Reconciliation, perhaps?

'Our meal-times were times to discuss politics and religion and we were regularly joined by the Gama Pinto brothers Rosario and Pinto, sometimes their wives and children, and sometimes Mboya came to eat with the others. We used to tease my mother that it just wasn't her food he liked, but that he fancied her!'

On Pereira's arrival in Kenya, the Goan East Africa Association delivered a letter of protest that criticised the Salazar government for not recognising the basic human rights and the human dignity of its colonial subjects.

Those Goans and the few local Portuguese who felt otherwise had the support of the colonial government. Supporting the boycott was the Kenya African National Union which attempted to stop all celebrations on the Coast, including those at Fort Jesus and Malindi. The provincial administration stomped on the KANU effort. The party retaliated by ordering all Kenyans to keep away from the ceremonies.

Pinto was joined in his crusade by trade unionist Mboya, the rising star of Kenyan politics. Mboya, who had a number of Goan friends, had said in Parliament that 'it was unfortunate that the Goans had chosen to stay loyal to Portugal, considering all the atrocities it had committed on its colonial subjects'. Ironically, Mboya would himself be the victim of an atrocity.

Many quite wrongly thought that any threat to their place in Kenya would not happen for many decades. It happened much sooner with the introduction of work permits and as 'Africanisation' and 'Kenyanisation' became real. They thought quite wrongly they could transfer their loyalties to the new owners of Kenya, not get involved, mind their own business and stick to enjoying their club life. Forget it. The Goans were not alone in this period of uncertainty. Like many whites and Asians they really wanted to stay in Kenya, but they were reluctant to commit to the country by taking on citizenship.

The Indian Trade Commissioner in Mombasa asked the local city council to ensure that all Indian flags were lowered in protest during the Vice-Premier's stay. During his visit, Pereira was regaled at the Nairobi Goan Institute, The Railway Goan Institute, The Goan Gymkhana, Santa Cruz Club, The Goan Tailors Society and at Goan schools in Nairobi and Mombasa. It was this unrelenting enthusiasm for the Portuguese guest that finally turned Pinto away from his community. The separation had come much earlier; the divorce was final during this episode. It was almost as if they were spitting in his face. I witnessed the conflict first hand on October 27 when I was outside the Goan Institute in Nairobi. There was a demonstration against the visit. Six people, mainly Africans I think, were arrested and detained after they crowded Pereira's car on arrival. Three more people were arrested at the Dr Ribeiro Goan School.

According to author Joao Sarmento, 'most Goans were anxious to be involved in the visit. Many wanted to get involved in organising dinners, visits and other social events.' It is fair to say some were actually falling over each other to bask in the Portuguese limelight. Consider this: the war between opposing Goan sides over Pereira's visit had a much more sinister motive hiding in the background. Goan loyalists were keenly aware of the almost explosive situation that existed in Goa at the time. They were vehemently opposed to any Indian intervention in Goa. Sadly, it was in the Kenyan Goan DNA to be prejudiced against their fellow Indians. The fragile and volatile political atmosphere truly frightened the Goan community, which at that time did not have migration to Britain on its radar. On the contrary, many Goans wanted to be buried in Goa. Hence, if only jokingly, many would say they were returning to Goa for their own funeral. The other reason for supporting the Portuguese was to keep the migration to Portugal option open and a number of Goans did just that but many left Portugal almost as quickly as they arrived. Goans never did understand the cynicism behind the colonial government's 'privileged class' status for the Goans. All it meant was that Goans unwittingly helped enforce the separate development principle by turning up their noses at fellow Indians and, naturally, the 'primitive savages': Africans. The Governor of Kenya, Sir Evelyn Baring, explained the racist policy to the Colonial Secretary in 1955: 'Up to 1923, the policy of segregation as between Europeans and other immigrant races followed as a measure of sanitation. The White Paper of 1923 recommended "as a sanitation measure, [that] segregation of Europeans and Asiatics is not absolutely essential for the preservation of the health of community", but that for the present it was considered desirable to keep residential quarters of natives, so far as practicable, separate from those of immigrant races'.

This separate development strategy had its genesis in 1929 when Britain secured for Asians a protected economic niche that reinforced racial separation with a class difference, thus encouraging antagonism between Asians and Africans and encouraging the probability that they would one day be seen as scapegoats. The sad thing about it all was that Pinto was absolutely and categorically correct: to continue living in Kenya, Goans had to commit to the country. They had to become Kenyans as opposed to a temporary immigrant tribe. As guests of the British colony, Goans had a privileged licence to be just that - privileged - because it suited the colonial government. Goans relished their position as the favourite brown-skins of the white colonials. However, there was no way on earth that the black Kenyan independent government would allow Goans to enjoy any kind of special position. As Mboya put it quite bluntly, 'If you don't like it, get out.' Most did. Sadly, there were many who took up Kenyan citizenship but, for various reasons, did not feel a part of the country and eventually left for foreign shores; this included many (or all) of Pinto's East African Goan League colleagues. I often wondered what happened to Rosario Gama Pinto until a former work mate sent me this note: 'After Pinto was assassinated, Rosario was told by a friend who was in the CID to leave Kenya quickly because he was earmarked and would be next. Rosario worked at the same office as I did and he quickly left the country telling everyone that he was going to Brazil on vacation. He never came back.'

On the other hand, there are many stories of Goans who became true Kenyans and who prospered beyond belief. Either way, there are no regrets just a little nostalgia for the Kenya we once knew. In hindsight, one would have to say that the Goan Overseas Association made a good investment in supporting Portugal. Just ask the thousands of Goans who hold Portuguese passports. For some in East Africa, the Portuguese document was their only way out. The current Goan population of Wembley and Swindon must surely include the Portuguese in their prayers, for without the Portuguese passport they might not have escaped Goa.

From left: Tom Mboya, Achieng Oneko, Joe Murumbi, Rosario da Gama Pinto, Peter Carvalho, Pio Gama Pinto. Photo *Louisa Heaton family album*

The assassination

Pio Gama Pinto had to die because he was perhaps the perfect African socialist in a Kenya that was probably 95 per cent capitalist.

Trading and bartering were natural to the large majority of Kenyans. Anything else was strange, therefore Pinto's socialist ideals threatened to spur on the first revolution. He was virtually at war with the capitalist conspirators, largely accused of land-grabbing by Kenya's first President Jomo Kenyatta and his 'Kiambu mafia' (there is plenty of written evidence of this, especially by the *Daily Nation*).

Pinto had almost nothing to his name. His wife, Emma, was the family's breadwinner. Their home in Nairobi's Lower Kabete Road was a gift from an admirer.

After Pinto was assassinated in 1965, Emma was shocked to find that there was no money in the bank account to pay the rent. With the work Pinto had done in organising and arming the Mau Mau and the wide-ranging freedom movements in Africa, especially those fighting Portuguese oppression, it was clear that he was the strategic brains behind any socialist drive towards power in Kenya.

Tanzania to the south was entertaining socialist ideals and Uganda to the north was heading in the same direction, as was the Sudan. Whispers of the 'communist' threat to Kenya - as opposed to an African socialist threat - were already gaining some momentum and it was not hard to imagine the involvement of the West, mainly Britain and the US.

As early as 1965, it was clear that Pinto was going to be a serious threat to Kenya's capitalist overlords, represented by the amorphous 'Kiambu mafia', and the US and British interests in the region. After all, in those early days of Kenya's Independence, most people did not care about the difference between African socialism and communism. Instead, political loyalties were drawn on ethnic lines. However, it was different among politicians. Odinga and Pinto were always dedicated to sharing the fruits of *Uhuru* equitably. As I have explained earlier, Kenyatta chose to appease the former colonialists and agreed to the "willing seller, willing buyer" principle on settler farm lands. Sessional Paper No.10 clearly sought to make Kenya capitalist. These two elements forced Pinto, in concert with Odinga and his parliamentary following, to challenge Kenyatta and the ruling elite. In the end, both lost out.

In this scenario, the thought did cross many minds that it was a matter of when, and not if, Pinto would be snuffed out. There was some sentiment that his continuing influence with the last remnants of the Mau Mau would perhaps save him. Wishful thinking, I thought at the time. Yet, the crystal clear bottom line was that he was a perceived threat to Kenyatta in particular and the 'Kiambu mafia' in general and he was viewed as working against Western influence in Kenya. The Kikuyu were in power, while the Luo - coalescing around Odinga - were desperate for power. You did not have to be a rocket scientist to conclude that a simple solution to the situation was the murder of Pinto. Getting rid of him would neutralise Jaramogi and any opposition to those in power and their Western supporters. It was as simple as that. I am sure even Pinto was aware of this.

Former political detainee and Member of Parliament Koigi Wamwere said that, "Initially, the struggle was between capitalism and socialism." The Kenyatta-Odinga rivalry culminated in a series of tragic events that began with the assassination of Pio Gama Pinto, a freedom fighter of Goan descent.

"He shouldn't have been the first one to be assassinated," said John Keen, veteran politician and Masai elder, of the young nationalist who was Jaramogi Odinga's strategist.

According to Wamwere, "Pinto was killed because he was seen as the brain behind socialism in Kenya." (*Nation*)

According to a tribute by his younger brother, the late Rosario Da Gama Pinto, the killing was impending. 'Pio was often threatened and even a month before his death was aware of the plot to kill him by prominent politicians. Although upset about the plot, he carried on as normal until his assassination.'

The then deputy speaker of Parliament, Dr Fitz de Souza, who reportedly witnessed Pinto engaging in a shouting match with Kenyatta in the corridors of the House, said later that Pinto was killed by the 'powers-that-be'.

'Prominent politicians' and 'the powers-that-be' is the euphemism used to camouflage Pinto's killers.

I suspect that the shouting match was over Sessional Paper No 10, which has been the subject of subsequent revision but at the time virtually legalised capitalism as Kenya's economic lingua franca. Pinto, at the insistence of then vice-president Jaramogi, was going to write amendments that would have been tantamount to a parliamentary challenge to Kenyatta's leadership.

There has also been an unconfirmed suggestion that the then VP Odinga planned to move a vote of no confidence in Kenyatta. Rosario, Pinto's brother who died in 1998, seemed to confirm this in the tribute which I have uncovered: 'Pio was murdered to silence him and put an end to his dream to implement socialism, the ideals for which the people of Kenya had formed government. Now that Independence had been gained and the armed forces' loyalty had been bought,' (my words: British soldiers were still in Kenya to provide further security) 'those in power considered it a convenient time to assassinate Pinto as a warning to other dedicated nationalists,' he wrote in the tribute entitled *Pinto, My Brother.*

After the assassination no one really spoke out or pointed a finger in public at the 'prominent politicians' or 'the powers that be'. Murumbi knew but said nothing. Instead he wailed at the very thought of his murdered friend. Murumbi was confident that he would have been able to negotiate Pinto's safety.

Odinga knew but said nothing. Neither did fellow Independence hero Achieng' Oneko or any of Pinto's Goan confidantes, except Fitz de Souza. He at least voiced the war of words between Pinto and Kenyatta. Pinto was confident that Kenyatta was not capable of killing him. Rosario noted in his writing that his brother had good reason for such faith. 'Pio had worked tirelessly for Kenyatta's release and had spent his last cent extending and refurbishing Kenyatta's home. In the process he had antagonised those friends who did not want Kenyatta released. Some of them went on to become ministers in the Kenyatta Government,' he wrote in his tribute. Rosario further said that Pinto made a great effort to 'improve Kenyatta's tarnished reputation'. 'He (Pinto) knew that the same 'divide and rule' policy the British used in India would be used to disunite Kenyans,' wrote Rosario.

Yet, it was unthinkable that anyone could get into a shouting match with the 'Father of the Nation' or insult him and live to tell the tale. In those days, no matter who you were, it was unheard of that anyone would insult even the simplest image of him, such as that on the Kenya currency. A few had already been deported for that very 'crime'.

At the outset, Pinto did not want the limelight of a high position, preferring to assign such glory to his trusted and talented friends like Murumbi, Bildad Kaggia, Fred Kubai, Jaramogi, Oneko, Pranlal Seth and others.

Pinto felt he could achieve more behind the scenes but changed his mind after realising that the only way to meet his goals was to be elected to Parliament. In 1963 he was elected to the Legislative Assembly and in July 1964 he was appointed a specially elected member of the House of Representatives. That was the beginning of the end for Pinto, a dedicated socialist, freedom fighter, journalist and son of Kenya. His place in Kenya's history will, however, not be erased.

For instance, Pinto broke the apartheid rules by entering European restaurants and hotels in Nairobi and Mombasa in the early 1950s. He and his friends would be physically ejected or coerced to leave by the police. As a result of his efforts, plus the changing political situation nearer to Independence, non-whites were finally allowed access to such places.

And when the Mau Mau found that they could not hold out indefinitely against the well-equipped British army, they fled into the forests and used Pinto as a go-between to request a ceasefire. Knowing that the settlers would crush the rebellion, Pinto approached the Government of India via its acting High Commissioner R.K. Tandau and asked that the question of negotiations be taken up at the highest level with the Colonial Office. The British Government's attitude was favourable. However, the local settlers who held high posts sabotaged this meeting. The security forces opened fire on the representatives of the Mau Mau. Pinto was detained under the

Emergency regulations as a scapegoat for the failed meeting. He was not allowed a proper trial or hearing and was denied legal aid.

He was held incommunicado and after a few days in Nairobi sent to Mombasa under heavy police escort. Pinto was later moved to Lamu Island and then Manda Island where hundreds of hard-core Mau Mau were exiled for years under terrible conditions.

Pinto was offered better facilities, but declined them on principle. He lived like the rest of his comrades, on maize-meal flour, rice, and fish.

'Our family sent him Sh150 a month - but he preferred to share the money with the needy,' wrote Rosario.

Pinto was promised an early release if he would confess but refused to give in, even at the threat of deportation. He was offered a one-way ticket to India which he again declined as he wanted a fair trial.

Pinto had opposed Asian participation in the establishment of the Asian Manpower Unit to quell the Mau Mau rebellion, making him a candidate for detention. The colonial government planned to establish three or four special combat units to bolster the Kenya Police Reserve. Asians, who outnumbered the whites six-to-one, were barred from participating in anti-Mau Mau activities because the British government feared a threat from their numbers in Kenya. Two units were eventually set up. The Asian community (minus the Goans who supported the colonial government) was divided. Indian members of the Legislative Council strongly backed the colonialists after an Indian trader and his wife and children were killed by the Mau Mau. Their deaths had a devastating effect on Asians. Others would later be killed but it was not clear whether they were all victims of the Mau Mau.

However, Asian traders in small towns and villages were accused of exploiting poor Africans and were hated. This situation remains to this day, albeit not as blatantly as it was in the colonial era: all part of the British divide and conquer plan. Thousands more would have died but for Pinto's intervention. The Mau Mau and the Kenyan political leadership respected him and valued his organisational and strategic skills. Later, he would make a huge contribution drafting important documents and writing speeches.

Pinto argued that these poor Asian traders should not bear the brunt of the attacks as their misguided leaders - some British stooges - were to blame. Not only did he obtain help and channel it to the families of the victims, he also paid for their children's schooling, food and clothing out of his own pocket.

Within the ranks of the Mau Mau in Nairobi, it was common knowledge that the Indian trader network - the world famous dukawallahs - carried messages and provided cash to help the fighters in outlying districts. At the beginning of the Mau Mau campaign, there had been strong-arming of the dukawallahs but it stopped quickly after Pinto's intervention. Pinto is reputed to have received considerable financial and in-kind help from several Indian diplomats to Kenya. His anti-British and anti-Portuguese exploits in India were well known to the Indian leadership.

In fact, he was in contact with and even met the then Indian Prime Minister Jawaharlal Nehru. Later, Prime Minister Indira Gandhi would also be made aware of Pinto's Indian and African nationalism. Some of Pinto's closest associates were Indians: the illustrious Pranlal Sheth, the academic and author Pheroze Nowrojee, the economist Sarjit Singh Heyer and others.

If not for Kenya, Pinto would have dedicated his life to India. I have a strong suspicion that India might have financed the Mau Mau through Pinto. I have no proof of this and it remains only a suspicion.

When the African-American leader, Malcolm X, visited Kenya in 1959, he found he had a lot in common with Pinto. They planned a common strategy to deal with the daily humiliation and indignities suffered by both Africans and African-Americans. Malcolm X was assassinated on February 21, 1965, three days before Pinto. Their murders are linked: both were considered dangerous to vested interests.

Pinto's was a family with deep roots in both India and Kenya. Rosario's daughter, Audrey Da Gama, said: 'My grandfather, Anton Filipe Da Gama Pinto, worked for the British civil service in Nyeri, Kenya, from 1919 to 1941. Pinto, Sevigne and my dad were born in Kenya, but educated in India.'

Sevigne Athaide, who lives in Mumbai, followed in his brother Pinto's footsteps and carved out an illustrious career in Indian politics, especially in Karnataka.

Rosario worked as an administrator for various companies in Nairobi and London. 'He and Pio attended the Problems of Portuguese Colonies seminar in New Delhi in 1961. They got a chance to ask Indian Prime Minister Pandit Jawaharlal Nehru for some university scholarships for East African-based Goan students. They were invited back for Goa's liberation celebrations,' Rosario's daughter, who holds the copyright to the tribute, said.

Pinto was invited to return to Goa to take a leadership role in the new Goa. He declined, saying that there were enough talented people in Goa and his priorities were in Kenya. 'As you can imagine, some friends and family members distanced themselves from Pio in order to protect their jobs. However, once he was elected to Parliament, the same people were happy to claim him as their own,' she said.

But after Pinto's death in 1965, the entire family felt unsafe. 'My father was also quite... angered by the silencing of his brother. This would have made him a target. In the end, my parents decided to leave quietly. Pio's death changed the course of our lives forever. We spent 10 months in Goa and then moved to the UK,' she said.

Her father, she said, was a compassionate and generous man and was probably more driven to throw himself into causes following Pinto's death. 'In later years, he had private audiences with Prime Minister Indira Gandhi of India. His objective was to obtain more scholarships for poor Goans. 'He also gave scholarships in Goa in his father's and brother's names. Education as a form of empowerment and love of family and tradition were central to his being,' she said. Rosario died in London in January, 1998 and his widow and children relocated to Melbourne, Australia.

Pinto's widow relives the day they shot him

Emma Gama Pinto fled to Canada with her three young children, two years after the assassination of her husband. She desperately needed to be in a safe place, far away from the scene of her nightmare. Within three years of arriving in Canada she lost sight in one eye. Now some 48 years later she is beginning to lose sight in her other eye and is in an Ottawa home for the aged. Although the family has not had closure on Pinto's murder, Emma is not bitter. The following is based on a conversation she had with US resident Benegal Pereira.

She arrived in Kenya in September, 1953. Her twin sister Joyce was already in Nairobi, married to Tome Mendonca. Rosario and Tome used to ride the bus to work and one day they hatched the plan to bring Emma and Pinto together. The two were married on January 9, 1954. The first time she heard mention of Pinto being a communist, she asked him and he told her he was not a communist but a socialist with strong Gandhian principles. That removed any doubt that might have lingered in her mind.

It was going to take a particularly strong and decisive woman to survive the perils that would befall her family over the next few years, beginning with Pinto's detention on June 19, 1954.

What were the early months of your marriage like?

During the first four years of my life with Pio, while he was in detention, I read a lot to try and understand why he was in politics for a country that was not his. It was just six months after we got married in January 1954 when Pio was sent to Nairobi Prison. Fitz de Souza took me to see him there. Soon after, Pio was moved to Fort Jesus and later to Manda Island in Lamu.

What was Pio like as a husband?

He was hardly ever there. Within the first six months, he told me 'you can't stay at home. Intelligent women don't stay home,' he said. 'Take a secretarial course and find a job. And take Greggs shorthand' (as opposed to the more popular Pitman's shorthand). Pio did Greggs shorthand and he said: 'One day you will able to read my shorthand if I need you to read back my notes.

So I enrolled at Premier College and started learning Greggs. I had hardly finished the course and had to go work because I didn't realise that he wasn't earning anything. He would come home at seven or eight in the evening. I would be quite annoyed because we had no phone and his parents were in Nairobi at the time. Pio and I lived in the servants' quarters of Fitz's (de Souza, Barrister and Speaker of Parliament) house and Fitz's parents were staying in the main house. (Fitz was in England studying, hence was not able to be at the wedding.)

At the time of the wedding, Joe Murumbi's first wife Cecilia and their son Jojo were staying with us. After finishing his school in India, Joe went straight to Somalia. Cecilia was the daughter of a chief. Murumbi could not come to the wedding because Pio, fearing for Joe's safety following the detention of important elements of the Kenya African Union, sent him to London. Joe was the KAU vice-president.

Did you know Pio as a political activist, supporter of the Mau Mau?

No. I didn't know the name, Mau Mau. (Elsewhere she says that Pio never spoke to her about politics, it was his way of shielding her). I knew he worked for the Indian National Congress in the Desai Memorial Building. I was not aware he was actively involved in the African political movement.

He told me only that he worked at the Indian Congress office.

What do you remember of that awful day?

On that particular day - we were living at No.6 Lower Kabete Road. The house had been donated to Pio. He had bought me a little car so that I could have some independence as far as transport was concerned. The new government was now nearly 14 months old and they had decided to get rid of all the English secretaries and Pio told me: 'You are going to be the secretary to Achieng Oneko, the Minister for Information, Broadcasting and Tourism.' Pio had dropped me off at my office in Jogoo House and had returned home to collect his Parliamentary papers. My car was being serviced. About an hour later, I was in Achieng's office, around 9 o'clock when my mother called me on the phone to say that Pio had been attacked and she was hysterical and I said: I will be home soon. I am coming home right away.

But I am a very, very calm person in any emergency. So I immediately phoned the Minister for Defence, Dr Njoroge Mungai, and told his office that Pio had been attacked and said please send the police there (to their home). Then I picked up the phone and rang Joe Murumbi because he would not have left the office because Parliament does not start until 11 am. He was the Minister for Foreign Affairs. He and his wife Sheila lived five minutes away from us. I said to him: Joe, Pio has been attacked, please go to our house.

Next, I ran into Achieng's office and said: Can I have your car? He said his car was in the garage for repairs or a service. Then I rang Odinga's office and spoke to, Caroline Odongo, Odinga's secretary, and said to her: Caroline, Caroline, can I get a car to take me home? Pio has been attacked. She said she would call me back immediately. She did. She told me Odinga's spare car was being sent round to the front of Jogoo House and would be waiting for me. Odinga was the first Vice-President of the country.

All the time, I assumed that Pio had been attacked and that he had been injured.

As I got to the gate of our house, I saw our car had been parked at the gate and as I got out of Odinga's car, I saw Murumbi arriving in his car.

As we walked past the car and into our home to find out about Pio, my mother said: he is still in the car, he has been killed. That was the first time I had heard that Pio had been killed. So we both dashed out to the car and saw that Pio's body had been covered in a pink blanket. My mother had asked our house servant, a nice young man called Waweru, to cover Pio.

Pio usually gave our 18-month old daughter Tereshka a ride from the back of the house to the gate from where she would be collected by the maid and walked home. When the maid got to the back of the car, she heard shots and she ran back to the house to get Waweru. She really did not see too much because she was terrified. By the time Waweru got to the car, Pio had already been shot.

Are you still angry?

No. Because of my reading of political matters I am aware that politicians lead very dicey lives. They are always walking a tightrope. So when Pio was assassinated I assumed it was part of the politician's life. It was shocking for me a new immigrant to Kenya that he was shot so soon. He had already been in detention for four years. It was tragic.

Did you feel cheated?

Well, I felt disappointed that someone who had worked so hard for freedom... in my readings, I read that bitterness is like a fire in the corner of a house that will eventually consume the whole house. So I was cognizant of the fact that I should never be bitter of the whole situation. It was a fact of life. Mahatma Gandhi was murdered...

Did you get much support from family and friends?

My twin sister Joyce lived just down the road from me. The people at the first private British company I worked for (International Aeradio Limited, engineers), I don't think they were sympathetic to Pio, but they were sympathetic to a widow. Joe and Sheila Murumbi took me to their home for two days. My mother stayed with the girls at our house.

On the day when we saw Pio's body in the car, Joe said let's get Pio inside the house. Because I was in shock I have no clear memory of the people there. Waweru and Joe's driver put Pio's body in the pink blanket and carried his body, not like a sack of potatoes, but something like that into the living room.

Fitz de Souza arrived at one point. I had not phoned Fitz. I don't know at what point Fitz was involved. Perhaps he found out from Parliament, which had been informed. (Fitz got the news at the High Court.)

Fitz was there when Pio's body was brought into the living room. I remember I sat down and they put the blanket down and I could see that little hole under his ribs. I was sitting with Joe and Fitz and I said: Gosh, Pio looks so pale.

And Fitz said: 'Get out of there, get out of the room.'

So that was my one and only view of Pio when he was brought into the home.

After nearly 50 years, do you feel that Kenyans have served Pio's memory well?

I think they are doing quite a bit to keep his memory alive. They have named a road after him and they also included his image in a commemorative stamp: Heroes of Kenya and included Mboya (a rising political star, also assassinated), Ronald Ngala (leader of people from the Kenya coast) and Odinga. The street in which we lived, Kabete Road, has been name after Pio. All the houses have been demolished, including ours and the whole area has been redeveloped. A large shopping mall has been erected.

What was Pio like as a Member of Parliament?

As you may have realised, I was more or less the breadwinner and Pio and I never checked our bank balance. I did not know how much we had until he was assassinated and when I went to the bank to get the money to pay our rent which was in arrears. There was nothing. And I had to pay Cecilia's rent as well...

I am a little confused, Joe Murumbi had two wives?

Yes. When he came back from England, he brought Sheila with him. As I said before, just after 1954, Pio sent Joe Murumbi via India to the UK to escape arrest. Pio was sending him information about the situation in Kenya, the Mau Mau, the detainees... so that Joe could advise the British members of Parliament who were sympathetic to Kenya.

Did you know India's High Commissioner to Kenya, Apa Pant, who said that it was Pio who introduced him to Kenyatta and Mbiyu Koinange and brought him into the enclaves of the Mau Mau?

Pio kept his political work completely secret from me.

On the night of Pio's assassination, his two best friends, the nationalist Pran Lal Sheth and the economist Sarjit Singh Heyer burnt every scrap of paper to safeguard Pio's local and international associates.

Why did they burn ...?

We have to speculate because Pranlal said that Pio was not only involved in Kenyan politics but also in African politics... countries that were just emerging. I guess they were concerned that Pio might have mentioned names and they were protecting these people, the politicians, dignitaries, that Pio had come into contact with.

I had no idea who they were because Pio never told me what he was involved in or the personalities. Pio used to have people from foreign countries come to the house and have meetings in his office but I was never involved. He never asked me to make tea or provide refreshments.

I just did not want anyone living in our home, even though we had a spare room. I told Pio we should protect our family. I said we had daughters and we must protect them.

How long did you remain in Kenya after the assassination?

I remained in Kenya for two years. I was waiting for the tombstone I was told was arriving from Italy.

Pio is buried in Nairobi's City Park cemetery, is it protected?

Not really.

Was he buried in the City Park cemetery for any reason ... most Goans were buried in the Langata cemetery?

All the arrangements were made by Joe Murumbi and Fitz de Souza. Fitz left Kenya soon after the assassination because he was afraid, he told me so in London not so long ago. He realised he might have been in danger. I think he was there for the funeral.

CHAPTER 18

FR HANNAN, PAEDOPHILE

I never imagined that I would one day take on the Catholic Church and single-handedly launch a campaign to get the Vatican and the Irish Congregation of the Holy Spiritans (commonly called the Spiritans and Holy Ghost Fathers) in Kenya to admit that the sin of pedophilia was committed by a priest who molested boys in his care as headmaster of the school in Eastleigh, Nairobi. If in 1950 someone in Nairobi had told me that Fr Hannan had sex with boys I would have laughed my head off. In those wonderful, innocent and naïve days the concept of a man having sex with a young boy did not exist. Very, very few boys were even aware of homosexuality. It was such a big secret it was as if it did not exist. I only came to know about it because my friends pointed out the resident gay who was the subject of much taunting and abuse. But a man having sex with a boy, or sexually molesting him: that would have been dismissed as rubbish. As a Catholic, my peers told me that even thinking such a thing might be considered a mortal sin.

Long before the 1960s Californian hippies declared free love, the African version had been alive and well for decades. Love was straightforward and sex was not unusual, just a way of life. Sex happened, guarded by various cultural taboos. Christian institutions were fundamental in the initial education of thousands of Kenyans. Unfortunately, these were also the darkest days in Kenya's history, perpetuated by the clergy engaging in child sexual abuse, molestation and the sexual abuse of men and women. A veil of silence existed, save for a few brave souls who spoke out.

For a child, the 1960s in Kenya was a time of pure ignorant innocence, sheer bliss. The average ten to thirteen year old knew nothing about sex. We did not even know that the white colonial government was evil to the Africans. We lived in a cocoon and God, the Great Protector, was everywhere. His images and those of the favourite saints lived in the altar that adorned the best room in the house. And every room had a picture of Jesus Christ, the Holy Family or any number of saints. You knelt on concrete or dirt floors and said the rosary every night followed by a good hour's litany of the saints and more. The local Irish priest was held in the highest esteem, almost revered. Bishops and archbishops were also revered, but without the familiarity the parish priest enjoyed. In Eastleigh Fr Hannan, who was parish priest as well as the headmaster of the St Teresa's Boys' Secondary School, was loved and admired by his flock like no other, except of course maybe the Pope.

A family was truly blessed and the envy of every other home in the suburb if the dashing priest with the sparkling blue eyes deigned to visit the family home. After blessing the home, splashing holy water in each room and leading the family in the rosary, he would say the Grace before meals, and would later join the man of the house for a drop or two of Scotch and a cigarette. He also spent some time with the children, especially the boys. Fr Hannan's visit signified that God Himself was smiling on them and their place in Heaven was almost guaranteed. To be blessed by the priest's visit to your home, to have the priest partake of your fare, brought a family closer to God. If you pleased Father, you pleased God. Brainwashing a young mind to do the bidding of any priest was practised by all, innocently, without a second thought.

Hannan was held in such high and holy adoration that to say anything against him meant that the owner of the evil tongue would be quickly treated as the resident pariah. To receive Holy Communion from Hannan during Mass was akin to receiving it from Christ himself. Most parents greeted him with their heads lowered, heads adorned with veils, sheepish smiles and their bodies were bowed in adoration.

It was an era when women wore black or white veils, rosary beads appeared to be an extension of the arms, and crucifixes and medals pressed with the heads of various saints decorated the women's necks. The rosaries and litanies were chanted as the family walked to and from church. In those almost traffic-free days nearly everyone walked to church.

In the 1950s, kissing a girl before marriage was a Catholic taboo (in Goa a chaperone was required during courtship). Touching her was considered a sin. I remember a priest in a sermon stating that evil thoughts began with holding a girl's hand. He also told us boys that it was not healthy to think about girls, and in the distant past when a boy met girl it was only allowed if an escort was present. In this respect, the Goans were five-star puritans. Even in the 1960s you did not see too many parents kissing each other or embracing lovingly even in front of their children. So the idea of a priest sexually molesting a boy just did not make any sense.

On the other hand, if someone had told me that the priest was sexually involved with a female teacher I would be more likely to believe that. He was a handsome, piercingly-blue-eyed monster with bucket loads of Irish charm. It was an era when some women swooned and fawned as those deep blue eyes penetrated their very souls. Some crossed the boundary and were soon enslaved by their sins of the flesh, their sin of having seduced the priest, but most were inoculated and vaccinated against such human frailty by the strength of their near-fanatical faith in Catholicism.

We will never know exactly how many Kenyan girls and boys, or men and women, were sexually abused or molested by priests. Their fellow priests, bishops, archbishops and the Catholic leadership protected molesters. It is also difficult to gauge how far back this activity actually goes. The most vulnerable were the orphaned street urchins in Kenya's cities, towns and districts. Orphans in Catholic homes may have also been abused. These sad innocents were lured by candy, a few cents, some food or soft drink. Virtually none knew what they were asked to do. In any case, if they did try to speak no one would listen because, in those days, it did not make any sense. There was more chance of believing that someone had sex with a domesticated animal than a holy priest having sex with another human, let alone a young boy or girl.

I began emailing hundreds of people and Catholic organisations able to throw more light on the case. After many months and hundreds of emails, an African priest responded, 'I am deeply disturbed by the story you have shared with me. I have forwarded the information to the right persons for immediate action. My deep sympathy and prayers to the victim.'

I jumped for a little joy because I had almost given up any hope of any contact from anyone in the Catholic Church. The ball really got rolling when a leader of the Irish Spiritans contacted me.

I had written to him: 'I hear a Christian soul screaming in the dark. It is crying out for help... help to ease the pain of more than 50 years. Pain caused by a son of the Roman Catholic Church, a son of the Irish Spiritan family. And you hear him not. Instead you choose to ignore the suffering soul. Is this what Jesus Christ taught us? Is denial and cover-up the new creed of the Catholic Church? There is plenty of evidence that Irish Catholicism, both in Ireland, USA and Africa, has become accomplished in denying sex abuse victims their natural justice. What gospel did that come from? I know that there are thousands of child sex abuse victims of priests who have been left hanging in limbo. Their civil suits for damages have been allowed to gather dust over the years. Lack of legal success has emboldened the church.

'Where is the holy grace in that? You hear a child cry but you turn away. What will you tell Christ on the day of your judgment? You are killing my soul and I do not have the tools and I do not know how to fight the devil in this war.'

He replied, 'I apologise for the delay in getting back to you. I was on leave when your email arrived. I am deeply saddened by the story of your correspondent and the abuse he suffered in Eastleigh, Nairobi. He mentions Fr. Patrick Hannan as the priest who abused him. The Irish Province of the Spiritans (Holy Ghost Fathers) absolutely condemns any form of child sexual abuse and we do reach out to victims who have been abused by any member of our Congregation and we try to help them in whatever way we can. Your recent email is the first information we have received of this particular case.'

He informed me had asked the Superior of the Spiritans in Kenya to investigate the Hannan allegations. He also provided me with a contact for any further questions I might have. I have never heard from them again.

My classmates regularly exchanged emails with ideas and opinions. It was during one of these exchanges in 2011 that Alex de Figueiredo first mentioned Hannan had sexually abused him. All hell, naturally, broke loose.

At St. Teresa's he did not study, he just scraped through. However, he says, 'Once I went to University in Canada I was finally able to enjoy school and ended up getting top marks. I was not afraid to go to school anymore. In fact, I became a teacher so that I could help children.'

It has never been established how many boys were sexually abused by Hannan at the St Teresa's.

It was not long before the once-religious young boy was ashamed to have been raised a Catholic. Looking back, Figueiredo's greatest hurt is that the Catholic Church in many instances condoned the behaviour of the abusers and, in many cases, even protected them from the law. He does not condone what was done to him but he has come to terms with that hell on earth and he is now able to lead a happy, productive, caring and sensitive life outside the church. 'Fr. Hannan is gone and he cannot hurt anyone anymore,' he says.

Figueiredo was wrong about his parents. He told his father when he was 24 in 1969. It was the first time in his life that he had heard his father swear. He was under the impression that his father had gone to the Bishop and had Hannan removed. His father had not. He wanted to confirm that so he asked him about it a few months before he died. 'His eyes filled with tears. I could see he felt he let me down and he felt awkward talking about it so I did not pursue the subject,' Figueiredo recalled.

He wished his father had never taken him out from the Goan-community-founded Dr Ribeiro Goan School. But then, he says wistfully, he would not have made friends who have been 'so supportive to this day like Skip,

Sultan, Edgar, Billy and Anthony, who has passed away'. However, not all classmates were caring. Some of the boys wrestled with their faith and were neither able to believe Alex's story or provide him with support. When first published in my blog, it tore the St Teresa's alumni right down the middle. Even in this day and age there were people who would not accept that Hannan was capable of the sexual abuse of young boys.

When Alex went to Hannan for confession, he was told, 'I can't hear your confession. We would have to stop what we do and I cannot do that.' Alex went for Confession to another priest, Fr Cremmins, who was also his Latin teacher and was angrily rebuked and received 'a severe penance'.

'From that day on he [the Latin teacher] made my life miserable. Every day he had me stand up first and quizzed me on Latin until I made a mistake. Then he would make me stand for the rest of the period,' Alex recalled.

He has stressed often enough that only reason he allowed me to tell his story was with the hope that some good would come of it. 'While you bring this subject to light my only hope is that it will make adults aware of the dangers that can surround innocent little children and that adults will be more vigilant. My concern is that it may take time for this to become relevant in developing nations. Had I received compensation from the church I would have used it all to help prevent physical and sexual abuse in Africa,' he said.

Alex went to confession in the Vatican. When he told the priest how long it had been since his last confession, the priest said, 'It is like the parable of the Prodigal Son. Why has it been so long?' Alex related the story of his ordeal and the 'priest started making excuses.' Alex broke into a sweat and told the priest, 'I am sorry I came. The Church has not changed,' and walked out. 'I was dripping with perspiration when I walked out. Maybe that is when I got rid of the demons.'

Finally, he said, 'I have pulled through and I think I am blessed because I now have a wonderful life. I do not go to church but I thank God each day for giving me such a great life.'

The news more than fifty years later that Hannan was a sexual predator who abused at least five boys ripped the Goan community apart. There were those who had always suspected something but, without proof, were unable to do anything, and there were others who turned on the victim, accusing him of making up the horrific story. Those Goans will go to their deaths never accepting that Hannan was such an evil person. There are many instances around the world of children telling his or her mother that the priest inappropriately touched them, and mothers beating the living daylights out of the child, or washing his or her mouth with soap and 'holy water' to cleanse the child of the evil within. The mother told the child not to speak such nonsense again. She repeated the message even more forcefully each time: 'Do not speak of such evil of the holy reverend father.'

Priests engaged in sexual abuse were known, but fellow parishioners turned a blind eye to their evil acts. As a last resort, the guilty priest was sometimes moved from parish to parish, then to Ireland or the United States where he continued to abuse boys or girls, depending on his preference.

This has been hardest story I have ever written. I did not know how to handle it and sought the counsel of a few friends. One said, quite rightly, that I should not go there. I would be opening up old wounds and old nightmares. Consider the fate of the parents, siblings and friends, he said. They had thought they were doing the right thing by putting their faith in the priest. The priest is dead. The victims have moved on. A second opinion was quite adamant, non-negotiable: we must support our schoolmate no matter what. A third opinion was that it was important to come out with the story to give other adults who might have been molested as children the sanctuary of telling them they were not alone. A fourth opinion suggested that the victim should decide if he wanted it published.

As a frontline journalist, the decision was a no brainer: publish. There is a case of the public good and there is an even bigger case for providing solidarity for the victims. Any newspaper editor worth his salt would publish without the slightest hesitation, as was the case in Kenya, Ireland, Canada and Goa. I do not write for any newspaper, I do not answer to any editor. Yet I have a responsibility to my schoolmate and others who might have been abused. Already one other victim has come forward. How many others are out there?

Most of the victims are in their 70s. Some will welcome the story, others will not. Others will vehemently defend Hannan and dismiss the accusations as lies. He was the man who took a four-classroom school and extended it to one of the best equipped schools in Nairobi. He did it by fundraising with the parents through whist drives, school fetes, raffles and help from the Catholic Church. It took many years but the parents were very proud of their boys' secondary school and large cathedral-like church. For all intents and purposes, Hannan was the best thing to have happened for Catholics of the Eastleigh parish. There will be many hundreds of parents and students who will be eternally grateful to Hannan. To the naked eye, he was quite a guy and even after he left St. Teresa's, many people kept in touch with him.

The sexual abuse of Alex de Figueiredo

Good taste and consideration for anyone who might have read my material has been the cornerstone of my career as a journalist. I am not a voyeur, nor have I have ever written any kind of pornography. On this one and only occasion I must depart from that. Child sexual abuse is a phrase that may shock us the first time we read or hear it. After being bombarded with the expression on television, newspapers, the internet and radio, we take it for granted. I am using graphic detail to illustrate just how some allegedly holy men can be and how they lure and torture the little children in their charge.

Hannan sexually abused Alex de Figueiredo from 1956 to 1961. Figueiredo was 12 years old when the sexual abuse began. Hannan phoned Alex's father that first Christmas and asked him to send Alex to school so he could set him some tests. Alex had been ill with chicken pox and had missed the crucial end-of-year school exams.

When Alex got to the school there was no one around, so he went to Hannan's office and after entering, Hannan shut the door. He asked him three questions and Alex answered them. Hannan was in a chair behind his desk. Alex was sitting opposite. Hannan asked Alex to come closer to him and when Alex got there, Hannan started tickling him. He then asked him to come around and as Alex stood beside him Hannan began playfully tickling him.

Alex says that Hannan stated, "'You are ticklish. Do you know where I am ticklish?'"

Alex replied that he did not. Then, 'Hannan asked me to try and find his ticklish spot. I thought that it was most odd for a priest to ask me to tickle him. I tried his ribs but he did not flinch. He kept on until I said, "I give up."

'Hannan said, "There is one place that you have not tried," and he took my hand and put it through the opening in his cassock and onto his penis. He then put his hand up my shorts and was playing with my penis. He did not ejaculate that time but on another occasion he did and I was shocked. I did not know what it was. It looked like pus.'

During the next five horrific years, Alex says, Hannan 'played with my penis and wanted me to play with his. He wanted me to suck his penis and I refused. I was so innocent and I was shocked that someone would suck a penis. Once, the priest was in a terrible state of sexual arousal. He looked at me with pleading eyes as he fumbled to get his pants down. Just as quickly he bared his naked arse to me. "Please f**k me", he pleaded. That was not the first time either.'

The five years were a complete nightmare. Alex could not tell anyone because he knew no one would believe him. He was Hannan's prisoner and there was no escape. Everyday brought a new hell. He absolutely dreaded getting up each morning. No one in the school of several hundred boys, teachers and other priests had the slightest clue what was going on.

'When I was older and we went camping he wanted me to f**k him and again I thought that it was filthy and weird that he would want a young boy to do that to a man. He once took me to this bed in the old house that was beside the church, where the priests lived.' Hannan never threatened or bullied him or used any kind of physical force. However, his other face was that of a cruel sadistic monster. Among his minor crimes was taking pleasure in whipping the daylights out of a child's naked bottom with a bamboo cane. He did this sometimes with a wet cloth on the bum or later rubbed salt into the wounds. Alex was afraid of him and of his strap which he used liberally on the naked buttocks of many boys.

In Nairobi, one mother had the courage to report the priest who sexually abused her son. The bishop to whom she reported the offence did nothing. The sexual offender continued abusing other boys. For the rest of her life, the mother carried a very heavy burden knowing that her darling son had been abused in such a monstrous fashion. The once-beaming smile left her happy face forever. There was some consolation in that her son was never again abused. He, too, lived a broken hearted life and went to his death with his heart carrying the shame of the sexual abuse.

Some Goan victims of sexual abuse by priests have since died, while others continue to wrestle with the nightmares.

The saddest of ironies is that one of Hannan's nephews wrote to me, 'Until I read this article Fr Hannan was regarded by me and my family as a kind of hero. I am deeply ashamed after reading about my uncle's abuse. I'm shocked and don't know what to think. I left the Roman Catholic Church several years ago after suffering physical and sexual abuse at the hands of Irish priests in school. I wish you well but feel so ashamed.'

Alex did not get an official apology from the Vatican. A priest did telephone him to tell him he had accepted Alex's version of events as the truth but, since Hannan had been dead a long time, nothing more could be done. Alex did not want any financial compensation but would have liked the Vatican to set up a fund to assist victims of sexual abuse by priests in Kenya. His wish was never granted.

Patrick Hannan (1921-1993) was born in Limerick, Ireland, on 25 August 1921. His first appointment was headmaster of St Teresa's Boys' School 1950-1960 and pastor of the church from 1956-1969. He then returned to Ireland and in 1971 he was appointed to the U.S.A, where he served as chaplain in Queen's General Hospital, Long Island, until 1973. From 1973 to 1989 Hannan worked in the parish and school of St. Theresa's, Hollywood, Florida. Hannan returned to Ireland in poor health in 1989, residing in Kimmage till his death 16 October 1993 aged 73 years. He was buried in Kimmage.

1957 M.R. De Souza Gold Cup (Kenya's premier hockey tornament) winners: Top Row: Adolf DeMello, Francis Gracias, Hilary Fernandes, Silu Fernandes and Henry Braganza. Middle Row: Philip Gracias, Reynolds De Souza, Alu Mendonca, the (late} Anthony D' Souza and Oscar D'Souza. Sitting: Saude George and the late Angelo D'Souza

Photo courtesy of Hilary Fernandes

CHAPTER 19

THE AFRICAN GOAN

There is an unwritten law in journalism that you do not denigrate the aged, the sick, or the mentally and physically afflicted. This same gene is part of the Goan DNA and from a very early age children are taught this. Even more emphatically, children are taught to respect their elders and often called the elderly 'uncle' or 'auntie'.

This is common throughout the world among close communities. In Australia, the aborigines practise it with a gusto that is refreshing. In choosing to perpetuate a mindless insult by another so-called writer, I do it with both disappointment and shame that a fellow Goan should stoop so low. Who the heck gives anyone the right to disdainfully call someone a 'dodderer' without good reason? Why is it that the pipsqueaks of this world who cause hurt by doing or saying or writing in this case the dumbest things? Or was it really a silly, fruitless exercise in riling the meek?

You have to be a contemporary of the dodderer to appreciate that he was once a warrior, a pioneer who was forced out of the comfort of his family home for nearly a century and transported to an alien country where he found no welcome but racist abuse and taunts. Worse, he was called a Paki while skinheads and white supremacists bashed him. He was for a long time a 'black bastard' at work or in the streets of England. Whatever the pain and the suffering, the dodderer persevered 'for the sake of the children'. Some could not take it and packed their bags for Goa, only to return a short time later. Being blessed with a good command and an excellent accent in English, the dodderer found it fairly easy to slip into mainstream English life both in the private sector and the public service. It was not long before the dodderers were commanding high salaries and high positions. It was also not long before the Poms were able to discern between the different brown skinned citizens. In Parliament, the dodderer and his tribe were recognised for their former colonial service, their quality of service, their loyalty to their colonial masters and, if not welcomed with open arms, they were accepted with hands across mouths and eyes.

The weather, unfortunately, was hard to handle. Having been born in a heavenly temperate climate, Britain's frozen winters were totally alien, especially for the older folk, soon to be called the dodderers. But they even overcame that, though never completely. There was some respite during the many visits to Goa where the dodderers lavished in sunshine and home. However, the Wimpy kids, the fish and chips generation, could not handle the pig toilets or the authentic curry dishes. The dodderers had to come to terms with that, too, and in the end sacrificed visits to Goa for the family's sake.

In the very early days of migration in 1968, Goan cuisine was rare and hard to come by, but it soon flourished as other brown-skinned entrepreneurs went about setting up spice shops, providing all the needed ingredients. It was also not long before families were supplementing their income by cooking food, especially Goan sausages, sorportel, samosas, pasties and a variety of other delights. It took some doing to achieve the flourishing Goan food industry which is lauded among the best of cuisines.

Perhaps the dodderer's greatest achievement is his children, who have blossomed into adulthood with university educations that once were thought to be beyond some Goans' reach. Today, the sons and daughters of dodderers compete with the best globally in the sciences, cyberspace, academia, nuclear medicine, highly specialized surgery, engineering of the highest calibre, music and every other sphere of life. Young Goans are among the most gifted people on Earth and many with Queen's

English and a variety of American and Canadian accents! These new Goans, however, are less Goan than the average Goan, not by intent but by automatic assimilation. For all intents and purposes, they are British, American, Canadian, Australian and European. They honour their fathers and mothers, give tradition a modicum of salutation but honour the ways of their birthright and the land of their birth. It is exactly the same in the US, Canada, Europe, Australia and New Zealand. It is only natural evolution. A friend from Australia who had visited England recently remarked that 'they sound like Poms, you can't tell the difference'. Exactly, they are Poms and proud of it.

The children of East African Roman Catholic Goans had that comical lilting Indian accent forced out by the colonial British government. They ordered that English was the only language to be spoken at home. No Indian or Goan vernaculars were allowed. There was a noble intent behind this would-be sinister edict. Some Goan kids were growing up as the butt of a thousand jokes as they directly translated English from Konkani. The results were hilarious just as they were in the case of Hindi, Punjabi and other languages of the Sub-continent. Goans born after 1940 (and some born before that) were the lucky beneficiaries of an English accent exclusive to East African Goans and they cherished it. In my own case, having been brainwashed somewhat by British and American movies and American detective and cowboy stories, I worked at giving full value to the letters L and R like the Scots but without the brogue. I developed a slight twang that pleased radio and television producers and has remained true despite the ravages of living in the UK. Sometimes I did sound more as if I spoke the Queen's English, or if I was an English Midlander, depending on who I was with.

In Australia, I have developed tiny bits of strine (Aussie lingo) and I am quite proud of it. I loved being on stage and being the master of ceremonies came natural to me early and my clear diction was my calling card. My youngest son Carl has taken emcee-ing to much larger stages and audiences and to his own unique dimensions than I ever could have. I marvel at the accents the young people spout these days. You know whether a Goan comes from Liverpool, Manchester, Scotland, Ireland, or London by his or her accent. In some cases the brogue is thicker than mushroom soup. There are also those young adults who are now blessed with all the language gifts that make up the Queen's English and, if spoken without life's human foibles, it is delightful. The US kids are a credit to the different drawls from different parts of the US. The same can be said of Goans from Canada, Australia, New Zealand, Europe and Asia.

Wherever they are, they pick up the accent because of the need to blend in and not stand out. It is a form of assimilation and no one has forced it on them; it is a subconscious thing. Only small minds from an ancient past will pick on accents as a negative. Accents should be celebrated in the same way the children of East African Goan dodderers celebrate academic and business success. Dodderers they may be, but they have gone through hell to give their children the best chances possible and the children have repaid the sacrifices of their parents by achieving outstanding results by any world standard. These super Goans may not be as Goan as their parents, or speak Konkani or love going to Goa. They may not even like Goan food or church anymore, but they are super human beings and now belong to the world. These are the new Goans.

Life in the UK was not a bed of roses. Some East African Goans did not want to leave Kenya, Uganda, Tanzania or elsewhere in Eastern Africa. They were forced to leave and for many years a brutal hatred of things African festered in their hearts, especially the Goans from Uganda who were forced to leave under conditions reminiscent of the Nazi era. The Ugandan Goans lost virtually everything, some even their lives as Idi Amin's soldiers sacked them from their beautiful country homes and careers. Most East African Goans slipped into mainstream English or UK life with relative ease, but they suffered all the pangs of racism that had once been reserved for the West Indians. Some Goans suffered injury from the Paki-bashing skinheads and the racist abuse powered by Enoch Powell and white supremacists. The East African Goan has endured many hardships, abuse and heartbreaks but has continued single-mindedly to make the sacrifices for the better of his children. The road to dodderer-hood is paved with a martyrdom of sorts.

The East African Goan dodderer deserves thanks and praise, not disdain or insults, for paving the way for other Goans to follow. Doddering I think, for most, begins at 65, or it could happen at much younger age for one reason or another. There is nothing elegant about growing old past 60 for many East African Goan dodderers. Their staple diet of fish curry and rice plus one or two vegetables, pork sorportel or chicken xacuti from the freezer, beef vindaloo, or lamb and potato curry has been replaced with fish grilled without salt and just a teaspoon of virgin olive oil, steamed peas, carrots, potatoes, beans, cauliflower, Chinese greens or a selection from God's garden harvest. And yes, lentils and four or five beans, that's where the farting comes from. Doctors tell me that the Goan coconut curries and alcohol, especially *caju feni* distilled from fermented cashew apples, was responsible for a higher than average incidence of diabetes among Goans and other Indians living along the Malabar Coast.

The rice and fish curry is still on the menu though in smaller portions and the basmati rice is low GI and cholesterol resistant to a small degree. There is also the no-salt smoked salmon with onions, tomato, lettuce, cucumber sandwich on 12-grain bread or the delightful canned salmon or tuna with onions, tomato, green coriander and chopped chilli sandwich. It worked great as a weight reducer for me. You are lactose intolerant after drinking milk for 68 years and you are seriously thinking about turning to soymilk for the porridge. Why, you may ask? Well a dodderer has got to do what a dodderer has got to do. Got to get that cholesterol down, got to keep those sugar levels to a minimum! Do not drink single malt scotch anymore. Cannot remember what beer tasted like. Once you binged on 16-20 pints at the local. Soon you are a reformed social drinker who now only drinks 2.5 litres of water a day. You are in the lion's den: your friends now have two beers where once they had three and four; one or two are forced to drink light beer and you sit there, the social alcoholic eunuch that you are and, like someone at a wake, you sip on that bottle of pure, unadulterated water. Your friends of 50 years don't know what to think. Some may even admire you for the willpower on display. They could never do that! Otherwise it is heart disease, diabetes, kidney or liver disease, cancer or some other such calamity.

You no longer look the tall dark lady-killer you once were. Once you were a soccer, cricket, hockey, golf, table tennis, badminton, athletics warrior and now your fleet-of-foot prowess is but a distant memory, sometimes not even that. Mostly you did your best work at the card table or at the races. More recently, the US casinos were a delight. You grew up in the shadows of Goan hockey and athletics Olympians. You were among the gods of your sports scene. Once you rocked! You jived, waltzed and tangoed with the power and grace of a gold medal skater. Today, you opt for economy of movement and space: you stand in one spot with your partner and generate some movement from the hip down and in your mind's eye you are at least making a very minor attempt to dance. No, the sweet bird of youth flew away many decades ago. Instead, you are 10-20 kilos lighter. Your skin is fairer and looks healthier (so you think). You will be 70 or 80 next month but you can jog a little on the treadmill at 4 kph, you are doing three minutes but aiming for six. You may be kidding yourself because shuffling your feet is not jogging. So, for the first time in your life, you are on the verge of becoming a gym junkie. Once you laughed at those old guys who spent hours walking laps around the football grounds at the Railway Institute in Nairobi.

Today, you push yourself just that little bit. Hey, at least your knowledge of the current pop scene is improving from the video screens at the gym. Your life is at the mercy of the specialists and vampires (blood tests) at the local medical centre. You see your cardiologist, endocrinologist, psychologist, psychiatrist and ten other specialists every six months. Today, life is full of tests: blood tests, urine tests, X-rays, MRIs, ultrasounds, CT scans, ECGs, stress tests, etc. Your heart is home to a pacemaker and blood flows through your arteries thanks to stents. I had a stent while on holiday in Goa not so long ago. These days some dodderers get their kicks visiting the physiotherapist or the Chinese massage parlour where manipulative fingers and machines ease the pain in the joints, the lower back, the upper back, the neck and the knees. Soon you will be looking to replace this or that. Imagine, you are in the market for spare parts surgery! And the funeral has become the dodderers' social club. Church and the good deeds it offers form your new sanctuary. Here you find peace amongst acquaintances of different racial backgrounds. And there is always a village feast somewhere in England or a *tiatr* (theatre) to catch with friends from long ago.

What the heck! No regrets. You accept that the damage has already been done and you only have yourself to blame. Loved it when you drank all that beer followed by a few shorts of scotch, every day! Worse, all those cigarettes you smoked such a long time ago. And that sorpotel, chicken skin-on xacuti, those wonderful vindaloos, prawn, crab curries, marinara chilly-fries, succulent pork curries, those extraordinary goat and lamb curries, pullao, heaps of basmati, butter chappatis, naans, yes you gave thanks and loved it all, especially those recipes for diabetes, those unforgettable Goan sweets. Now you dodderer, dodderer you, you put up your hands in resignation and say: I'm happy to go when I am called, I have no regrets.

Regrets, you have a few. Being the last of your generation from East Africa where the umbilical connection with Goa was generally strong, you still dwell on some old-school hopes and aspirations. You accept that mixed marriage, even with Muslims and Hindus, is a matter of supply and demand... the children tell you it is only because of love. Once you might have killed or packed your daughter off to Goa or a nunnery, today you ask your friends: what to do? You find solace in 'as long as they are healthy and happy'. You forget that this particular DNA gene was cut a long time ago, when the young people quit on religion. You say: I guess that is evolution.

I am delighted to be a Goan of East African origin. There will always be something Kenyan running through my veins because I owe Kenya a debt of gratitude for giving me life, a career and the experience of many wonderful and magical moments. Similarly, my DNA can only be Goan thanks to my father and mother, even though I speak very little Konkani and that with an accent. I am comfortable with the Goan in me and the Goan in my friends and acquaintances. I am also comfortable with the Goan in my children, who are more Aussie than Goan or Pom or Kenyan. They have their parents' DNA and nothing else Goan. They are cool with that.

You seek out old friends from the old country because you share a common East African gene: a lifetime of memories, shared events, sport, growing up, births, marriages, deaths, loss, achievements, nightmares, dreams,

Goan food and a million other specks of life in an African paradise where we thought we were in heaven on earth. All this before the shanties invaded Eastleigh and went viral all over Nairobi, like the favelas in Rio.

The East African Goan, as the label suggests, is a breed apart. There are a million things that bind us together forever. We shared in the joys of birth, marriage, of growing up poor and not knowing it, propped up by hundreds of friends who were in the same boat. We shared what little we had, as did our parents. Those that had a bit to spare did it with discretion worthy of sainthood, mainly through fear of the evil eye. We saw our loved friends die and we buried them. Others we pulled out of car wrecks that had taken the lives of others. We went through the nightmare of recovery together and we all became victims of the aftermath. The memories of the lost loved ones bind us together forever. We shared broken hearts and dreams. We shook our heads at the heartbreakers and soon made up once the healing was done. We raised children and shared their First Holy Communions and Confirmations with our inner circle of friends and family. Tears of pride rolled down our cheeks and our friends were there to put an arm around us and turn the tears to smiles.

Our parents saw us grow into adulthood and marry and continue the cycle of life. We share a love of God, the church, the school and the club. We chose our clubs according to the like-minded friends who were already members. So we joined the Railway Institute, the Goan Institute, the Goan Gymkhana and the Tailors Society reserved for trouk, Konkani speakers and fans of *tiatr*. It was not long before tailors' children deserted their fathers' club for the RI or GI, the Mombasa Institute, the Kampala Goan Institute and similar institutions. At these clubs we began our education in the social mores of life. We met girls and fell in and out of love.

We danced cheek-to-cheek, held hands momentarily and secretly. We tasted the first kiss that was no more than a fumble of lips, French kissing came much later with experience. We bought the girls Babycham, Wincarnis, gin and tonic, Bacardi and Coke, the lager shandy and a glass of wine, preferably Portuguese Mateus. With a girl in your arms, eyes closed you kissed her lightly on the lips, cheeks and forehead and you sighed a gentle sigh of wonderment. We spoke to the parents of our girlfriends for the first time and, if we were lucky, we had an adult conversation.

Sometimes we got invited to dinner. For the son of a tailor, this was a different lifestyle and, more often than not, you were intimidated by it, you feigned working late or some such honourable decision to turn down the invitation. And if you wanted to take a girl out and were too afraid of the draconian parents, you asked a special kind of guy who could charm the old folks to ask on your behalf. But if the parents had a habit telling boys to 'come back when you have your university degree' you sometimes gave up the love of your life.

We gave no currency to the gossip and wounding words from the women of low esteem and we cared even less for the denigration by caste, although a few did succumb due to a tyrannical father-in-law to be. Especially those who believed very firmly that the sons and daughters of carpenters, tailors, motor mechanics, clerks, accountants, public servants, should marry their own kind, as well as from the relevant north-south Goa divide as well as the all-important financial or education status. Children of the poor did not have to worry about that. Their education would be limited to secondary school for the boys and secretarial college for the girls and they were happy with that.

Some would argue that there was one club that was the home of the imagined Goan upper class, something that has been relegated to a sad past. The club provided us with all our heroes and role models and they were mostly superstar sports men and women, many of them current or past Olympians. We played tennis, badminton, hockey, cricket, soccer, table tennis, darts, snooker, billiards. We played sport hard, sometimes we drank hard, foolishly, and even more foolishly we fought amongst ourselves. We had fought the good fight and there would be another day, another challenge. We had learned some of life's lessons with a black eye or two but we had also earned some mutual respect. We also became members of the 'club' so that we could avail ourselves of the facilities for our weddings, whenever they would be.

We shared the pain and trauma of being denied work permits, in effect the 'get out of Kenya' kick. We held the painful farewells and drank a few Tuskers to drown our sorrows. Will we ever see each other again? That was the question of loved friends as they were dispersed to the four corners of the world and that is why we all come to London or Toronto to meet up with our soul-mates, blood brothers and sisters of sorts, but above all the unique Goan tribe from East Africa. Today we seek out old friends to find out how they are, how their folks are, any news from Kenya, Uganda, Tanzania or Goa? Heard from anyone in Canada, US, Australia, New Zealand? We are of one tribe, bonded together through shared life experiences and in the twilight of our lives we hurt together just as much as we love and laugh together. More importantly, we cherish each moment shared.

In Sydney, Australia, I meet every Friday with Tony Reg D'Souza, Loy D'Souza, Felix Nazareth, Cajie Miranda, Leslie and Andrew Scott and Terry Pereira (Peter Cook's (Railways) son). We are all from Eastleigh, except Felix who was a member of that other club I mentioned. Now we live within 10 minutes of each other. Harold George D'Souza from Mombasa, who lives 40 minutes away, and a whole bunch of other East African Goans occasionally join us.

What is even sweeter is that the young adult brood and their partners sometimes join the old men, bringing to the table fresh ears for our well-worn stories and jokes. My friends' wives also join us from time to time. When he is in town, we are also joined by the mirth and merriment of Kenyan Drake Shikhule and his wife Jo-anne. We do this come what may, rain or shine. Absences are frowned upon... in jest. These dodderers have a great time although our drinking habits are on the wane. The ravages of a deliriously happy past seem to taking their toll. Some of us have cut down on our usual three pints of beer to a couple of light ones. Random breath testing is one reason; taking care of health business is another. But there is no letting up on the sharp one-liners or the piercing, laughter-rendering retorts. The Friday Club is known the world over. Now only Terry works full-time. We have nothing to apologise for. The Eastern African Goans gave much to their countries of adoption. Most important of all was religion and education. They saved their pennies and helped the Irish priests build churches and schools. In East Africa, these great institutions were dotted in the many towns. Wherever there were a few Goans gathered then, Catholicism and Catholic school education flourished. This was the greatest contribution to the colonial countries, so much so that emerging Africans preferred the Catholic education system to the public government schools.

Goans in post-independent Kenya

What started in 1963 as a steady exit by Goans who felt that there was no place for them in an independent Kenya reached a crescendo with the exodus in 1968. Before that there had been a steady trickle of Goans returning home or families sending wives and children to the UK. The steady trickle continued to increase with the introduction of the work permits, the Africanisation police and the so-called Kenyanisation policy which was introduced to force Asians to become Kenyan citizens. In 1968, thousands left Kenya.

After 1968, some families sent their wives and children overseas for safety and hung around until it was also their turn to leave. After 1975, the once mighty Railway Goan Institute shut down for lack of patrons. The Goan Institute and the Goan Gymkhana, once the exclusive realm of middle class Goans (GI) and Brahmans (GG), was home to ghosts of the past and any non-Goan who wanted to join the club. Caste, class, village, colour, religion or position did not matter anymore. Although most clubs opened their doors soon after independence in 1963, there were few takers.

I was a young parliamentary reporter and had the privilege of watching Fitz carry out his Deputy Speaker duties. He was always ice-cool and precise, with an uncanny mastery over parliamentary standing orders. There were not many occasions when MPs argued with the quiet Goan. He had a great teacher, though, the wise Sir Humphrey Slade, the Speaker. I thought he represented the best in white folks and carried the unwritten banner on his forehead that not all white men were evil bastards. The sad thing was I cannot ever remember speaking to Fitz. I was the prisoner of other post-independence topics. In my own case, Kenya gave me a career that took me into the halls of power in many countries and showed me a world that I could not have even imagined. From leaving school at 13, to becoming Chief Reporter and an investigative reporter, my journey did not come easily. However, from the earliest times, as I came into close contact with men who would become the greatest powerbrokers in Kenyan politics in 1960, I knew Kenya was not my country and there would be no permanent place for me even though I was born there. I would never enjoy the kind of editorial freedom I had tasted in Britain and other parts of Europe.

My two brothers chose to remain and people like Daniel arap Moi and Njoroge Mungai tried hard to change my mind. But while I was there, I did what a good journalist does: sought the truth. I must confess that I did not have the guts to report all that I had discovered. I could not remain in a country under constant threat of deportation or a bullet aimed at my head. I left in 1974.

Yet everyone, including Kenyatta and his cabinet ministers, thought I was a Kenyan citizen, to the extent that I went as part of official Kenyan delegations to various countries. Most African heads of state and their ministers recognised me as a Kenyan. I look back at the land of my birth with nothing but great fondness and even greater heartbreak as corruption and crime continues to fester close to its heart. I fear for its future. Perhaps there is one group of people who deserves Kenya's collective applause: the Goans that remained. I am not sure that those who stayed after everyone else had left did it for reasons of commerce and business, or that they could not fathom living anywhere else, or because some of them were genuinely dedicated to the betterment of the country if not the people. Whatever the reason, the eternal survival instincts of the Goans have allowed them not only to prosper but also to become one with other Kenyans. Some mixed marriages have signalled the infancy of assimilation. Some, if not all, of these very successful Goans have ensured their children left the country.

Yet one non-political power couple stands out: the multi-faceted Felix Pinto and his table tennis legend wife Jane Pinto had committed themselves to Kenya through a range of businesses as early as the late 1950s. He and his family have made an immense contribution to post-independence Kenya. Here are a few grains of Goan heritage who persevered in business, creating jobs, contributing to the education of young Kenyans and Kenyans with disabilities, creating opportunities for individual advancement, caring for the environment including the national parks and animal sanctuaries. They have managed to succeed, sometimes under frightening and challenging times, with the same quiet dignity and poise that was the hallmark of generations before them. I for one, of those who left 'home' for the safety of foreign shores, have always saluted you. You have always lit the flame of remembrance and protected the heritage of the good name Goans have enjoyed throughout the generations.

There is one footnote in history we must not forget: the architect Braz Menezes won the competition for the country's independence decorations that transformed Nairobi in 1963. He was among the first Goans to become a citizen and start his own firm and he led the way in reforming the approach to low-income housing projects in slum areas. With his partner David Mutiso he transformed his firm into the largest truly Kenyan one. Their high point was being selected to design the United Nations Environment Program headquarters. The firm of Mutiso Menezes International still exists today even though the original partners have left the firm.

As always, in all our endeavours, good, bad, or ugly, the final salute must remain with the women, often the greatest heroines of the Goan home and the community collective. They were the foundation of the community as the homemakers of each family. I doubt there is a single family that does not owe its greatest debt to the mother. Where would our fathers have been without their wives' fortitude, faith, strength of character and as empresses of their domain, although in those early days the man was always the master of his domain. Mothers universally were God's own wonderful creation. Even though, in those times, they walked in the shadows of the husbands.

Where, I wonder, would the cabinet ministers, permanent secretaries, heads of government and other senior marshals of government have been without their devoted, dedicated and utterly, utterly confidential Goan secretaries? These women were the real Goan heroines in the run up to Independence and were even more entrenched and silently powerful after Independence. Their bosses found them absolutely trustworthy, otherwise how could they have been entrusted with both national and private information, sometimes of the highest secrecy and of the most sensitive kind? Goan secretaries were no less head-hunted by the private sector and until their departure served with incredible success, so much so that when some of them migrated to Britain, the transition was often seamless. It was the wife who often found work first before the husband. Alongside the secretaries, I would add the teachers, nurses, midwives, radiographers, lab technicians, doctors and the many other professions women graced in a beautiful country.

Teachers, both male and female, deserve their own pages in history. I have never stopped admiring them and that is perhaps one of the reasons why I loved school, especially English, so much. Goan teachers were among the jewels in the crown of Goan progress. However, after independence, they played a much more vital role in developing the hearts and minds of young Kenyans for future leadership roles. One of my good buddies, Tony Reg D'Souza, did exactly that. At the famous Mary Hill Catholic School in Nairobi, he taught young boys who would eventually be in the leadership of the country and titans of local industry. Many years later many of them still remember Tony, who now lives in Sydney, Australia and we meet every Friday for a beer!

Among the men are those who manned the Customs and Excise departments in Mombasa and at various airports. These men in white protected the country with a diligence that is reserved for heroes. Here as well stand the Goan men and women who made sure the railways were run to the highest efficiency: on time and with a First Class that was the envy of others in Africa. Goan chefs and stewards and waiters made sure the food was world class and the service memorable. Here again an army of Goans trained Africans to succeed in a seamless transition.

Perhaps the most flamboyant of the Goan professionals were the legal set. To this day they continue to do Goans proud. And before ready-made clothes arrived, Goan tailors were in high demand and had a reputation for excellence bar none. Most of them returned to Goa after independence. If nation building did not involve politics, the Kenyan Goans matched the other migrant tribes. But I say again: not collectively, but individually. As a community they built schools, churches, housing estates, and social clubs, gave alms to the church and the poor and helped St. Vincent de Paul care for destitute Goan families like mine.

Goan secretarial colleges were responsible for churning out Goan secretaries to the highest standards. I went to Goan-owned Premier College in the city to learn short hand and touch-typing. Got the touch but lost the short hand bit.

Dr Ribeiro Goan School in Nairobi and the Goan School in Mombasa were perhaps the truest epitaphs for Goan contribution to education in Kenya. It has been one of the great achievements of the community and there are thousands, albeit a vanishing breed, who will never forget it. There were also a couple of housing estates that were to the Goan credit.

Goans and Asians, particularly the mighty Indian Bazaar spice and clothing moguls who ruled the economy, were labelled as exploiters. Treated even worse were the shopkeepers in the remotest parts of Kenya, the dukawallahs. Asians constantly had the abuse of exploitation hurled at them to the point that it became a black Kenyan mantra. Political opportunists repeated this in front of thousands of people at rallies for independence, regardless of whether it was true or not.

There is no doubt that in the early years, Africans were treated somewhat badly as is the want of colonial Africa of that period: 'they are not like us...'; 'they are savages'; 'their gods are witch doctors' were some of the kinder sentiments expressed.

However, there is one group of people that the Kenyan government owes a particularly huge debt of gratitude and these were the Goan civil servants. Whereas once their ancestors ruled the seas in the cabins, bars, dining rooms, as waiters, stewards and chefs, this vigilant band of Goans ruled the civil service, sometimes imperiously but always with loyalty, honesty, dignity and a steadfastness that was reminiscent of the last soldier standing in any historic conflict. Mervyn Maciel will, I am sure, pay great homage to his fellow clerks. From early on, most of the 'brown Portuguese' employed as clerks by the British were called 'Indian Baboo clerks' by some.

Various governors of Kenya including Sir Evelyn Baring had often pointed to 'their fine reputation for loyal service' and to the fact that the most trusted member of the district staff was the senior Goan clerk. It was easy for the Goans to believe in this image and thus consider themselves not only a class above Asians but also the 'favourites' of the colonial government. They were quite proud of their newly inherited 'status' and when they returned home to Goa they would emphasize the difference in their lifestyles, adopted from their contact with the Europeans and some would even speak in broken Swahili with each other. From Kenya's dust, the country's DNA had entered the Goan bloodstream, and for generations to come Goans would happily shout about their Kenyan connection. However, while they did not want to be called Indian or Portuguese once they had migrated to the UK and parts overseas, many were happy with the Portuguese label.

As the Goans waited with heavy hearts, sobbing and tears and trepidation for their future, they assisted in the training of Africans to do their jobs and thus facilitated the transfer of business from the Goans to the newly independent Africans. The few who took up Kenyan citizenship provided short-term longevity of experience in their jobs. They were the go-to experts for the new employees.

Equally, Goans in the medical field did the same. Some doctors remained several years longer until there were suitable replacements. A similar trend followed in the private sector. In virtually every sphere of production, manufacture, agriculture and animal husbandry, Goans played a pivotal role in the early years of Kenya's independence. In every sphere of life, except politics.

It was this devotion to their God that provided them with the faith and strength to be generous to a fault. There were some exceptions of course. As the final page was being written with the exodus of a majority of the Goans, it's ironic that this might have been their finest hour when the sun went down on colonial Kenya.

Exodus with tears into the unknown

Winston Churchill in a communication to the founders of the Nairobi Goan Institute stated, 'The British Empire is big enough to shelter the law abiding and peaceful Goan pioneer, a good citizen of Portugal and to protect him in all his activities in British East Africa either as a Government employee or otherwise.'

The Goans who had to leave Kenya made the decision to remain Portuguese, British, Indian or nationals of another country. They rejected the option of a Kenyan citizenship. If they could not become 'African', they could not commit their lives and the lives of their children to an African country. They had to go. Some, like me, made up their minds very early that they would be moving on. I have already explained why I had to leave… in a hurry.

However, even many of those who took up citizenship sent their children overseas. After the children had settled in foreign lands, their Kenyan citizen parents joined them. A few brave souls who would not have felt at home anywhere else continued to live out their days in their Kenyan paradise.

Tom Mboya, while speaking in the Kenya Legislative Council, sounded one of his many warnings to the Goans. 'There are some Goans and Goan associations in this country. I respect the Goan community. I notice that some Goans and Goan associations went out of their way to declare their loyalty to Portugal.

'Indeed, there are Goans in this country who wish to be loyal to Portugal, then I say, you have no business being in Kenya. They cannot be loyal to Portugal as well as Kenya. Loyalty to Portugal means loyalty to the acts of that regime, means accepting what they are doing in Angola and Mozambique, particularly to their policies and system. If that is what the Goan community in this country wants to be, let them know from now on they will have no place in this country.

'They must declare their position publicly and clearly where they stand. We have many of them in our Civil Service, some in high positions and if their loyalty can be doubted they have no place in our civil service. They must ask categorically if they are loyal to Kenya or Portugal. That is my warning to the Goan community.'

I think on July 21, 1961, also in Parliament, Fitz de Souza said, 'Goans in this country are very clearly told if they do not support the Portuguese policies they would be deprived of their Portuguese passports.

'I want to assure the Goans in the country that the African people and the party I am associated with Kenya African National Union are not the enemy. They fully realise the contributions the Goans have made and will continue to make in the future.

'Those Goans who are tools of the Portuguese administration, those Goans who are trying to compel their fellow brethren to support Portuguese obnoxious policies, those Goans will not be tolerated. And particularly where a Goan occupies a position in the civil service and claims loyalty to any government as barbaric as Portugal cannot be trusted in the service of this country.'

If you left Kenya, it was because of the choice you made, even though you were forced to make it. In 1963, Jomo Kenyatta urged all Asians to support the ruling KANU party. He said in a speech that he and M.A. Desai had 'worked as brothers for the rights of the Asian and the African.' Kenyatta said that he had sat with the great Mahatma Gandhi and Jawaharlal Nehru and had planned the future of their respective countries. Kenyatta said that he hoped that Asians would join in building a Kenya in which Africans and Asians 'live together, work together and plan together'. He said his government would 'protect their businesses' and 'they had nothing to fear.' There was a strong belief among Asians that those Asians who did not support KANU would be evicted and deported. Kenyatta said anyone guilty of doing this would 'be punished worse than under the British.'

The late legendary US Civil Rights activist and the first African-American appointed Justice of the US Supreme Court, Thurgood Marshall, was invited by Jomo Kenyatta to the Lancaster House Constitutional Conference to assist with the writing of independent Kenya's first constitution. Marshall was very keen on equal rights for both the Asians and Europeans in an independent Kenya. To that end he incorporated a bill of rights in the constitution. In July 1963, he visited Nairobi to see how his bill of rights was being exercised. Below is an authorised and generous excerpt from Mary L. Dudziak's fascinating book: *Exporting American Dreams: Thurgood Marshall's African Journey (OUP USA):*

'At the end of their first day in Kenya, Marshall and Berl Bernhard (Marshall's travelling companion, the US Civil Rights staff director) attended a reception and dinner in their honour at the home of Tom Mboya, who now held a cabinet post in the new government. Marshall fulfilled his promise to the Indian shop-owner. (Earlier in the day in Nairobi, the two men had seen a sign in a shop window: "Forced to close". The Indian owner told them he was being boycotted. Marshall told the shopkeeper he would raise the matter with the Prime Minister that night.)

'Bernhard recalled, "About halfway through the cocktail hour, Thurgood got a hold of Kenyatta and said: 'Jomo what the hell are you doing' and I thought, my god, ... and he said: 'I spent all my time busting tail in that wet place in London a constitution for you with a bill of rights. And you don't go around taking people's property without due process of law. And I've only been here one afternoon, what is the first thing I see. (sic) You're beginning to make it impossible for Indians and Pakistanis to stay in Kenya and operate their business. What are you going to do about it?'

'Bernhard described Kenyatta as a very impressive man, "very cool, very elderly." Kenyatta told Marshall they were looking into it. Marshall was not mollified. "No it's not 'looking into'," he replied. "It's doing something about it."

'He called Mboya over and said to him, "Your responsibility is to see that see that despite what the Prime Minister wants to happen, that we are going to protect the property rights in the country.'

'Tom Mboya said, "Well we are going to do that, Judge, and… "Marshall cut in: "You're not doing it."'

I am not sure if there was another occasion in history when someone stood up to Kenyatta on the issue of the Asians in Kenya. Several months later, however, Thurgood criticised Asians for not taking up citizenship. Asians feared that citizenship would not protect their jobs, their businesses or protect them against discrimination and deportation. That is exactly what happened.

The 1968 exodus to the UK was a heart-breaking episode in the lives of the Kenyan Goans. Many thought that the day would never come when they would be forced to leave Kenya. They thought: 'We will serve the new government as well as we served the colonial government. If we leave, who is going to do the work? The country will collapse in a short time.' It did not.

Night after night they boarded aircraft bound for the UK. You could hear people crying and sobbing in the airport's departure lounge. There was a lot of anger and abuse. There was a lot of fist-pumping in the air. In the end, they left with heavy hearts. It was heartbreaking watching the household employees sobbing uncontrollably as they said farewell to their former employers. They had little idea what was waiting for them at the other end. They knew they were not wanted. Advertisements by cities like Bradford, Leicester and others made it clear: 'Don't come. We don't want you.'

I went to Leicester, Birmingham and other parts of the British Midlands. I also visited Bradford. The message to the Asians in Kenya was the same: 'we don't want you.' Leicester was a broken city after textile manufacturing crashed in the UK. The city and its suburban inhabitants were in the doldrums. Many did not know when they would find work again. Leicester already had a mostly out-of-work West Indian population which was fighting its own race relations battle. In 1968, the people of Leicestershire were very insular. Not many ventured outside the Shire boundaries and this had been so for generations. They did not have much idea of the world outside or the rainbow variety of nations. It was a standing joke that many local thought they needed a passport to get to London. And if you mentioned Wales or Scotland, they would ask, jokingly, what country is that?

It was not long ago that the late firebrand Member of Parliament and leading anti-Asian migration guru, Enoch Powell, was speaking of 'Rivers of Blood' that would be running all over the UK. There were no rivers of blood, but in those very early days, Asians were attacked and beaten by skinheads, many of them devoted supporters of the gospel according to Enoch Powell and other white supremacists like the National Front. 'Paki bashing' became a new British pastime. All brown skins were called 'Pakis'. They could not tell the difference. However, the Asians including the Goans did overcome. Ironically, Leicester, Birmingham, Bradford and many suburbs of Great London are prospering because of the South Asians. But in those early days it was particularly dark times for the new immigrants. Imagine a mother with three school-age children in the middle of the great metropolis. But help did come both from state institutions and kind Britons.

While they continued to make a new life for themselves in their new country, the Kenyan DNA was strong in their blood. There were those who had put Kenya completely out of their minds and were never to return there. The majority, however, yearned for the old country and would return on holidays or they would be jumping for joy every time a Kenyan won a gold medal on the international and Olympic athletics. So much so that many still wear to this day those distinctive T-shirts with the logo of the Kenyan beer Tusker. It was once a favourite beer and thankfully is available in many parts of the world.

The Kenya DNA was alive and well.

Many years later, in 1974, I migrated to London then moved to Leicester. By then the racism had died down somewhat but there was no fraternizing.

For example, I went to the Wyvern Arms pub every day for a whole year and a half before someone actually spoke to me. When the kid did it was difficult to understand the Shire accent. He asked and it sounded like: 'jiyachuuk errars'. I told him I could not understand what he was saying. He lifted the darts in hands and gestured throwing them. What he said was: do you chuck arrows. From that day I was an accepted member of the pub because I played darts, snooker and pool and became a representative member of the pub teams. I used to meet the pensioners every Sunday morning for a game of dominoes and we each bought a round. That friendship meant that I never had to buy any vegetables. Fresh greens were delivered to my doorstep free of charge.

I never experienced any kind of racism during the four years we were there or the many times I visited the British Isles before. I guess I was lucky.

The vanishing Goan

Currently there are households where fish curry and rice are no longer the exclusive meal on Friday nights. What is a Goan without his fish curry and rice, their staple diet for hundreds of years? In about 15 years that trait will completely disappear outside of Goa. Only migrants from Goa will persevere for a little while. In 30 or 40 years' time, the Goan gene will probably have died out completely outside of Goa and with it interest in Goa will also continue to dissipate.

In 2015 only 25 per cent of the population in Goa was Roman Catholic. How soon will it take the Christian religion to disappear from Goa itself, since Catholic Goans continue to migrate to distant shores? Especially since thousands have availed themselves of Portuguese passports and continue to create new Goan ghettos in British suburbs.

Tragically, not many Goans in the diaspora speak their mother tongue Konkani. There is a real disconnect with real Goan culture. When I write of Goans I am referring to the 100-carat authentic Roman Catholic variety, 6am/7am Mass with mum, of course, before work or school, Angelus at midday, Benediction in the evening, a rosary and all the litanies in the world while kneeling on a concrete or mud floor, confessionals on

Saturday afternoon and the resultant three or four rosaries for all those evil thoughts of puberty, novenas for this and novenas for him or her, for souls you know and did not know, a statue of this one and that one, the procession from one home to the next and the endless prayers, a prayer to this saint, that saint, that other saint and, of course, my patron saint, your patron saint... always the prayer: deliver us from evil. You would think that living was a never-ending battle with Mr Devil. Sadly or not, the devoted and the devotion are vanishing, especially outside of Goa. But they did leave us with good manners, godliness, goodliness, etiquette, decorum, honesty, loyalty, trust, a marriage for life (that is questionable as a good thing), a passion to succeed and give the children everything they did not have, a love of music and dance, an eye for the arts, dress and style and, of course, a cuisine so exclusive it could only happen in Goa.

As a journalist, I have always felt freed from all the taboos and prejudice of the Goan kind. I was fortunate enough to be born poor of a tailor family and the only way was up. The evolution of freedom was happening all around me. My Goan friends came from different castes and classes of the Goan landscape. Whether our parents liked it or not, we were unstoppable. The Silent Generation and the one before it were infested with all the prejudices of separatism, class, caste, inter-tribalism, racism and prejudice by religion. Who in their right minds would put a daughter, sister, or niece through the kind of torment mothers once did, saying: 'My God, My God, what have you done to us? What kind of devil has taken you away from us and Jesus?' (Tears, wailing, temple beating and chest thumping ensued). 'What will people think, what will people say about us? That we did not bring you up properly? We took you to church every day? We were going to find you a nice Goan Catholic boy; you were not ready yet, no? A Muslim, a Muslim, a Muslim is a devil. He does not know God. You have disgraced your father, your family and the Goan name. How will I be able to show my face outside our home? How will I be able to go to church?'

Enter the father, defender of our faith. 'You are no longer a daughter of mine. You will not look at my face or talk to me. Wash her in holy water, rub some garlic on her and call Coutinho, he will know what to do, salt

and chillies, whatever. Ask the priest to come and exorcise her. He will
get the devil out of her. Say a few novenas, give a few masses. Write to
Goa; tell them to pray at our church. If everything fails, we will send her
to Goa and the nunnery in our village. That will take the devil out of her.
You stay with her for six months, we will manage here. Tie her to the bed
and make sure she does not run away, she may kill herself. And they will
blame us. Take her to the doctor tomorrow; make sure there is nothing
growing inside of her. If there is, you know what to do. Do not talk to
anyone else about it, especially not your brother or your sister. You know
what big mouths they have. And we will not go to the club for a few weeks
or at least not until we return from Goa. You know it is your fault. You
were not a good mother otherwise this disaster would not have happened.'

Meanwhile the victim would be thinking, what have I done that is so
wrong? I am 14 years old. I love Sharif. This is my life you are destroying,
my soul you are smashing and my heart you are crumbling. You are killing
me! Please stop this pain! I am only in love! I am only in love! I may not
marry him and I will commit no sin with him, so what is wrong? I have
not even kissed him. We do not know how. God, what kind of God are
you? Sharif just saved me from those horrible Goan boys who were teasing
me. Is it sin to be nice to someone who is nice to you?

The boy's father would respond, 'I have spoken to Sharif and he tells me
that nothing happened. He only walked her home from school. But I can
see a young boy's love in his eyes. It is the first awakening of manhood,
nothing else. So we are sending him to a madrassa in Islamabad. His
brothers have convinced him he has to go. My wife is heartbroken. She
does not know what she has done wrong. This country is difficult for our
boys. Girls have their faces uncovered, almost naked at the shoulders and
legs. These things are too much for a young boy. Yes, there is no point in
taking chances.'

The girl's father would reply, 'Memsahib and I have decided to send Ellen
to Goa and that should be the end of that. What can we do? They are
children and we try to bring them up according to our gods. What else
can we do? OK. Everything is good.'

If the situation involved a homosexual son or a lesbian daughter, the parents' suicides would be just around the corner or one of them would be in an asylum. Fortunately, this prejudiced, homophobic Roman Catholic persona has vanished.

The Goan caste system, too, is vanishing, at least in the diaspora. But slivers of prejudice remain which is the only reason some Canadian Goans saw the need for an organisation called 'The Sons and Daughters of Tailors'. I expect, like the vanishing Goan, that it is a fad that will fade away. But it was not too long ago that mothers told their sons to keep away from a particular girl because her father and mother would not tolerate it because they were a different caste or in a different class. After all, he was only the son of a lowly shoemaker and she was the daughter of educated parents who were reasonably well-to-do. We cannot sit at the same table with them, she would tell him. For her to be with you would bring great shame and disgrace on their house and our people will not like their high and mighty ways, especially when they will always be looking down on us. We, each of us, must stick to our own kind. Too many young Goans were driven to exile, to suicide or a life in living hell because of this kind of prejudice within. Fortunately, this Goan has almost completely vanished.

Fortunately, there is one Goan who is not vanishing: the recent migrants from Goa to Africa, the UK, Canada, US and elsewhere. A hard-working species, reminiscent of the original migrant somewhat but more committed to building new homes in Goa, supporting the people who remain behind and forging a beautiful future for their families. These are Goans of two continents; happy to be toiling away with the firm knowledge a retirement awaits them in Goa. I hope this Goan is around for many decades to come. This Goan has a lot of pride in his or her achievements and the security of a future in Goa and overseas.

There is another Goan Catholic emerging from the rubbish tip of prejudice. The African Goans, especially the East African clique, tend to hang together and are forced to mix, by the necessity of numbers, with Goans who have migrated directly from Goa, from other parts of India and Pakistan and from the Gulf countries. These intra-Goan prejudices fortunately break down when inter-marriage comes to the rescue.

In the bad old days, those piercing thorns of prejudice always seemed to surface with questions. 'Where do your mother and father come from? What is your father's profession? What does your mother do? Why, your father could not afford to keep her home? What is your village? Do you all have a house in Goa? What is your profession? How many degrees do you have? How much do you earn? What are your assets?' They never ask, "are you a practising Roman Catholic?' Fortunately, this is also a vanishing Goan. It is vanishing even more when a different race is involved. These days none of these types of questions are raised.

The wonderful thing about today is that none of that nonsense is relevant, in as much as being or not being a Goan is relevant. The young Catholic Goan has no hang-ups whatsoever. They are gender neutral, religion neutral, nationality and ethnicity neutral, colour neutral, language neutral and plain old could not give a stuff-neutral. Free at last, free at last. A friend married a Muslim boy. He is a gentle, doting soul and totally in love with her. He is everything that she dreamed of in a soul mate, a friend, a lover, the father of their children and her husband. Before she married, she had to convert. Her mother does not care, only her daughter's happiness matters. His parents dote on the granddaughter but they had heavy hearts when he told them he was marrying a Roman Catholic (infidel, shaitan (devil)). Today, she is the daughter they wished for their son. No worries, no problems, love rules. I love 'em both, love 'em all.

More recently, one of my most favourite young people married an Aussie girl. I love this kid because he is a special kind of person. He is blessed with gentleness and an innocence that is bereft of anything ugly or untoward. He is one of life's quiet achievers. Their wedding was a sensational day and night. Goans are blessed with a fine taste for beer and scotch and have a pretty good set of pins and hips on the dance floor. Besides health restrictions, we will eat most anything, just like white Anglo-Saxon Aussies. We made a whole bunch of new friends that day and celebrated a whole bunch of other lives. I saw a whole lot of Goan baggage go out a welcome window. That day, I felt that being Goan was irrelevant. That day, the Goan had vanished and it was a good thing too.

There are too many mothers and fathers and grandparents who might be turning in their graves for the way things have turned out today. In those beautiful, innocent old days, a fair-skinned damsel was a prized catch as much as a dark-skinned African, African-American or a Caribbean maiden is a hot catch now. Marrying a Muslim, a Hindu, a Punjabi or a black man: they would have not have dreamt about it. It would have been a nightmare for a people who were taught that they were *Portuguesa,* not even Goan. Fortunately, that prejudice is well and truly dead and buried.

Every day is a beautiful time for the world, at least some of the world. It is particularly true for my part of the world, Australia. My country is blessed with having a few serious problems and lots of minor problems, mostly of man's own making. It is indeed a land of opportunity. Like everywhere else, integrity and honesty are at the mercy of those who make it their business to corrupt the world. But generally, Australia seems a country just as much at peace with itself as most places in the world. In most places of the world, you will find young Goans at peace with their lot. They are the new Turks on the block except they do not mix with boys in the hood. The hood is no place for them. These are the freest Goans anywhere. In fact, being Goan has very little meaning for them. They have shifted their world so many times that they are now in a different world where Goa and Goans do not exist. There is very little chance that their spouses will be Goan. They do not move in Goan circles and do not have the opportunity to meet potential Goan life-mates. Very few Goans anywhere in the world have second thoughts about their children marrying a non-Goan, especially people of white skin. Even the former taboos of not marrying blacks (Africans, African-Americans and West Indians), Muslims, Sikhs, Punjabis, Indians in general, etc., are disappearing, at least outside of India.

It is in the lofty spheres of achievement that Goa and Goan become rather irrelevant and insignificant in the larger scheme of things. For one, very few of the old-fashioned Goan Catholics will come into contact with them, interact with them or become part of their scene. Konkani, Goa, etc., might as well be in another universe. This is also true of the other sub-species at a much lower level who have come to accept their surroundings, the culture, life as being their own and they see themselves as no different than anyone else in the street, the suburb or the city. They are only acting naturally, making themselves at home in an environment that is comfortable. Listen to them talk. The Queen's English was never before given such an exquisite lilt or the various British (the Scottish brogue, for example) accents pronounced with such panache (such as Liverpudlian or London's variety of Cockney) that more often than not it is just sweet music to listen to. This is even more so in the US, Canada, Europe and the world at large. More often than not, these new Goans will marry non-Goans and it is here that the vanishing really begins.

As you walk through the corridors of life in US, Canada, Europe, Australia and South America, where the assimilation (or, rather, where the intruding colonial population has replaced the indigenous population) is often complete, the dominant ethnicity is slowly losing its unique lustre. The spices of multi-ethnicities are diluting the single strains. In cruel times, they would have been referred to as a nation of half-castes. The Indian in the West Indies is less of an Indian and almost all Caribbean, with the black American part being dominant. This is a classic example of assimilation. In Europe, however, the reverse is probably true. The African part of the West Indian is being dominated by the European. The result is, like in Brazil, fairer skinned half-castes. Often the golden glow of the skin is sensational.

Indian half-castes, Anglo-Indians, migrated in great numbers to foreign shores where today there is very little Indian left in the DNA. The bottom line is that the world's ethnicity is changing. A Jew is no longer a Jew, he or she might be Jewish, but not an uncontaminated sample Jew. The same can be said for many White Anglo Saxons and those whites in Europe, Canada and the US. Even the Ku-Klux-Klan patron saints are no longer totally white without a speck of black. In reality, there is no such thing as a pure race. With Goa's largest population located outside the Indian Sub-continent, Goans are subject to all the changes affecting a shifting world.

It is the same for other sub-continentals. Not everybody can handle the mental trauma of an arranged marriage in India, and local overseas Indian girls are frowned on as not being the real thing. So mixed marriage through love, necessity of demand or necessity of sex is a natural trend.

This is why so many Indian surnames have Christian first and middle names. It is even more difficult to tell who really is a Goan when the issue of the marriage has a Smith, Jones or Brown for a surname. Sometimes this has been necessitated by the economies of availability: not enough Goan girls or boys. Some traditions, especially religion, have had to be sacrificed on the altar of marriage. Can any Goan of pre-baby boomer days imagine their daughter marrying a divorced white Anglo-Saxon in the Church of England, or some other non-Catholic branch of the Christian church, or a temple, *gurdwara* (Sikh temple) or mosque? But it happens. After all the questions, what relevance does Goa have in the greater world? The new generation has to chart its own course. Enveloped by the myriad cultures in Britain and Europe, born Goans have taken to their adopted cultures like fish to water. There is little to no room for Goa. Within a few decades the slightest trace of the East African Goan will have disappeared.

Right now the changing of the guard is happening to the Silent Generation. They are dying out. They were the last guardians of the memories and traditions of an old Goa. The baby-boomers will also be gone in 20 years or so. With them will go the last vestiges of the Goa that their parents and grandparents once knew. With Gen X and Gen Y and the generation after that, whole generations will be lost to Goa. Britain, Europe, US, Canada, Australia will replace what was once Goa. It will soon be a vanished population.

This is a mighty tsunami wiping away a whole country resident overseas and with it will go its history, its theatre and music, traditions and everything else. Perhaps, the only thing to survive will be a modern version of a few dishes from its traditional kitchen. That is all. Otherwise, the so-called real Goan will be a stuffed relic in a museum somewhere. Goans in Goa will finally realise that in the bigger scheme of things they are simply Indian.

Of course, the vanishing is not restricted to Goans. It is a global thing.

The following is an editorial published in the *Catholic Mirror* (Nairobi, Kenya), in March 1968.

'Goan Catholics

'The spotlight in recent weeks has been turned full on the exodus of many Asians from Kenya. Among those who have departed are a number of Goan families from Nairobi and other centres in the country. Their departure must necessarily remind us of the extraordinary contributions the Goans of Kenya have made to the Catholic Church and Catholic life in this country. They came here bringing with them a tradition of Catholic worship and family life, which stretched back more than four centuries to the great apostle of their homeland, St. Francis Xavier. In their own country - an area surrounded by non-Christian communities - they had developed that Christian tradition. It centred on a great devotion to the central act of worship of the Church, the Sacrifice of the Mass and the Blessed Eucharist. It found strength in their love of Mary, the Mother of God and St. Francis Xavier. The older generation passed on their faith to those who followed them and many a missionary in Kenya in the last hundred years has had reason to thank God for the example of Catholic life of this people. Their loyalty to their faith and their unhesitating generosity in the material support of the Church and its spread to others are too well known to need emphasis.

'One need but mention a few of the monuments to this generosity: the Holy Family Basilica in Nairobi, St. Francis Xavier's Church, the Boys' and Girls' Schools and the St. Teresa's Church in Eastleigh, Parklands Church, Dr Ribeiro's Goan School. They were generous to a fault when it came to giving to God, whether that giving involved the sacrifice of their time and comfort in working for such societies as that of St. Vincent de Paul or the Legion of Mary, or delving into their resources to build churches where God would be worshipped or schools where their children would receive a true Christian education. It is only natural then that the Catholic community, comprising people of every race, should regret the necessity that makes many of these fellow Catholics leave us in Kenya. The Church will be poorer, spiritually and materially, for their going, but the countries to which they go will be the richer for their coming. Those who remain will, we know, continue the Goan tradition of loyalty to their faith. Those who are leaving will carry with them the thanks of their fellow Catholics and missionaries and the prayerful wish that all will go well for them in their new homes. To all, whether they go or stay, might be applied the words of Pope Pius XI regarding another small Catholic race, the Irish, whom persecution and economic necessity compelled to leave their homeland a hundred years ago: "Like God's pure air, they are everywhere; and everywhere they are doing good."'

We lived a utopian life in Kenya. Amid the Mau Mau fighting for their land and the resultant colonial atrocities against the Kikuyu and other black people in Kenya, Asians lived a relatively peaceful life. There was some concern, but not enough to pack the wives and daughters off to the safe havens in India and Pakistan. The British and other settlers were in a terrible state of fear as the white farmers and their employees were in the gun sights of the Mau Mau. It was even worse for the 'loyal' Africans who were to die in the hundreds if not thousands at the hands of the Mau Mau as part of the latter's fear campaign.

Generally speaking, brown skins and other similar foreign tribes did not involve themselves, because it was not their fight and because they were in awe of the colonial masters. Mainly, they had been conditioned to not even think for a moment of the plight of their fellow Kenyans. True, some did make something of an effort to show a little concern for their cooks, nannies, gardeners and other domestic staff. In some cases, Kikuyu employees were sent back to their home villages from the main towns and cities, even though this was a cruel blow.

A few years before the fall of the Boer empire in South Africa, attempts were being made to formalise through legislation an evil system called 'separate development' or apartheid. It was almost like an Aryan or Nazi conspiracy to keep all the different races in their respective ghettoes with the exception that the whites would get the choicest bits. Fortunately, the attempt failed and with it so did the apartheid system and white dominance. It is little known that the British successfully achieved the evil separate development system in Kenya: Africans lived in huts around their small farms, Asians, Goans and other non-whites lived in their designated areas. The whites lived in the best part of the towns and took over the best farmland. Growing up in Eastleigh I had a little interaction with the Sikhs, Hindus, Muslims and one or two Arab, Gujaratis, Cutchies, Borana or Somali families. I had absolutely nothing to do with any white kids. They did not live in my world and they were not aware of my kind. Our fathers came into contact with the whites as servants on a higher social rung than the Africans.

Goans were given preferential treatment because they were not likely to upset the social applecart. The favoured treatment was really another piece of the divide and rule strategy. The Goans were of course preoccupied with their God, their social clubs, sports and community-related charity works, including the building of schools where the community had congregated around a Catholic Church.

Our parents tolerated other brown skins but only just. There was never any question of assimilation. They would rather celebrate death than marriage to a non-Catholic. Even marriage to a white person was frowned upon vehemently and put the family in complete community disgrace. There was not even the thought of marriage with the 'savages', the Africans. Some inter-marriage had taken place in the very earliest days at the coast, for lack of Goan females, and in the hinterland.

CHAPTER 20

EGBERT FERNANDES

On Thursday, November 6, 2014 Goans around the globe joined the hockey fraternity to mourn the passing of one of its great sons: the dashing centre forward, Egbert Carmo Fernandes. He was 73 years old. In 1960, at just 19 years and 63 days, he was the youngest Kenyan hockey Olympian to don the No. 9 shirt and begin an illustrious career, which earned him the respect of his hockey peers, the affection of his admirers the world over and the pride of his family, his Olympian brother Edgar and sisters Edna and Ellen, all hockey players of international note. According to his sister Ellen, Egbert passed away peacefully at 7:30 pm on Thursday 6 November 2014. While he was undergoing treatment for a growth in his oesophagus he took a turn for the worse. 'We received a call from my sister Edna, who was at Egbert's bedside at 6 am Monday November 3, telling us that they were moving Egbert to palliative care that morning since Egbert had made a decision for no further treatment. He did not want to prolong his suffering and he was quite specific about that. Egbert was administered appropriate drugs until his passing.' Egbert was among a rich vein of Kenyans who achieved stardom as triple hockey Olympians (Rome, Tokyo and Mexico), played in countless internationals and made even more appearances for his club, the Nairobi Goan Institute, the only club he played for in Kenya. He played like a dashing gazelle in full flight, like a cheetah, the flashing hunter, a little Nureyev as he twisted and turned, dummied to right, dummied to left, flicked a pass in either direction, or stretched like a giraffe to push that puck just out of reach of the opposing full-back to whack in yet another goal. It is no exaggeration that he was not just poetry in motion but a very intelligent forward. While doing all this he had to outwit his opponents to prevent them injuring him or giving him a quick whack on the ankles or shins. With the exception of Jack Simonian, or one or two others, most of the Kenya hockey team inherited their hockey genes from India or Pakistan and those two countries continued to dominate until the very end of the 1960s. Kenyans were really challenging and were soon respected by the best in the world. It was all in the speed, flick of wrist and cunning, producing the unexpected legal hit that was as unstoppable as a bullet.

Kenya was ranked 7th in Rome 1960, 6th in Tokyo 1964 and 8th in Mexico 1968.

Egbert and Edgar were born in Kisumu and moved to Kiambu around 1951 and to Nairobi around 1952. Both Edgar and Egbert debuted for Kenya in 1958. Edgar was cut from the run-in squad for the 1956 Olympics in Melbourne, Australia. They could not play in Kiambu because there were no flat, grassless patches of land. In Nairobi, there was a ground at Dr. Ribeiro's Goan School, a better ground near the Railway employees' quarters in Park Road and a little patch of dust in Ngara. Hockey came very naturally to brothers Hilary, Leo and Nereus Fernandes, Edgar and Egbert Fernandes, Sylvester Fernandes, Saude George and Aloysius Mendonca, some of whom got their first taste of the game at the Dr. Ribeiro Goan School but it was fine-tuned on a small patch of Kenya *murram* situated conveniently between the Government and Railway employees' quarters in Ngara. It is here that individual genius found the time and space to experiment and bloom. At Dr. Ribeiro's they were guided by Kenyan hockey legend Anthony De Souza. After finishing school, they learnt more from their club mates before graduating from the finishing school of Kenya and learning under national coaches like Hardial Singh.

Hilary went on to become the architect of Kenya's winning streak and Leo joined on the Kenya team. Edgar Fernandes was the thinking man's Kenya half back. He was sheer class. Alu Mendonca, one of the most elegant left wingers, was recognised as perhaps the best player Kenya ever produced.

If Edgar was sheer class, then Sylvester (Silu) Fernandes was the larrikin genius on the other side of the field. He played some unorthodox blinders in his time. Saude George is one of Kenya's few double international goalkeepers. The hockey world respected his courage and his calm, cool approach to the game. This Ngara mafia's skills were further enhanced when they joined other great Kenyan players like Avtar Singh, perhaps the most capped player of all time; Surjeet Singh Jnr, a classy centre half; Amar Singh, who was a joy to watch; Reynolds De Souza, a charming, gentle forward with an uncanny killer instinct for scoring or delivering the killer pass; Surjeet Singh, senior and elder statesman of the game with Pritam Singh; as well as the crafty Santokh Singh Matharu. The pedigree of all the Kenya hockey teams was almost at its best and Egbert thrived in this exalted company.

The Ngara mafia was indeed a very close-knit group and Hilary tells the story of Egbert picking him up every morning on a pedal bike. They happily went to school, Hilary operating the left pedal and Egbert the right. One foot up somewhere on the bike, they had not a care in the world.

Who could have imagined in those early days that this scrawny kid would be the only Kenyan to be nominated for an Olympic World XI (nominated after the Olympics)? Of everything he accomplished, one memory stood out for all time. Edgar explains, 'His greatest memory of the best game we ever played was when we beat India in 1964 in two tests, lost two and drew one on their home soil. But at Jabalpur we beat them 3-0, Egbert scoring 2 and me 1, as I played at inside right alongside him that year.' In his other life he worked in finance at the US Embassy in Nairobi. Egbert was transferred to Canberra in 1973. Edgar and his family joined him there the same year. When the most popular Goan player married the No.1 Kenyan women's hockey star, it was the stuff of dreams. They were blessed with three children and two grandchildren.

In most things, Egbert's life imitated his hockey. He was decisive and resolute, executed simple but direct plans and knew exactly what he wanted to do. As the cancer took hold, Egbert made it clear that he did not want to linger bed-ridden in the intensive care unit. He made it clear that he wanted to go as quickly as possible and did not want to suffer or be propped up by a cocktail of drugs with only one result: his ultimate death. He was resolute and decisive and left this earth on his own terms. RIP hero, mate.

One of the many, many wonderful Kenya beaches: Diani Beach
Photo courtesy of FB I love Kenya Original

The author, Silvano Gomes, Rudolph Fernandes, Tony Reg D'Souza, Gilbert Fernandes and Steve Fernandes. Photo: Azhar Chaudhry

CHAPTER 21

THE JOKERS

The Mau Mau emergency meant little or nothing to the Goans who lived in the main cities and town centres of Colonial Kenya. There was heightened concern for those who lived and worked in the outlying districts. There was special concern for Goans because they were considered lackeys of the colonial power. Goans were 'favoured' by the British and went about their business as only Goans could, with not a care in the world. Goans enjoyed the full tapestry of life and everything the magnificent Kenya offered to them, within limits, of course.

I really came into contact with the Goans after I became a journalist in 1960, and then with Goan sporting types. I did not join a Goan club until 1966. Until then I had hung around my Seychellois and Mauritian friends, mainly because we had a band going and all the members were Seychellois. It was in 1963 that I ran into a bunch of guys who to this day remain imprinted on my memory with the fondest and funniest of times. Our gigs were almost non-stop at clubs, sports, parties, dances and more dances. The principals of what became to be known as *The Jokers* were: Rudi Fernandes, Tony Reg D'Souza, Pio Almeida (for a short while), Steve Fernandes, the late Anthony Coco Cardoso, Gilbert Fernandes, Tony 'Fatso' Pereira, ad hoc member Rowland Rebello and yours truly. The unofficial godparents were (the late) Ben and Julie Pereira, mainly because they were daft enough to host Christmas breakfast (after the midnight dance) at their place. There were a bunch of juniors who included Norman Da Costa, Silvano Gomes (until they became senior members), Neville

Pinheiro, Diamond Mike, Albert D'Souza, Albert Markit, Jules Fernandes, Edwin and Ivy. They started hanging around late in the picture, as did a whole bunch of other people. Angelo Costabir was a respected irregular member, there were many like him and yet more who claimed membership in *The Jokers* were really frauds to be kind. Rudi, Steve, Fatso and Coco were all teachers and Tony Reg was our intern, still finishing university and soon to join the teacher ranks. They must have made fantastic teachers because their former students speak fondly of them. Tony Reg became a walking encyclopaedia and knew virtually every single Goan in Kenya. He was an extremely popular guy who often acted as intermediary between a difficult set of parents and nervous wannabe beaus. Norman, of course, went on to become one of Africa's greatest sports journalists.

It all began in a pretty convoluted way. Rudi was a year ahead of Tony Reg and Pio was a year ahead of Rudy, all at St Teresa's Eastleigh. Steve came and joined Rudi. Meanwhile Coco was finishing off at Dr Ribeiro's. Coco's value was that he was pretty well known at the Goan Institute for his snooker and table tennis ability, and because he had a car. Tony Reg lived in the Government Quarters in Ngara opposite the Teacher Training College where Steve and Rudi would end up. The two used to drop in at Tony's place for snacks and later on when Tony moved to larger quarters across the road they would come and spend the night there. Tony and Rudi's friendship would be further cemented when both lived across from each other in a block of flats in Eastleigh. While Steve and Rudi were finishing off College, Tony was accepted at Strathmore where he met Donald Gonsalves and Winston Verbi, ex-St. Teresa's colleagues.

The initial core group was Tony, Rudi, Steve, Pio and Coco. They were all teachers who, with a little help with the three groups of students at Strathmore College (Kanu, Kadu and APP -African People's Party- the three main parties in Kenyan politics), began organising parties and Coco used to transport all the girls from their homes. The parties consisted of just a record, some soft drinks and maybe a beer or two. They also recruited some erstwhile members of the Sandy Makara gang from Pangani Chini, such as Rudi's brother Lenny, Jules and Diamond Mike Fernandes, Philo Mazor, Geoffrey, Sandy, Gerald, Sally Ahluwalia (who taught all the boys to dance in between hundreds of cups of chai made by the wonderful Macharia), George Alvares, Dennis and Darrell Pereira, Brian Fernandez, Steve and Walter Rodrigues, Ralph and Tim Fernandes, Desmond and Peter Andrade, George and James Alvares as well as Leslie Scott, Ashley Pinto, Neville Pinheiro and a bunch of other guys.

At this stage, Gilbert and his DKW joined the group and he was made very welcome. Before that the guys went everywhere by bus or walked. This public transport was very well utilised on Saturdays as the guys cruised Government Road and Kimathi Street, starting from the top at Keby's, past the Tropicana, Woolworths, the New Stanley Hotel (Thorn Tree Restaurant), past National Mutual, left past the bus stop, past BMC and left into Government Road, past Channi's pharmacy, Standard Bank, a whole bunch of shops and left into Kimathi and then starting the whole thing all over again, cruising to catch the eye of a chick or two.

After Rudi and Steve started working, Tony was heading for university and they graduated to having a drink at the Tropicana restaurant, sitting alfresco and doing a bit of armchair cruising. All manner of friends and acquaintances and wannabe-*Jokers* used to congregate at the Tropicana, which also put on a stunning lunch, before the boys headed for the Railway Institute. I used to be a regular at Sans Chique, the Lobster Pot, the Thorn Tree and the Tropicana and it was here that I met *The Jokers*. With the exception of Coco, who was thought to be a member of the Goan Institute, none of the other guys were members of any of the three clubs. Yet, during the school holidays they would all meet at the Railway Institute until some twit or two dobbed them in. This climaxed in the classic incident when a guy who later became a great friend barred *The Jokers* from coming into the club for the New Year's Eve Dance. War was declared on Marcus Braganza. Fortunately, it was never consummated, and instead the guys decided to come through the front door and apply for membership of the RI.

Meanwhile, Ben Pereira had a difference of opinion with the Goan Gymkhana and he decided that he would take his business elsewhere. He took it to the Railway Institute and he and his wife Julie were both adopted by *The Jokers*. Edwin and Ivy, who used to pop in during the school holidays, were also adopted. Silvano was not an official member to start with but his girlfriend's parents, especially her mum Olive, were friends of *The Jokers*. As I wrote earlier, the Hornets apparently had a difference of opinion with the Railway Institute and decided to go solo, bringing a whole new bunch of guys into *The Jokers*. Only the streetlights and tiny candles at the bar lighted one of the parties we had. Discretion of the highest calibre was achieved and no one was any the wiser about interactions between the groups of consenting teenagers.

The Jokers had one philosophy: to party and party, all except for Rudi Fernandes, who had long before found his true love and we waited patiently for him to name a date. Rudi's other claim to fame was practising his debating skills in the early hours of the morning off Ainsworth Street with his bosom buddy Tony Reg. Their daily habitat after work was the Railway Goan Institute. Their Saturday habitat was the Tropicana Restaurant by day, the Panafric, Swiss Grill Room, or wherever there was a dance or party. Again, with the exception of Rudy, none of the guys actually had dates for their nights out. Silvano was already going steady with Dola, as was Arnold with Carmen. Diamond Mike was chasing Cynthia and has been happily married for several decades now. At a dance, for example, they would make a brief appearance in the hall, retire to the bar, decide who they were going to dance the midnight special and last dance with, book the girls and carry on drinking. Now and then they would surface from the bar to meet dancing obligations with mums, other relations, or to protect one guy's choices for the night. More often than not, I used to hang a camera around the necks of Gilbert and Tony Reg and get them to accompany me to official journalistic dates to enjoy the drinks and the views. Coco had a car, a Triumph that was meant to seat four comfortably but usually took anything up to 10, especially when Gilbert was not around with this gleaming DKW.

The girls loved Gilbert, our own version of the great Elvis Presley. They swore he did not only sing and dance like the King but Gilbert also looked like the King. It did not wash with the guys, but the girls loved it. Anyway, Gilbert was a very popular guy. He was also charming to all the mums.

Gilbert accompanied me to parties outside Nairobi, especially in Kericho, Eldoret, Nakuru, Mombasa, Malindi, the White Highlands and many more. And it was not only because he had a car that he was my special friend. Hundreds will say it and I will deny it each time. To this day he has remained a special friend. Steven Fernandes is another special person in my life. This is a special kind of guy with a devil may care attitude, a hockey nut, fishing nut, Tusker nut, pull-your-leg nut everyone it seems has a Caito story to tell. He was a fantastic athlete and an all-round fun guy who thought he was the resident expert on betting on the horses and gambling at cards. Gilbert was another card shark with Tony Fatso. Most of the guys would get together for marathon card sessions at Limuru or Kiambu during the long weekends. Fatso was a teacher and he would ring-in his Indian colleagues into the betting ring. And of course, all the guys played for a beautiful hockey team called the Hornets. I will never know what possessed Norman and Silvano to ask me to coach the team. I had an absolute ball and it was a great team if I say so myself. Hockey Superstar Hilary Fernandes was the real coach, or at least he was the special strategic consultant who helped us with niche planning issues. You know that is all bullshit.

One year we took the whole team to Mombasa where we were to play the Mombasa XI, which included all-time greats Pritam Singh (in my book the greatest of them all) and Franklyn Pereira among others. En route to Mombasa, not even 20 miles out of Nairobi, Polycarp and Steven binged on everyone's packed dinners. So when we discovered that someone had thieved our food we had to make do with what we could buy at the various stations late at night and it wasn't much, probably a lot of mandazi (like a doughnut without a hole), charcoal grilled corn and some vegetables. There was no Wendy's in those days. Anyway, we had to get our own back. We lost very narrowly to Mombasa but had a great time socially. The next day before we boarded the train I arranged with a friend of my mother's to pack Goan finger food for the boys and this we hid from Polycarp and Steve. My mum's friend was pretty well known in Mombasa and her food was out of this world.

About 40 minutes outside of Mombasa, the two overgrown ankle-biters were clamouring all over me. 'What's for dinner?'

'Nothing.'

'What do you mean, nothing? You are the coach and you are the manager. You should look after us.'

'Oh, yeah, like you guys did with our food?'

'Bloody hell, this is not right, this not good enough!" And they went away, complaining.

It was twilight when we approached Voi, one of the larger stations, and I noticed Steve and Polycarp standing on the steps of the carriage, readying to get off. Get off they did, like gymnasts executing perfect landings, straight into the arms of the waiting policeman, who promptly booked them into the cells for illegally getting off a moving train. Earlier when I had asked what they were doing, both had replied in a chorus of 'corn beef sandwiches, corn beef sandwiches'. That is how Polycarp got the name 'corn beef'. The station master was a guy called Menino. I had been in a fight with him in Nairobi. He had not forgotten and when I tried to plead for the boys' release, he simply said 'piss off'. So I asked Hilary to do the pleading and that did the trick and a pretty shaken up pair were retrieved from jail.

Video cameras had not been invented in our heyday. I guess that is one reason why there are so few photographs of us growing up: there were no instamatics, disposables or digitals and hard case cameras were pretty expensive, especially those Kodak Brownies.

If we had been able to record for posterity then we would be viewing our fishing trips to Athi River, Machakos, Stony Athi, Dandora, Ruaraka and various spots upcountry along the Tana River. Our friends in Kisumu and Entebbe introduced us to fishing in Lake Victoria. Lake Rudolf (later Lake Turkana) created unbelievable memories, especially landing the greatest fighting fish, the tiger fish. Lake Turkana also had some of the largest Nile

Perch in the world. But most of the time we had to make do with tilapia in the rivers and ponds fairly close to Nairobi. They were a brilliant fish for *recheado* or simply plain fried. *The Jokers* were also part of the Samaki (fish) Club, which had other Railway Institute members including John Goes and Philo Mazor, both of whom were pretty good at throwing the *pagelle*. My lasting memory is of Mazor teaching the late Derek D'Mello to throw a net. I suspect that was the last trip to Stony Athi, at least for me.

These Samaki Club safaris were brilliant, albeit a little regimented. A dedicated barman, Estess Martin never gave you your change back which went into the club's coffers. Various mothers provided the guys with a variety of ground spices both dry and liquid. Mazor, Diamond and one or two other guys were chefs. The rest consisted of the first shift that made coffee and large, thick corn beef sandwiches and a second shift that cleaned all the fish. The menu consisted of several curries, especially the beer curry and a variety of fried fish with the *recheado* at the top of the tree. Those were magnificent, carefree days: lots of jokes, lots of laughter and lots of pranks. Steven was always at the bottom of one or another. This was the sweet bird of our youth and I am sure we are richer for it, even though in distant lands we miss it. At least I do. Similarly, I miss our picnics with everyone on a back of a truck, singing, singing and more singing and a picnic basket to die for!

We went to Keby's for *faludas* (Indian ice cream based drink), the Ismailia Hotel for those fantastic samosas and potato bhajia, pakorah), Snow Cream for coffee and ice-cream, to the Embakasi airport waving base after the dance for coffee and to watch the planes take off, to Maru's in Riata Road for bhajia and that fantastic tamarind chutney, to Singh's bar opposite the GI for crumbed drumsticks and lamb cutlets. We loved Salim, who made those fantastic kebabs outside the RI and of course Mittaiwallah, who still produces the greatest Indian sweets in the world. We went to the movies at the Theatre Royal, Empire, Capital, Kenya, 20th Century and the mighty Drive-In, the lovers' haven, and some even ventured to the Odeon and the Shan. One year Vincent Gunputrav and I hooked off from school every Wednesday at 2 pm to see every single episode of Flash Gordon.

I have already mentioned the Swiss Grill but there was also the notorious Sombrero Club, the piano room at the PanAfric, the wonderful Equator Club where the late Max Alfonso used to jam with the band on his harmonica. If that was not enough there was always a quick trip to Mombasa, Nakuru, Eldoret or Kericho. We are spread around the world but folks are happy to remind us of those post-puberty crazy days of love and fresh air.

Fadhili Williams' *Malaika* was the first song that captured most hearts in Kenya and the rest of East Africa and Africa. Before that, Asians (mainly Goans and a few Khojas) and Europeans rarely danced to 'African' music. *Malaika* broke the ice and was followed quickly by *Taxi Driver, Bus Conductor, Harambee Harambee* (the Kenyan slogan to work together, pull together) and the rest, as they say, is history.

The Starlight Night Club opposite the Panafric Hotel was the first multicultural venue but the whites were mainly tourists, British soldiers and US volunteers. It was also a reasonably respectable place for picking up business ladies and I don't mean the commercial kind. Besides me you would rarely see a brown-skin but you would see lots of journalists, especially on a Friday or Saturday night.

Among the first clubs to be dance-exclusive were the Equator Club, Starlight Club (my favourite), Equator Inn and the pioneer Sombrero Night Club. The Equator Club, while it lasted, always had the best musicians and music from jazz, rock n roll to pop, to soul. It was hotter than hell. It would be a very long time before rock n roll and 'The Twist' would seduce black Kenyans. It was left to a few Goans, lots of Sychelloise and Mauritians.

The Swiss Grill in Westlands was for lovers, people looking for love or those who were planning to make love. The music was wonderfully modern although there was a large helping of Dean Martin.

On the dance floor, beside Fadhili Williams and his band and Charles Hayes' recording stars, the hottest bands on the earth were the Bata Shoe Shine Band, Inspector Gideon and the Police pop band, and Pascal and his

Congolese rhythms. Other bands were the Rhythm Kings, the Typhoons, Amigos, the Bandits, the Shiftas, Scorpions, Cooty's Band and a few bands from the Coast and the various bands Henry Braganza sang with. The Goan bands tried to play music from Goa as well as the remnants of old and boring British tunes. Being cheek to cheek at midnight was the only saving grace until Bill Haley and Comets, Elvis Presley and the likes of Otis Redding, Sam and Dave, Chuck Berry, Sam Cooke, Aretha Franklin, Clarence Frogman Henry, Ray Charles and everyone from Tamla Motown taught us to dance the devil's dances: rock n roll, the twist, the blues, soul and everything wonderful that happened after 1960.

The Europeans danced the night away at Rotary and Lions clubs events, the Impala Club, the Railway Club, the Muthaiga Club, the Parklands Club. Whites only please. Adultery welcomed.

I produced two spectacular entertainment shows: one at the Nairobi City Hall with about 96 participants; the other to mark an anniversary at the Railway Goan Institute. I was also a pioneer compere on VOK music TV shows. My work as an investigative reporter took me away from all that. I managed a band called the Wheelers (Steven Rodrigues, Vernay Arissol, Lewis Arissol, Maurice 'Kanada' D'Silva, Benjamin Lopez, David Lobo and Robert Cecile) from the age of 13.

Courtesy of FB site I Love Kenya Original

CHAPTER 22

THE BATHING OF THE MIND

September is one of the best months to visit and tour Kenya. The mornings are fresh without any chill and the evenings are sublime. In between dawn and dusk there is gentle warmth that opens your pores and lets out tiny sprays of perspiration. It is a kind of exhaust for the body.

Dawn: 6:06, sunrise: 6:26, sunset: 6:32 dusk: 6:53. So you get 12+ hour days and a bonus dusk of 21 minutes. All this is very important, especially if you are heading out on your first safari. So there you are all cuddled up in the warmth of your bed at the Amboseli Lodge. You fall in love with the lodge straight away and get a little peek at Mount Kilimanjaro. Still it is an awesome sight, taking your breath away. It feels like there is something divine in the air. Before dinner, you go for a drink with the guys at the tented camp. They are all seated around a huge bonfire; someone is playing a guitar, all the drivers and staff are singing away. It is another memorable experience. Get back to the lodge, rush a shower and a change of clothes and 'reserved' is the best seat in the house in the specially-built balcony to watch the animals at the water hole and salt lick down below. After dinner I settle into my special chair but give up fairly quickly because I am about ready to drop into the sublime, cat-purring sleep. I am happy, tired and delighted to be alive. Dawn at 6:00 means out on a pre-breakfast game run by 6:30 at the latest. A perk-you-up morning tea or coffee in your room before you hear the gong go, the knock on the door and a gentle voice saying, 'please wake for game run, the animals are waiting to greet you.'

On the game run from Nairobi I visit three prides of lions. The driver brings us so close we could touch them. Lazy, aren't they? Good, everyone remembers to hold their breath, otherwise the lions would have caught the human breath and cubs would have started fidgeting and the adults would have moved them on. God, the cheetahs are a sensation, first stalking their prey and then running it down like speeding bullets. I saw that on television once, did not believe it could actually happen right in front of my eyes. How lucky I am, what speed, what grace, what majesty, sorry about the prey. I guess that is what life is like in the savannah. People do it, too. They call it War. Or they call it murder. I saw elephants, lions and buffalo yesterday. Today I hope to see leopards and rhinos to complete the must-see Big Five. We should have made a list, what else did we see yesterday? Zebra, giraffes, gazelles, eland, impala, wildebeest and those other things, the bat eared foxes, looked so cuddly. I must make a list today, I told myself. On the way to Tsavo East and West there is a great treat in store: Mzima Springs, home of the mighty hippos. What a sight that is going to be!

And so it goes on! And you wonder where the day went as you sit sipping your first drink just after 5 pm at Tsavo Lodge. You began the day with a champagne breakfast by the river. What a breakfast! You saw your first leopard and rhino and a bunch of other animals. But what takes your breath away is the brief encounter with hippos at Mzima Springs. As the name suggests, the watering hole with a resident herd of hippos is fed from a nearby spring. God they are huge, aren't they? Very quiet, very serene.

After picking up your things from Tsavo East you head for another game run and a bush lunch. There is nothing bush about it: prawns, crabs, lobster, hams and roast lamb, pork, beef and lots of salads.

You shower and are hungry but first there is the important tradition of pre-dinner drinks. Take it easy, it is going to be a long night, I don't know how much sleep we are going to get. After dinner I meet Joe Kavirondo, the man in charge of the animal orphanage at Tsavo (West) Lodge. At the moment the orphanage has three baby elephants, two black rhinos, six gazelles, two giraffe and a bunch of other smaller plains animals and two orphaned lion cubs whose mother was killed by poachers. Aren't they evil, the poachers, I mean? Did you see the elephant carcasses, with the ivory tusks ripped off the heads? How sad, how inhumane. I will be heartbroken about that for the rest of my life. Joe's mother was a Maasai and his father was a Kipsigis hunter from the north.

Some animals have an instinctive fear of Joe. He is a sort of human anti-baboon spray. Joe has to just enter an area where the baboons and monkeys are making a nuisance of themselves and they take off like their life depended on it. The Maasai Mara game lodge used to employ a Maasai warrior to keep the baboons out of their dining areas. After dinner we are all seated around Joe.

'Welcome to Tsavo Lodge. I hope you will enjoy your stay enough to want to come back. I want to talk to you about the next few hours at the viewing from where you will be able to see a procession of animals who come for their daily drink, mud bath, frolic and, of course, the all-important salt lick. You will see the elephants come, have a drink, take a protective mud bath against fleas and other insects and spray protective dust on their bodies. They will leave once they have had their fill. The lions, zebra, rhino, cheetah and other plains animals will follow them until every species has had its fill. This procession is repeated every night.

'There is one rule you must not forget: do not talk, sneeze, cough or make any kind of human sound. The wind is likely to transfer the human smells to the herds below and they will stampede. You will have spoilt it for everyone. Very late into the night we are expecting a visit from a couple of leopards. One of my colleagues will be going around the lodge with a gentle gong in hand. We have put up several game baits in the trees. You are sure to see a leopard or two tomorrow. In fact, if the animal gods are good to you, you might even see a leopard family we have been keeping an eye on.

'There is a special way of making the next few hours absolutely unforgettable. Your thoughts are your own. It is your very own private suite to the world. As you become one with the environment all around you, two things happen: your eyesight becomes sharper and your hearing keener. I do it as often as I can. There is a kind of magic out there. It is not just eyes that see, or your nose that smells, or your hands that touch, it seems as if every part of your body is doing any one of those tasks. It would seem like an out-of-body and into wilderness experience that makes you merge with everything around you. You are the night, you are the wildlife, you are the insects, you are the music of the night, you are everything and you are completely at peace with it all. Try and see if you can catch that exact nanosecond when dusk becomes twilight and twilight becomes night. The photograph above comes close to catching one of those moments.

'You may not notice it immediately, but you suddenly feel utterly and completely relaxed, at peace, you are home. There is a kind of languid feeling in your body, the limbs seem at rest. You feel it first in your shoulders. The head seems to come to rest, completely at ease, on your shoulders as the night goes on. Oh, that drink in your glass never seems to end, it is always there. First you hear the sounds of the animals. You play a game with yourself trying to identify each species. In the far, far distance you can hear the roar of a lion or two, or even the stampeding footsteps of a plains animal, perhaps someone's dinner.

'So you stretch your legs in abandon. You feel good about yourself. Never felt so alive at this hour of the night, you tell yourself. But it is your own personal window into the world that you find so narcotic, as you watch for the departure of dusk, the arrival of twilight and, eventually, the dark of night. The night sounds change... listen, listen it is the orchestra of the night, a billion, trillion insects playing their nightly symphony. You have to listen carefully. Don't try to analyse it, just go with it.

'We call that the whole experience: the bathing of the mind. Please enjoy the experience of a little bit of Africa, loving life to the maximum.' I feel truly fulfilled. Tsavo West, you are my heaven.

We stopped off in Voi, another overnighter, before gently arriving in beloved Mombasa. We went to Malindi but the white sands had disappeared in a flood. Watamu Beach Hotel is even more beautiful than I remembered. Off to Masaai Mara, Mount Kenya Safari Club, Tree Tops,

Secret Valley, The Ark, Mount Kenya, Nyeri, Nanyuki, Aberdares, Lake Baringo, Ol Donyo Sabuk, Lake Nakuru, Lake Naivasha, a plane trip to Lake Turkana before heading for Tanzania, Arusha, the Serengeti and lots more.

EPILOGUE

With Sincere Thanks ….
I am Goan.
I am Kenyan.
I am British.
I am Australian.

I am a man of many parts, from many places but right now the whole of me is Australian. Many events, many people, many, many places, much, much luck, some coincidence, many surprises, all of these ingredients have fashioned my life. Until the last sunset arrives, I will be eternally grateful for being blessed with the family I have had and the life I have led. As the cliché goes, I might have done one or two things differently, but then again, there really isn't very much I would change.

Being born in Kenya was perhaps the greatest blessing of all. What a country! The spectrum of life is a creation of myriad trillions and more of specks. Each speck, good, bad, or ugly has its own space in the universe of things but Kenya will always remain my earth mother and one which I was privileged to have loved with all my heart. I have lived all my life like a knife through a block of butter. I have not looked back or laboured on the past, but have lived in the moment and relished the coming of the tomorrow. In my rear view mirror are few regrets, if any. The Kenyan dust runs through my veins and resides in my DNA, which means my body form will always be Kenyan but, while I have left my heart in Kenya, my soul belongs to my country of adoption, Australia.

The Goan in me will only die with that last sunset. I have lived my life on a line I once heard in the movie *South Pacific* in which a Pacific Island princess falls in love with an American and tells him: 'I will always honour the ways of my father but I will also respect the ways of the new land I have adopted'. As I moved from country that is what I have done: I continue to honour the land of my father, Goa. And I commit my all to Australia, as I said many times, this country gets my bones.

I also enjoyed our brief sojourn in England and will always be grateful for the vast amount of help I received from that country, especially in facilitating and hosting the many study trips I did from Kenya. One year I was flying for a brief trip to Paris the next day and I did not have any pages left in my current passport. The Foreign Office was able to get me a new passport in a few hours. They also set up meetings with the prevailing cabinet ministers and backbenchers of interest as well as arranging visits to various parts of the country, Wales, Scotland, Ireland and Northern Ireland, and independently many countries in Europe. And, of course, there were visits to the chairman's boxes at the various London soccer clubs. Thanks a million.

In Sydney, Australia, one of the first new friends I made was Richie Gonsalves, ex-Karachi. I met him at a card table and later got to know his wife Dorothy and their sons pretty well. They introduced me to Ben and Vivien Almeida. The late George and Cynthia Fernandes joined us and these four families did most going-out things together. Richie was a very, very funny guy who only drank Black Douglas Scotch and if you did not pour yourself a decent drink, he complained 'do not dirty my glass.' Ben is a great cook and is renowned for his biriyani. George was our resident fixer-upper and always willing to lend a hand. It broke all our hearts when he and Cynthia died quite young. I also hooked up with ex-Kenyans George and Sheila Pereira and their sons Colin, Clive and Carl. While George was a quiet achiever, Sheila was always the life of the party, especially with her Konkani songs. John (deceased) and Ivy Mascarenhas (ex-Uganda) were first time acquaintances. John was very dedicated to the local Goan cause. Alban and Laura Rattos, Richie Rattos, Eddie Rattos (all ex-Uganda) brought a huge range of interests: fishing, music, cricket, darts and plenty more. Tony and Eleanor D'Souza (ex-Karachi) were a gift. Eleanor organised the women's group, which put on the social events of the Goan Overseas Association during my tenure as president. In this respect I was also aided by Tony and Gloria Vaz, George and Dawn Dias, Les and Rineth Scott, Andrew and Claudia (deceased) Scott, Tony and Phil Fernandes, Mal and Margaret Ferris who are very special to my family, Cass and Mona Dias, Harold and Hazel D'Souza, Paul Francis, Patrick and Elsa Pinto, Mervyn Pinto, Anton 'Caramar' Fernandes, Leo and Piety Rocha, Caj and Bernie Miranda, Maggie Soares, Felix and Hazel Nazareth, Victor and Monica Nazareth, Willie and Betty Fernandes, George and Cynthia Peres da Costa, Pat (deceased) and Bertha D'Souza (great supporters of the Goan Association), Lyle Sandford and his late dad Frank and John Muir (New Zealand) were some of the people we met in our early years in Sydney. Much later I hooked up with childhood mate Tony Reg and his wife Rebecca D'Souza and his brother Loy. Terry (Geeta) also joined our Friday Club.

I will remain indebted to Denis Muller, once chief sub-editor of the *Sydney Morning Herald*, and his family who looked after us when we first arrived in Sydney. Everyone at the *SMH* was terrific and I enjoyed my time there as I did at *The Australian, Good Weekend Magazine, St. George and Sutherland Shire Leader* and at the Caltex Refinery at Kurnell, which changed to a petrol farm.

I have woken up each morning and my prayer has been: thank you, God. It is great to be alive, in Australia. Thank you.

These days I bathe my mind watching the wonders of Sydney, Australia.

I have been privileged to have been a newspaper reporter, blessed with the ability to ask why, when, where, who which, how, to observe, to analyse, to articulate, to seek the truth and to present the balanced facts. I am a member of another vanishing breed. Soon the laptop will be switched off and I will give my aching neck a rest.

That's all folks.

The famous Collegians hockey team (Photo: Trifa De Souza)
Back row: Bertha Fernandes, Melita Caido, Alvira Almeida, Flora
George, Mavis Pinto. Middle row: Late Nifa De Souza, late Peter
Barbosa, Sister Trifa, Michael D'Souza and Edna Monteiro. Seated:
Marjorie Pinto, late Alba Mendonca and Sister Christine Pereira.

Trifa De Souza would have been one of the first Goans to represent Kenya at the Empire Games in Cardiff in 1958 unfortunately she arrived in Cardiff only to find that her Portuguese passport (Portugal was not part of the British Empire) disqualified her.

Lightning Source UK Ltd.
Milton Keynes UK
UKOW01f1627041016

284440UK00002B/350/P